OP

ORIGINAL PLUMBING

THE BEST OF TEN YEARS OF TRANS MALE CULTURE

EDITED BY AMOS MAC & ROCCO KAYIATOS
FOREWORD BY TIQ MILAN

FEMINIST PRESS
AT THE CITY UNIVERSITY OF NEW YORK
NEW YORK CITY

Published in 2019 by the Feminist Press
at the City University of New York
The Graduate Center
365 Fifth Avenue, Suite 5406
New York, NY 10016

feministpress.org

First Feminist Press edition 2019

This book was made possible thanks to a grant from New York State Council
on the Arts with the support of Governor Andrew M. Cuomo and the New York
State Legislature.

First printing May 2019

Library of Congress Cataloging-in-Publication Data is available for this title.

ISBN 978-1-936932-59-7

To the trans people who came before us—
you were our lighthouse.

May this collection light the way
for the next generation.

CONTENTS

FOREWORD

In 2004 I had a moment of recognition that made me realize I wasn't alone. Up until then, I didn't know that being a transgender man was possible. I knew that I was unhappy and self-conscious, humiliated when I was read as female and disheartened that I couldn't find the space to be who I needed to be. I was masculine presenting but still being seen as a woman, which made me feel invisible and wrong. At that time, I understood gender to be static and set in the stone of genitals or gender roles. I didn't know gender could be fluid—transforming and self-determined by anyone who dared to define themselves outside of expectation or performance—until I met Nico.

It was a slow Friday afternoon, and I was working the happy-hour shift at Meow Mix, a lesbian dive bar on Manhattan's Lower East Side. Mix was small and dark, with just a few barstools around the dance floor, and usually smelled like old beer with a faint hint of vomit. In walked a short guy with a dirty-blond goatee and a stack of flyers. He had shy, squinty eyes and quarter-sized gauges in his ears.

"Hey, I'm throwing a fundraiser here next week. Mind if I put some flyers on the bar?"

"For sure," I said.

He spread them out across the sticky black bar and tacked a few up on the wall. I grabbed one to see what it was all about. On it was a photo of the shy guy at the bar, shirtless with his arms across his chest, smiling and looking off into the distance. The headline read:

HELP OUR BUDDY NICO SAY, "*TA-TA*, TA-TAS!"
A TOP SURGERY FUNDRAISER

Top surgery? What the hell is that? I thought. I looked at the flyer then back at him. Then again at the flyer then back at him.

"Holy shit? Are you . . . you used to be a girl?"

Back then we didn't have the same decorum and affirming language around transgender people like we do now.

He giggled and politely corrected me. "I'm transgender."

That day changed everything. The veil had been lifted and a path to manhood emerged. There was a way for me to be the person I saw in my mind and felt in my heart. After that fateful meeting, I was committed to finding transmasculine community. I went to support groups for trans men in the Bronx and invite-only meet-ups in Brooklyn. I talked to hundreds of transgender men of color in Yahoo chats and Facebook groups until the wee hours of the night to feel seen, reflected, and real. We asked one another questions, not to invalidate people's truths, but to be complicated by them.

We shared information on doctors and surgeons. We talked strategies of coming out to family and friends, being stealth or disclosing at work. It was vital information that we weren't getting anywhere else, especially for the guys who weren't in large progressive cities like New York or Los Angeles. We needed this online communiqué because the discourse around LGBTQ people was still mostly gay and lesbian. Transgender people, especially trans men, were extremely marginalized, as organizations focused more on overturning sodomy laws and passing marriage equality than protections for trans folks.

At the same time, transgender men have been working in the background of human rights movements. We've toiled away in LGBTQ organizing, fighting for our rights to have access to safe, affordable gender-affirming surgery and nondiscriminatory health care. Trans men like Kylar Broadus, Jamison Green, and Imani Henry have been working for the visibility of transgender men and nonbinary folks when many gay and lesbian organizations weren't creating space for us or prioritizing our needs. We've been vocal about a trans guy's rights to birthing, parenthood, marriage, and the option to be low or no disclosure if we choose. With little to no visibility, we've been here since the beginning. Fighting, scratching, and clawing to be seen and be respected.

We've also always been hot as fuck: beautiful, fluid, and multidimensional—complicated and provocative. Somebody needed to take notice and give transgender men the photo shoots and good lighting that we deserved. Photographer and writer Amos Mac teamed up with artist and producer Rocco Kayiatos to do just that. Together they created *Original Plumbing* in 2009, the only quarterly dedicated to transmasculine culture and aesthetics. They showcased trans guys of different body types, races, and a multitude of masculinities: some femme, some gay, some macho; leather daddies and family men. Manhood was our playground of possibility—not some stiff notion that could be undone with the slightest of ease. The beautiful thing about transgender men is that we make masculine identity our own. We make it layered and complicated.

Being transgender isn't the center of every trans guy's identity, but it creates a specific lens for life, community, and self-awareness. Although being a trans person comes with its share of sacrifices and hardships, there is freedom in being self-determined in how your manhood can show up in the world. We create new blueprints of masculinity and remix the old ones. Cisgender masculinity is often limited to a binary set of experiences and has been starved of complexity and flexibility. *Original Plumbing* reached into the nuances of self-determined masculinity with stellar photos and in-depth interviews.

Being trans is movement building, and our aesthetic is a boundary-pushing protest in and of itself: the audacity to be sexy—the chutzpah to believe in the ability to create manhood and masculinity that is ours—is a revolutionary act. In every issue, trans guys from Brooklyn to Germany could feel seen, validated, and a part of something bigger than themselves. *Original Plumbing* was the example that so many young trans guys out there needed. It was the zine that made them know that they weren't a freak or wrong or unworthy. *OP*'s every feature and issue recreated moments of recognition and possibility like the one I had that sleepy Friday afternoon in an empty bar, but for thousands of transgender men all over the world. There is a shared experience of coming out, figuring it all out, becoming who you were meant to be, and paying it forward to the next guy who is misunderstood and isolated. Many of us have been that isolated kid. *OP* was proof that we could live and be beautiful and loved. It also brought the global transmasculine community together under common experience while highlighting our individuality in a way no other publication has been able to duplicate. The guys featured in the issues of *OP* came from all walks of life: Artists and writers. Skateboarders and activists. There were scores of trans men who were living their best lives, showcasing the unapologetic ownership of an identity and authenticity many of us would have literally died without.

In 2010 I was invited to be part of issue five, the Fashion Issue. I'd seen Rocco perform and was always impressed with his work, so it was an honor to participate in such a groundbreaking publication and I jumped at the chance. It was also to be my first photo shoot as a transgender man. I knew that if there were any publication I should come out in, it was this one.

I'd done shoots and interviews before, but being in front of Amos's camera was different. He was open and smiling, and seemed just as excited as I was to be doing the shoot. I didn't have to worry about intrusive questions about my body or traumas around coming out. Amos and Rocco understood that my transness was the lens that influenced my style and swagger rather than the focal point of my expression. The photo shoot was quick and seamless. The photos were gorgeous. I still have one hanging on the wall today. It was one of my proudest moments as a writer and public figure.

The issue release party was unreal. It was sweaty and crowded, and had Brooklyn bursting at the seams. There were hundreds of people dancing and drinking. Go-go boys and girls grinding on top of speakers. Groups of transgender and genderqueer folks posing under the bright lights of a photographer's camera flashing in the darkness of the dance floor. Couples and "throuples" making out in corners, hugs and smiles all around. People of all gender identities and of every hue celebrating that night like it was their last.

Most folks take for granted the importance of being reflected. They don't give a second thought to the power of representation or, conversely, the implications of being rendered completely invisible at the mercy of people's imagination and misinformation. To be reflected in media and culture, in a way that is authentic and true, gives us the space to dispel whatever myths or stereotypes someone may have about transgender people. It invites our allies to understand who we are and do their part in shifting the cultural landscape toward acceptance and inclusion. Visibility also sends signals to other trans folks who have been ostracized by family or forced to be no disclosure under threat of violence and discrimination. *Original Plumbing* was a way of telling other guys that we are indeed living, loving, and thriving all over the planet. *OP* was the original celebration. It affirmed transgender masculinity in all its modes and possibilities. It substantiated the cool confidence of individualism that so many of us walked with in the world. We shook up the boring binary ideals with our genderfucking raucousness of kinky pansexuals. We were different. Our gender was couture and sexy.

Amos and Rocco captured our good side. They were the first to understand transmasculinity not as a bland copy of cisgender men but something new, deliberate, and, dare I say, better. They saw the culture we were shaping and the new inroads to manhood we were creating. What they did with *Original Plumbing* was monumental and will be an iconic piece of LGBTQ history for decades to come.

—TIQ MILAN

Photo by Lydia Daniller

PREFACE

When we first started *Original Plumbing* in 2009, it was for two reasons: to feed personal, creative freedom, and to create something that was a necessity. Virtual platforms for self-representation didn't exist then like they do now. The trans male community was basically invisible. We knew there was a need for something like *OP*; that, at its simplest, it would be entertaining, and, at its best, it could save lives.

After spending years organizing community events and performing around the country, bringing trans men out to his shows, Rocco had a long list of contacts under his belt. Amos had a passion for art books and storytelling stemming from his photography, and a deep understanding of how to aesthetically elevate a self-published project. One fateful day, while Amos was shooting Rocco for a trans photo series, a partnership between the two was magically formed.

We wanted to make a print magazine, not a digital one, because we saw it as an art project and a potential time capsule of trans male

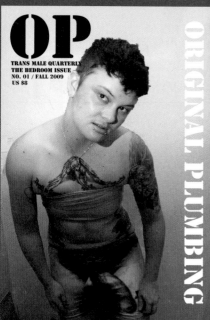

OP

TRANS MALE QUARTERLY
THE BEDROOM ISSUE
NO. 01 / FALL 2009
US $8

ORIGINAL PLUMBING

OP

TRANS MALE QUARTERLY
THE HAIR ISSUE
NO. 02 / WINTER 2010
US $8

OP

TRANS MALE QUARTERLY

The Health and Safer Sex Issue
NO. 03 / SPRING 2010 / US $8

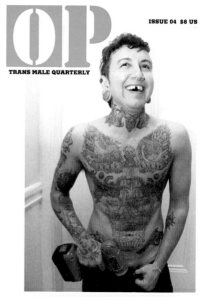

OP

TRANS MALE QUARTERLY

ISSUE 04 $8 US

WORKIN' STIFF

culture. With print comes something to hold on to and flip through, to rip up and hide under your bed, to lose in between novels in your bookshelf. Amos was inspired by zines that spoke to a sometimes-underground, often-artsy world, like *BUTT* and *S.T.H.* (*Straight to Hell*), and never stopped collecting glossy teen magazines like *Teen Beat* and *Bop*. As pop culture lovers, we were motivated to create something specific for trans guys. *OP* was intended to be a space where we could share other trans people's stories without making it "Trans 101" or exploitative: a snapshot of the community, made from within the community. Neither of us were ever at a shortage for ideas and future visions for features or themes. And for ten years, *OP* continued to be the premier publication by and for trans men.

Original Plumbing launched at a time when the world at large seemed to think that print was dead. *OP* never felt the ramifications of such a sentiment; the first edition, The Bedroom Issue, sold out before it even left the printers! The immediate response from potential readers and media outlets was electrifying. Still, we'll never forget those early days of *OP*—spending long days, and even longer nights, setting up our "office" in coffee shops or in one of our bedrooms. We'd feed off each other's energy for days at a time, scripting ideas for future issues, making lists about potential collaborations, and brainstorming how we could impact the larger landscape of trans representation in media. We were passionate, but we were DIY: Our trips to the post office were infamous. We'd lug Ikea bags packed with hundreds of magazines—often hand-labeled, always in manila envelopes—to ship all over the world. Postal workers loved to hate us, and we never did figure out a way to streamline the process of mass mailing. (We're artists, leave us alone!)

With each new issue of *Original Plumbing* came release parties all over North America, which inspired more dance parties, Pride events, bookstore readings, and even the "Trans Dating Game!" featuring Rocco, who channeled the energy of a vintage game-show host onstage at the Stud nightclub in San Francisco, with trans men as the focus. *OP* events followed the tradition of the magazine—creating real-life trans male spaces, beyond the pages and into the world.

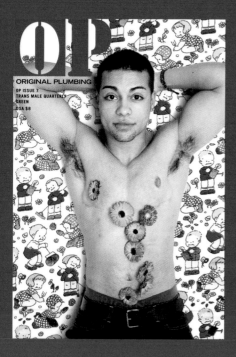

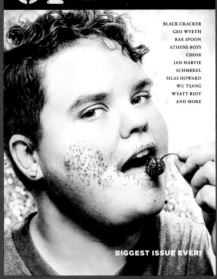

OP ORIGINAL PLUMBING

TRANS MALE QUARTERLY
ISSUE 9 / **ENTERTAINMENT**
USA $8

BLACK CRACKER
GEO WYETH
RAE SPOON
ATHENS BOYS
CHOIR
IAN HARVIE
SCHMEKEL
SILAS HOWARD
WU TSANG
WYATT RIOT
AND MORE

BIGGEST ISSUE EVER!

TRANS MALE
QUARTERLY
USA $8.00

THE JOCK ISSUE
ORIGINAL PLUMBING

10

Spring 2013 / Issue 11

OP
ORIGINAL PLUMBING
Trans Male Quarterly
$9 US

THE
HERO
ISSUE

HONORING TRANS HEROES OF THE PAST AND PRESENT

OP
FALL 2013 / ISSUE 12
ORIGINAL PLUMBING
TRANS MALE QUARTERLY
$9 US

PARTY

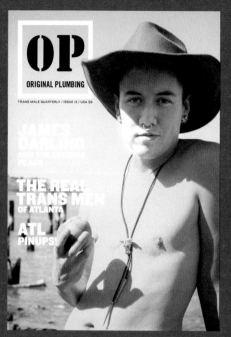

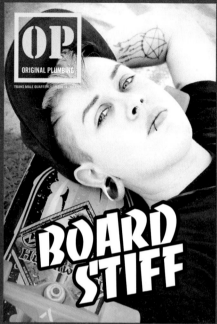

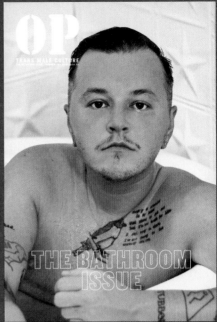

As language and identities shifted over the years, the pages of *OP* featured work not only by those who identify as FTM, trans male, or men of trans experience but also many who are nonbinary, genderqueer, and transmasculine of center. It's difficult to take a step back and see how far the trans community has come regarding visibility since the launch of *OP*'s first issue ten years ago. Yet, while vocabulary has developed and the trans narrative has gotten louder through platforms like Instagram and YouTube, we are still a marginalized community. Scrolling through any major media outlet will show you that trans stories are still largely told by cisgender people and folks from outside the community.

When we started *OP*, we had no idea we would make it to twenty issues. Or to ten years. We're not planners. We're fly by the seat of your pants–ers. We do things instinctually and guided by our desire to make a difference through art and expression. If we'd thought about what *OP* could've become for longer than a second, we probably never would have made the magazine. That's just how we work: fast, hard, and unapologetically. Whether you're just learning about *OP* today or have been a reader and supporter from the beginning, we thank you for taking this trip with us.

This book—a collection of our favorite moments from each issue of *Original Plumbing*—is dedicated to so many people in our community. It is dedicated to anyone who ever picked up a copy of *OP* to find themselves, to trailblazers who shared their stories publicly, and to those who build community just by showing up. It is dedicated to those working on the front lines of the trans civil rights movement, striving to make this world a safer place, and to all trans people living authentically, and especially to those who strive to do so. By existing, you're changing the world.

Love,

AMOS MAC & ROCCO KAYIATOS

OP

TRANS MALE QUARTERLY
THE BEDROOM ISSUE
NO. 01 / FALL 2009
US $8

ORIGINAL PLUMBING

WHY ORIGINAL PLUMBING?

Whether or not we hang on to our original plumbing is up to us, but for the trans guys that do, "original plumbing" is a term often used when referring to our genitals, junk, business, family jewels, bits, the "downstairs" parts. It is the aim of *OP* to shoot true diversity in the FTM community; in size, age, body, surgery, hormone use and non-use, because it is our belief that surgery and hormones don't necessarily make the man... It's more than just that. Maybe it's an attitude, a swagger, a limp wrist, or just an awareness of one's self. Needless to say, there is not just one way to be a trans man.

What initially began as a zine to showcase photographs I had taken of various trans men in the community quickly snowballed into something much larger. Trans guys from all over the world started pitching ideas and wanting to help out and it was clear to me that we were ready for a magazine like this to exist. I was tired of waiting around to see an accurate representation of the trans male community in magazine form, so with the help of some friends and tons of inspiration from the people around me, I present to you the first issue of *Original Plumbing*: a magazine for trans guys, made by trans guys.

Issue #1 is the Bedroom Issue. What better way to get to know someone than to hang around in their personal space and ask them questions while they lounge in next to nothing? As this is the initial issue it seems only appropriate that the theme is focused on getting to know the first *Original Plumbing* models—Elijah, Cyd, Tuck, and Jay R—while you get to know us as a magazine.

Thanks for reading, and see you in the winter for *OP* #2, the Hair Issue, where we will obsess over the hairy, the hairless, and everyone in between!

Amos Mac
Editor In Chief

xoxo
Amos

COVER MODEL: Cyd Nova; photo by Amos Mac

ELIJAH

"I got these shorts a long time ago; a friend made them then my girlfriend's mom hemmed them for me. I only wear them on special occasions."

Photo by Amos Mac

FUNKY BISEXUAL

TUCK

"UNLIMITED TEXTING"

Knowing that texting is Tuck's preferred mode of communication and the admitted way he "woos" women, we decided to interview him via SMS.

ROCCO: So, you're a porn blogger by profession, you get paid to write dirty. Do you talk dirty in bed?

TUCK: No, I freeze up verbally in bed and all I can do is grunt. I love being on the receiving end of nasty talk though.

R: Do you like being on the receiving end of other things in bed?

T: Damn right. Ever since my first shot of T I've been an anything goes kind of fucker. Also I'm pretty much just a man-whore that loves sex any way I can get it.

R: So would you call yourself a sex addict?

R: Cause I would.

T: I'm not a sex addict. I know this because I found trans bed death whilst dating a foxy blonde for two years. I wanted to die but I never strayed.

T: On the other hand. My life revolves around anal. My work is porn. I think about sex all the fucking time.

T: My jokes are heavily sexual and I am fortunate enough to get laid consistently.

T: You only think I'm an addict cause I keep trying to shower with you.

R: I love showering with you.

R: As your good friend I know this: Sex is a PRIORITY. If you go a couple days without you say it has been forever and are afraid it'll never happen again. Why?

T: I love showering with you. You know why I freak out? It's the exact same as having a half empty pint of ice cream.

T: What if the store stops selling Ben and Jerry's? What if I never get ass again? I would die. I would become a monk or become Goth and hiss at people on the bus.

R: If you had to choose between sex or ice cream?

T: That's incredibly tough. I guess I would choose sex and then eat more cookie dough.

INTERVIEW BY : ROCCO KAYIATOS
PORTRAITS : AMOS MAC

R: What do you look for in girls you have sex with? And what type of girls do you like to get into relationships with? Is there a difference?

T: For sex I'm wide open. I love girls of all flavors. Busty thick girls. Pocket-sized waif girls. Girls I don't even like! I mean I have to somewhat find them attractive now that I don't have beer goggles.

R: I know, you need a girl that can give you a good double fisting from time to time.

T: Ha no but I need a girl that loves everything in bed. I hate being limited.

T: When I'm in love I'm a totally different person though. I morph into a well-behaved monogamous boy within five seconds and spend my time baking and spooning.

R: Since you are single and you bake and spoon with me—am I your girlfriend?

T: I wish you were my girlfriend. Or I wish I was your daughter. Actually I wish I were both.

T: I wish you would triple fist me.

T: Really I just want a smoking hot busty brunette girl to wed and make babies with. Using my nineteen-year-old nephew's sperm of course.

T: Don't make me sound too twisted or I will never find a wife.

T: I just don't want to end up watching bad porn in a Tijuana flat at the age of 80 like my father.

T: Let me see it first heh.

R: Sorry I was gone for a sec. My roommate ordered pizza and they gave her the wrong one. This one has nothing but clams and cheese on it. I ate some. Am I gross? It was kinda gross, but good. It's still pizza.

T: I can't believe you ate clam pizza.

R: I know. Am I disgusting? Would you have eaten it? Come over I have more.

T: I would never eat it. But I don't eat water animals anyway. I have a headache and I'm full. You should put in there that if I actually like a girl I'm an awkward nervous wreck. And sweat too much.

TALKIN 'BOUT A TRANSFORMATION: 24 HOURS ON CRAIGSLIST

BY HANK T.

AS someone who has found their last several dwellings, jobs, bikes, rideshares, and many, many, many long walks on the beach via Craigslist (CL), I am here to share my critically savvy eye for effective CL branding. Unofficially and not surprisingly, it appears that San Francisco reigns supreme for no-strings-attached (NSA) hookups with guys assigned-male-at-birth (I like to call them GAMABs... and that makes me GAFAB!). Sadly, I no longer live in San Francisco and, in fact, recently moved to Minneapolis, where CL does not seem to have nearly the same cultural salience (see Table 1), but writing about the glories of hookups in SF makes my current celibacy a little less painful.

If we use CL San Francisco as a case study, maybe we can learn a thing or two. First, let me share with you some effective marketing strategies based on my random survey of ads yesterday. Not that I want to advocate ageist or otherwise unsavory politics, but I am struck by the fact that most of the 35 ads seeking sex with GAMABs posted their ages, and those ages ranged from 21 to 37. Hmm...no one over 40 looking for sex, eh?!

Many of these ads emphasized the author's youthfulness and masculinity such as boyish good looks, muscles, tattoos, and facial hair. There was one explicitly genderqueer ad, while others used an entirely different strategy and emphasized their "tight [front] hole" or "dripping pussy" and "boobs." I suppose it depends upon whom you're trying to attract—one who's more attracted to masculinity or one who associates the height of sexual pleasure with female body parts...or simply a GAMAB that's as hot and horny as you are. Maybe you don't care what or whom your GAMAB prefers, but at the risk of reinforcing the binary you may want to create two separate ads—one for each target market if you will.

Beyond the land of milk and honey, I chatted with some guys living in the apparently drought-stricken cities Chicago and London (neither made the top 10) to see what they think the barriers are. Our London lad reports that he recently posted two ads, "two weekends in a row and left one up during the week as well and ALL of the replies I got...were from [GAMABs] thinking I was MTF even though I explicitly said I was not. I explicitly said I was not. On the flip side, the concurrent ad I ran where I did not disclose got loads more responses (though eventually nothing came of it…)."

My Chicago informant actually met his partner through CL! However, that match took them both out of circulation. He says many GAMAB-loving guys are similarly partnered and, thus, not cruising. He has also observed that guys are "using other sites including Manhunt, Adult Friendfinder, Bear 411, etc.," and some guys are too scared to cruise online for fear of their safety. The good news is that, increasingly, GAMABs are posting for GAFABs (again, see TABLE 1).

Perhaps we might all engage in a collective exercise and answer one of these ads or create one and increase visibility and possibilities for action. On a cautionary note, very few ads posted by GAMABs mention "safe sex" explicitly. So when you come across a hot ad that only mentions "disease free" or "clean," you may want to clarify what is meant by this. Cheers!

*based on a sampling of CL ads (search term, "FTM") one fine day in August 2009

TABLE 1: Top Ten Cities for Hookups with Non-Trans Men via Craigslist*

Rank	Metro Area	Ads by GAMABs	Metro Area	Ads by GAFABs
1	San Francisco	16	San Francisco	35
2	Atlanta	16	Portland	13
3	New York	14	Atlanta	12
4	Philadelphia	14	Los Angeles	12
5	Portland	9	New York	9
6	Seattle	8	Philadelphia	9
7	Phoenix	7	Seattle	7
8	Los Angeles	3	Washington, DC	7
9	Dallas	3	Minneapolis	6
10	Boston	3	Boston	4

JAY R

Photo by Amos Mac

"Last year my sister walked in the room when I was talking to my mom and told her I was going to turn into a boy 'and get a dick and everything.' My mom looked at me and said, 'You better not just come home and randomly show me your dick. Tell me ahead of time!'"

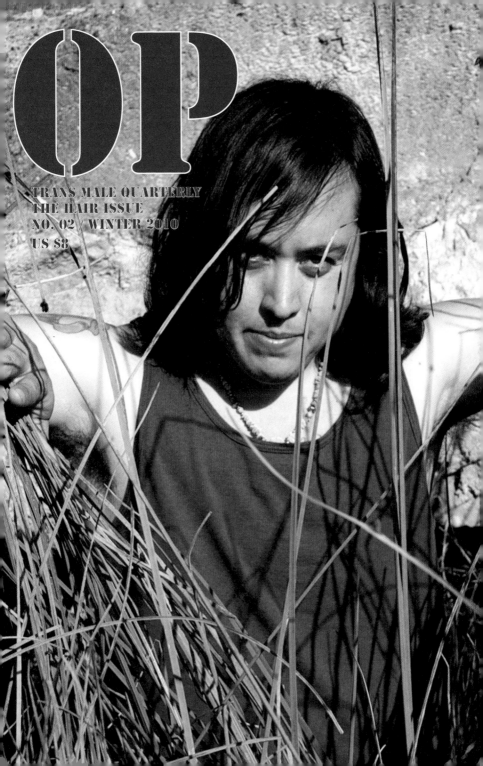

OP

TRANS MALE QUARTERLY
THE HAIR ISSUE
NO. 02 / WINTER 2010
US $8

LETTER FROM THE EDITOR

A lot of trans guys early in transition who choose to take hormones obsess over hair growth, counting their newest facial hairs, keeping journals to document the days, or perhaps even making a YouTube video or six to document the excitement as each new chin hair pokes through. It's a given that the newness to things such as the growth of hair is a subject close to many of our hearts. But what happens when that excitement goes away and becomes old news? How do we maintain the hair that we already have and what can we expect as we age?

In the Hair Issue we tackle that subject and dive a little deeper. You'll notice Rocco weave the subject of hair *loss* through different interviews, a consequence we often don't think about before we start to take the hormones that masculinize us. Also in this issue, a guide to manscaping, and stories from several distinct voices on how the subject of hair has affected their lives post-transition.

On these pages you'll meet our second round of models: Khane, a Brooklyn barber who buzzes intricate designs into the heads of people all over the five boroughs and beyond; Ayden, an adorable Bear from the "mean streets" of Canada; Dylan, a Zumba instructor who allows me to drape him in faux fur for artistic purposes; and cover model Chris, a silky-locked "Criminal Queer" whose filmmaking keeps the community on its toes.

In our spring issue we'll be tackling the subject of trans health and safe sex. We'll discuss herbal ways to aid a transition without taking testosterone, how to prepare your body for surgery, and safer sex practices for guys like us. Can't wait!

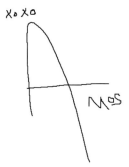

XoXo

Amos Mac
Editor & Photographer In Chief
Original Plumbing Magazine

COVER MODEL: Chris Vargas;
photo by Amos Mac

PARIS EXISTRANS 2009

Words and photographs by Elliot Foxprince
Interview translations by Jane Cope

"Mme. Bachelot! More Work with and for Trans' and Intersexes!"

Existrans, a group for trans rights and visibility, organizes a march every year for transgender and intersex people. It originated in Paris in 1997, with about only 60 people in attendance. In 2007 a march was organized in Madrid, Spain, and by 2008 the cities of Brussels, Bilbao, and Lisbon also joined in.

Currently, there are marches organized by Existrans all over the world. This year's Paris trans march was a call to the French Minister of Health and Sports, Roselyne Bachelot, to do more work for trans and intersex people of France. (Mme. Bachelot had removed trans identity from the list of long-term psychological illnesses this past May, but the local trans community insists she still needs to do much more.)

On the morning of the march, we gathered at the base of the Church Saint-Jean-Baptiste de Belleville, and the crowd quickly grew in number. The march began on Rue de Belleville with megaphones and high spirits. We poured through the streets of Belleville, with photographers buzzing all around and crowds growing on the sidewalks to see what the commotion was about. I felt an overpowering sense of belonging. The people around me, although they were shouting in a language I don't speak, were shouting for MY rights! For OUR rights!

For the rights of every person who struggles with his or her gender, for the rights of every person who doesn't fit a binary.

Toward the end of the route, the Rue de Belleville curved, and from the top of the hill I could see the Tour Eiffel standing tall in the distance. It hit me right then that I was actually in Paris, that I was a part of something larger than my own personal gender struggles, surrounded by people just like me, standing up for myself. Everyone around me was chanting and cheering, and for the first time in my life, I felt good about myself, so proud of who I am and who I have become.

When we reached the end of the march, we stood together at la Place de la République—trans men, trans women, genderqueers, gender-fuckers, cisgendered people, allies, and onlookers. Minutes after arriving, we were directed to lie down and have a moment of silence in memory of all the trans people who have been killed just for being different. It made me want to cry. The whole event was likewise overwhelming. It's very important to realize that although we are all different in so many ways, we can still stand together and fight for our rights as individuals and as a community. I felt nothing but love surrounding us in the park at la Place de la République, and as we marched through the streets of Paris.

FLORYAN

Age: 19

From: Ile-de-France, department 92

How do you identify?
I identify as a bio-guy who's just developing. However, I do announce my status as trans to advance the larger cause.

Is this your first march?
It's my fifth or sixth. I've been a co-organizer for most of these years, except for the first year. This year, I've been more involved than ever because I'm almost finished with school.

How do you feel about the trans community in Paris?
We're pretty closely knit, but we're not visible enough.

BRUCE

Age: 27

From: Just outside of Paris

How do you identify?
Trans. My identity moves around a lot.

What pronouns do you prefer?
Male, but it depends. I prefer "he," but I like being called "she" as a sissy boy by my fag friends. I don't want to give up my fag and feminist sides.

Is this your first march?
It's my fifth. There are more young people and more trans boys, pirates, and queers now. There are also a lot of young new people in the new trans group, Outrans.

How do you feel about the trans community in Paris?
It's really starting to move! There are a lot more young, energetic people now. There are also new ways to identify as trans and more visibility. It's unfortunate that politics haven't followed suit. For example, if you don't take hormones, you can't get legal papers. I feel sad that you have to conform to a normative way of being transgender to get legal papers for hormones, a psychiatrist, and surgery.

KAY

Age: 31
From: Toulouse
How do you identify?
I identify myself as a transboi, a transgender person. I've never been a girl, although I've been put in this box, but I'm not a guy either. I'm not trying to become a guy, even if now people who don't know me see me like that. I have a trans identity!

How do you feel about the trans community in Paris?
I don't know if there's a trans male community in Paris. I mean there's a kind of trans' community in the way that people who are activists in one way or another (could be art also) know each other but there are a lot of trans people who disappear after their transition. And within this community, mixed with transgender and queer people, there are clearly more and more trans guys. And apart from that there's no real trans male community in Paris. The Outrans Association was founded by trans guys this year, but I'm not sure they're creating a community because there are also cisgendered people in the association and I know a lot of what they're doing and I really don't get this impression. In France the community is more a mix about trans', queers, activists, feminists, and some others who are around.

ANAKIN

an organizer for Existrans

Age: 23

From: Paris

About the march...
When it comes to organization, everyone does small things. The collective is large. The march represents lots of different backgrounds and lots of different ways of being trans so sometimes it can be hard to get along. It's positive overall, though, because we can work for common goals.
How do you feel about the trans community in Paris?
I feel like people feel safe to transition here. People feel a lot more confident in themselves as the community becomes more and more visible.

CLO

Age: 32

How do you identify? As a tigger!

What pronouns do you prefer?
Mostly male. I don't care if people I know say "she."

Was this your first march?
No, it's my third or fourth! I came here first as a dyke and was shy. Now it's my march!

How do you feel about the trans community in Paris?

I live in the Marais, the gay area of Paris. It was awful because for several years I was in the dyke community even though I'm not a dyke. In the past 2 years though, I've met queer family and other trans guys. In the beginning, this was exciting and we became a family quickly. After about 6 months, everyone began physically transitioning. This was hard for me because I don't want to take hormones or have surgery. But it's okay because they're friends and we can be different. It was just hard for 1 or 2 months because I had to figure out we're not exactly the same. I'm 32, I've already made my transition.

LOU

Age: 18

From: Paris

How do you identify?
I don't identify myself, it's simpler.

What pronouns do you prefer?
Whatever.

Is this your first march?
No, it's my third.

KHANE
THE BROOKLYN BARBER

"Even though I identify with the trans community, I also identify with the butch community. When I barber I use 'she' because it's important to me to use that pronoun in this male dominated profession. There are 'female' barbers, but I don't see them getting notoriety. That's why I take every opportunity to do interviews, barber in public, and post photos to show that female-bodied barbers do exist and are just as good if not better than persons identified male at birth."

TAILS OF A KNOTTY BOI
ASHER O. KOLIEBOI

"Jamaica, Jamaica!"

The words hit my ears like darts. My body tenses and I feel my ears getting hot. Before turning around I already know who the culprit is: a white, twenty-something, upper-middle class suburbanite. Trying to ignore the calls I keep walking. The heckler continues.

"Jamaica, Jamaica!"

Who is she talking to? I am not Jamaican. I turn to face my perpetrator. She puts her hand to her mouth and exhales an imaginary cloud of smoke. I flare my nostrils and grit my teeth as I storm away in a mixture of embarrassment and rage. The simple stroll in the mall with my father has turned into a life-altering event.

> *But hair, simply my hair, was one aspect of discrimination I did not know I needed to be prepared to handle.*

Radical change has been a constant theme in my life. Yet, while embracing my race and challenging gender stereotypes I never considered how big of a role my hair would play in my transition and people's perception of my masculinity. Growing up black in a predominantly white neighborhood, I witnessed my father being pulled over or followed in stores, so I had a good idea of what to expect when I decided to transition in 2004. I knew my dark skin and thick frame might make me vulnerable in a society that thrives on criminalizing black men. But hair, simply my hair, was one aspect of discrimination I did not know I needed to be prepared to handle.

Long before I began my journey in gender fluidity, I embarked on a journey of racial self-discovery. As I began to educate myself about the experience of people in the African Diaspora I could not help but look in the mirror. The chemical relaxers I had used to straighten my hair for the past eight years did not jive with my newfound radical understanding of race and racism. Similar to the internal dialogue addressing my gender identity and expression I would have a few years later, I began to question what I had been taught about beauty and changed my appearance to reflect my politics. I believe the physical is political. In August 2003 I cut my hair and began growing dreadlocks.

Six years later, my long, vivacious dreadlocks cascade down my back like a charcoal waterfall. Though the decision to start locking my hair has been liberating, it has also been bittersweet. Since choosing to take testosterone, my hair has been a source of controversy. My coiffure establishes my position as a radical afrocentric warrior, a visual representation of my resistance to the forced enslavement and colonization of black bodies.

Though I may view my hair as a public symbol of resistance to white beauty standards and white normativity, I am often boxed in by the trite and antiquated stereotypes relentlessly hurled at black men. I am often perceived as intimidating, a criminal, exotic, or in some cases effeminate due to my choice of hairstyle. People also see me as a weed smoking drug dealer.

A white guy on a bike approaches me as I am walking home from a club. I try to ignore him as he struggles to catch up with me. "Hey man," the winded rider calls after me. "You know where I can buy some weed?" Full of liquid courage I whirl around and scream, "Why would I know that?" Startled by my answer he glances at my shoulder and exclaims, "Because you're a big black guy with dreads."

My courage fades and I go home to sulk. What is most painful about incidents like this is they are not isolated, but, instead, ongoing reminders that no matter how many degrees I have or how many smiles I dole out while walking down the street, I will always be viewed as a dealer or thug. These incidents serve as a reminder of the very present and real value placed on black men's bodies.

Transmasculine communities have always been an unwelcoming space for my mane. Since choosing to transition I have visited countless websites and thumbed through many zines with "passing" tips that urge trans men to "go for a short-back-n'-sides cut." Such suggestions do not take into consideration black masculinity, black hair, or its cultural significance. Like all masculinity, transmasculinity is not a monolith. Cutting my hair and wearing a polo shirt, like the tips suggest, not only erases my individuality but my radical racial identity as well.

AYDEN

"My hairy body is a very frequent topic of conversation amongst pretty much everybody. I think they have the perception that my body hair is some kind of magic, like unicorns."

DEAR TESTOSTERONE

CHASE RYAN JOYNT

Dear Testosterone,

I fear there has been a grave miscommunication between us. Prior to embarking upon this journey together, I was under the impression that we had a specific plan of action. Seeing as we've had many years to prepare for this partnership, it comes as a great surprise to me that we have become so fractured. So in the interest of clarity, I thought I'd write you about some of our most pressing issues.

I realize I might have made some assumptions here (and we all know where that leads), but I must admit that I was kind of hoping that you would have dropped my voice and/or broadened my chest PRIOR to providing me with an exorbitant and unmanageable amount of ass hair. Would it have killed you to say, "Chase, just so you know, when this nice lady sticks that needle into your thigh, your ass will soon be transformed into a Chia Pet"?

On that note, I'd also like to mention the fact that I no longer seem to have pubic hair, but rather something more like an epic pubic labyrinth forest.

Not only is this mildly to moderately embarrassing, but it's causing my poor leg hair to have a serious identity crisis.

How is hair expected to survive when some days it feels like ass hair, and other days it feels like pubic hair—but all the while it remains in the same place on my thigh? Some clarification on this front would be deeply appreciated.

With everything I've asserted thus far, it may appear that I am ungrateful for all that you have "provided" for me. And I don't believe this is the case, however, in light of the Great Hair Parade of 2008, I should probably also mention that I'm having some further concerns about the thirteen chest hairs you have so graciously bestowed upon me.

Why must they be so long, like braided-hair-on-a-ten-year-old-

girl long? The admittedly useless length of these hairs only further underlines how much effort you could otherwise be putting into my SIDEBURNS.

I thought I made it explicitly clear that I would take the voice cracking, I would take the backne (thanks for that), and I would take the moody temperament of a perpetually misunderstood thirteen-year-old—but only if IN EXCHANGE for some rockabilly-sportin'-motorcycle-ridin'-Elvis-mother-fucking-Presley sideburns… yet you have mysteriously given me nothing. And I am not impressed.

I understand that this letter might come as a shock to you, especially considering how adoringly we once used to speak of our love. But I do still hold great hopes for our future and sincerely hope that you might consider the above and make some adjustments accordingly.

Yours,
Chase

DYLAN

30, OAKLAND, ZUMBA INSTRUCTOR

Dylan wears a faux fur coat from Thrift Town.
Photographed on San Francisco's Tire Beach by Amos Mac.

WHAT'S **YOUR** FAVORITE PART OF BEING A TRANSSEXUAL?

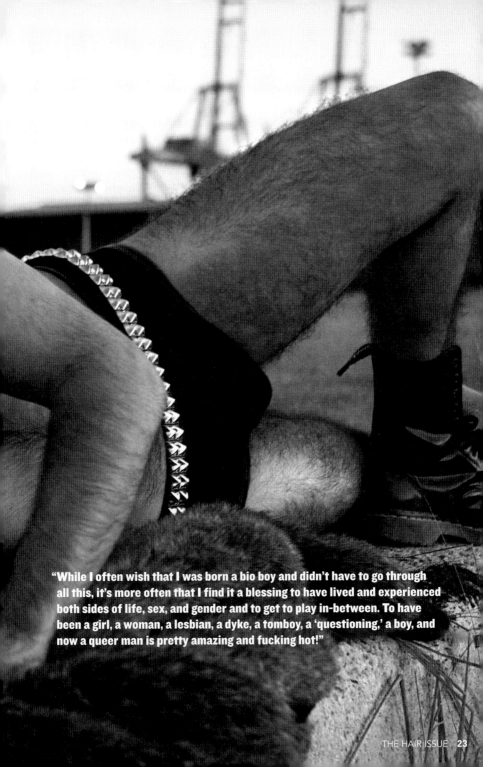

"While I often wish that I was born a bio boy and didn't have to go through all this, it's more often that I find it a blessing to have lived and experienced both sides of life, sex, and gender and to get to play in-between. To have been a girl, a woman, a lesbian, a dyke, a tomboy, a 'questioning,' a boy, and now a queer man is pretty amazing and fucking hot!"

THE CASE FOR MANSCAPING

JOSHUA KLIPP

For the purposes of this article, "manscaping" is defined as:
The grooming of testosterone-induced body hair from the neck to the nether regions.

WHY MANSCAPE?

Most trans men spent the better part of their youth and young adulthood envying cis dudes' ability to grow body hair. But now some of us—with hormonal enhancement—are finally able to grow it ourselves. Given the effort that body hair growth takes, the reasonable question begs: Why the hell would we want to shave it off?

Three compelling answers to this question:

1. In general, those who love us also love it when we manscape.
2. Manscaping is an indicator of self-care and self-love.
3. Manscaping displays the goodies, your junk, the giving tree, Tiny Tim's topiary, your bits, that you're hung like a horse… fly. You get the idea.

Working backwards from number 3: A transman friend and I recently discussed our private parts and he asked me, "Am I a freak?" Unfortunately, it seems that many trans men harbor this secret fear. The best advice for anything that terrifies you: Take it head on. Turn it around and take mad pride in your body. Trans men are hot, sexy, and it's time we stop apologizing for what's in our pants and start showing it off. How to start: Manscape it. Trim back that bush and go stand in front of a mirror. Look at it. Love it. Touch it. Encourage others to touch it as well. And while you're at it, notch down the fur crawling out of your shirt collar and bursting out of your armpits like a bad weave, too.

Which brings us to number 2: Manscaping as an indicator of self-care and self-love.

It doesn't require a lot of fuss; any trimming makes it look like you care. Manscaping will also: (a) make your muscles look bigger (including the love muscle, as covered above);

(b) increase sensation on your skin; and (c) improve your hygiene. Doesn't take a rocket scientist to know you'll smell better if your deodorant faces a smaller uphill battle. And as we know, smell means just about everything when it comes to our lovers.

And this brings us back to number 1: our lovers… who love manscaping.

A recent poll of admirers of trans men (including men, women, trans women, and other trans men) revealed that:

- 88% find manscaping to be a turn ON.
- Of that 88%, manscaping preferences fall into the following order of priority: back hair, below the belt, chest hair, armpits.
- 60% of lovers of trans men have assisted in the act of manscaping (and most said they'd do it again, and again, and again).

Numbers don't lie: manscaping is sexy—even the act of doing it is viewed as potential foreplay. The majority of those polled weren't into a smooth body shave, but preferred a nice even trim. And reasons given for why manscaping is so important include: nice view, easy access, and shows off muscles.

If you were waiting for some proof that manscaping is hot, now you have it. Next up: how to do it.

CHOOSE YOUR TOOL

At the Walgreens electronics counter, the clerk opens the glass case and awkwardly lays out my requested manscaping tool options. He first hands me the Philips Norelco box, adorned with a photo of a smiling, hairless man standing under a streaming showerhead, and says, "Dude, that is so gay." After making a few notes, I stash my steno pad and tell the clerk, "I'll take the gay one."

HOW TO MANSCAPE

Now, how to put these tools to use?

Under no circumstances do I endorse the nuclear, down-to-the-skin manscaping method. At least not regularly. It might be kinky fun for like, one night. But you'll pay for it over the next month. Between the itching, razor bumps, and ingrown hairs, once is enough to have a really good time and learn a valuable lesson.

Photo by Amos Mac

Back hair: You'll need help, but apparently, according to my poll, people are excitedly standing by to aid you. Funny (trans)man comedian Ian Harvie has offered to carve a Boston Red Sox letter "B" into a hairy back (or ass), so that when the hair starts to grow back in, it'll "look all aged or antiqued, or like ivy on a wall." So tasty, I'm picking hair out of my teeth already. Recommendation: beard trimmer, 2–3 guard.

Chest hair: I prefer an even 2 guard. Joe Gallagher of Joe's Barbershop suggests a 3 guard on the pecs, 2 guard on the abs, and leave the treasure trail thick. Solid advice from a former Mr. Leather and the guy I trust with my pate. Joe says you can even try shaving the hair on your stomach in the form of abs. But don't try this on a beer gut. No one will fall for it, unless they're super wasted.

Armpit hair: Most trans men probably had shaggy armpit hair long before transition anyway. But now, hygiene factors in. I like to take it down a couple inches with scissors, then clean up the edges with a beard trimmer. Be careful, and use a comb if necessary (but do not use your roommate's comb).

Nether regions: This is a tricky but important area. Depending on the strength of your tool, you may need to manually trim before going in with the weed whacker. Stay focused. One moment of distraction can lead to worlds of pain. Start with a 3 guard, then take it down to whatever makes you happy. BE CAREFUL. Use mirrors. Brush off frequently to check progress. Take your time. Give yourself at least 15–20 minutes of uninterrupted time, and be able to shower afterward.

Clean up: While manscaping is hot, hair trimmings are not. Do something good with your hard-earned scraps. Use it as mulch, compost it, donate it to the local drag king crew. Whatever you do—clean it up. Do not leave it for your roommates or lovers to find stuck to their toothbrushes, in between their toes, or wedged into shower caulking. Be clean, be shaven, but be nice, too.

So in conclusion, I believe manscaping is definitely the way to go. But don't take my word for it—try it yourself. If you don't like it, shoot yourself in the ass a few times and it'll grow right back. But do me a favor and try it just once. You'll look sharp, smell good, and end up loving your beautiful, sexy body even more.

CRIMINAL QUEER

INTERVIEW ROCCO KAYIATOS
AMOS MAC PHOTOGRAPHS

Filmmaker Chris Vargas has been making queer cinematic madness for the past decade. He constantly stirs up controversy within the LGBT community across the globe with his boundary-pushing and hilarious films—think Christopher Guest does radical queer anti-assimilation.

CRIMINAL QUEER: CHRIS VARGAS

Rocco: Introduce yourself and tell me a bit about who you are and what you do.

Chris: My name is Chris Vargas, I am 31 beautiful years old, originally from the San Fernando Valley in Southern California and I currently live in Oakland and make movies and videos with my friends and lover.

Did you go to school for filmmaking or is it a hobby that has become a way of life?

Well, I made my first Super 8 film *Road Rash* while I was slowly pulling it together in my mid-twenties at LA City College. That lil' film has traveled, playing in LGBT film festivals across the world. Then I finally transferred to UC Santa Cruz and majored in Film and Digital Media; now I go to UC Berkeley where I am making more videos. So I guess it's both a hobby and a way of life. In the past six years I've only had to work one year not doing something related to queer film/video, so my hobby became a way of life. Or rather, not working became a way of life, and film and video has allowed me to pull that off.

So since you don't have to work a day job, what is a typical day like for you, be honest...

Well, recently I've been waking up at a cool 11 or 11:30, which I am not proud of, and I either pull myself together to get to class at 1 p.m. or eventually mosey on over to my studio where I pretend to edit the movie *Criminal Queers* that I am working on, but mostly I check my email obsessively and google myself.

That seems like a good use of time. What is the most interesting thing you have found when googling yourself? Also, tell me about *Criminal Queers*.

From googling myself I have realized that I am not as famous as I thought I'd be by 30 and that Chris Vargas is a good DJ. But then I get to page 3 or so and I realize that lots of people don't really like my movies, mostly *Homotopia*, but I anticipate *Criminal Queers* will have the same reception. It is a movie about abolishing the prison-industrial complex. *Homotopia* is about not getting married, and a lot of gays are not trying to hear about that!

You take on such controversial and intense subject matter, so of course you would see an intense reaction to it. Do you agree with that old phrase "No press is bad press"? Because at least your work gets people talking and thinking. Have you ever gotten into a fight with someone at a screening?

I do agree that "no press is bad press" and there is a lot of potential for me and my collaborator, Eric Stanley, to get sued for our next project but we're all "bring it on!" And, yes we have gotten in many a fight over *Homotopia*, but mostly we've had really good (if sometimes heated) conversations about rethinking this rabid push in California, and all over the nation really, to get married. I mean, my mom even said to me, in so many words, that marriage should be abolished for all people.

Why do you think you guys would get sued? Also do you think it is possible that we would see marriage abolished in our lifetime?

Well, I'd rather not talk about details lest I incriminate myself and others. But, watch out for the movie and you'll see. We may or may not have been deceptive in our intentions to film at a certain iconographic LGBT organization's retail store in the Castro.

And about abolishing the institution of marriage, probably not. And frankly, I'm over trying. Sometimes I wish that gays could just get married already so I can stop hearing them whine about it all the time.

You and your boyfriend would not get married though, right? Or would you?

No way. Maybe some hippie-goddess commitment ceremony with no state license involved, but even that is pushing it. We sort of talked about doing it when we went to Vegas, just because according to my documents I am female and we could actually do it. But then we just made a video about it and we got it out of our system.

OP

TRANS MALE QUARTERLY

The Health and Safer Sex Issue
NO. 03 / SPRING 2010 / US $8

LETTER FROM THE BEDROOM OF THE EDITOR

Dearest Reader,

Is it just me or does the title the Health and Safer Sex Issue make you think of a class you're forced to take in high school? Lucky for you, this is not high school! This is, in fact, a transsexual magazine that shares with you various viewpoints decorated with hot photographs that you may or may not want to rip out and hang on your bedroom wall. That being said, for issue three of *Original Plumbing* we've found five dynamic trans guys that share their health and safe sex experiences with the world, and a crop of new writers that tell us what aspect of health is specifically important to them. Even some of the most squeamish topics are presented in a light that a lot of us can relate to, or at least giggle at.

One thing I'd like to put out there for all of us who live a life of the transmasculine persuasion is the importance of keeping an open dialogue about the future of our health. For various reasons the health lives of trans guys, specifically those who are middle-aged and beyond, have not been fully documented for very long. This leaves the younger generations with a lot of "what ifs" when it comes to the future, especially regarding our lives on and off of hormones. For the sake of the guys that follow in our footsteps it's up to us to be aware of ongoing health issues we encounter and to communicate these patterns with each other.

For those of us on hormones, how will we feel in 20, 30, 60 years? Will we be able to take hormones into old age? If we no longer can, how will it effect our well-being as old men? It's important for us to ask ourselves (our therapists, herbalists, doctors, and each other) these questions, just as it is crucial to check in with our own bodies on a physical and emotional level consistently. Testosterone is powerful stuff. Talk about it.

Be well. See you in late summer with the WORKIN' STIFF issue!

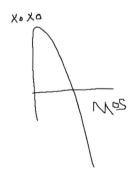

XoXo

Mos

HEALING HANDS

My name is Saul Lorenzo Silva. I'm a massage therapist,
I'm an artist, I'm a go-go dancer, I work as an administrative consultant
at a nonprofit, and I'll soon be a personal trainer.

Photo by Amos Mac

" I constantly strive to grow—mind,
body, and soul. I've done and
continue to do a lot of self-healing
work. I read a lot of books on
Buddhism and struggle to make
meditation a regular part of
my life. I make art, which I find
very healing. And I've worked
really hard with my family and
friends around my transition. My
interpersonal relationships are
very important to me."

A HOLISTIC APPROACH TO TRANS HEALTH

Jacoby Ballard

Conversations about trans health—even within our community—often remain focused on access to respectful allopathic care (hospitals, doctors, nurses, etc.), hormones, and surgery. But there's so much more to trans health, just as there is so much more to anyone's health than the symptom-management approach and major interventions of allopathic care. As an herbalist, health educator, and yoga teacher, my approach to transgender health is about treating the whole person, which may include addressing trauma from a transphobic society, dissolving scar tissue from surgery, opening intercostal muscles often shortened by binding, nourishing the liver that processes hormones, figuring out how to maintain an erection while on estrogen, and more.

Working and teaching within trans communities, I have found many myths about herbs, as well as a general lack in community knowledge about how herbalism may specifically benefit our health as trans and gender nonconforming people. While this forum offers only a cursory introduction, feel free to contact me for more information!

Transitioning through Herbs

There is a myth that herbs can be used to transition. I have researched this extensively in the last five years and found that herbs can slightly masculinize or feminize one's appearance, but do not have the power of allopathic hormones to transform one's secondary sex characteristics. I am often asked about the effects of "Phytoestrogens" and "Phytoandrogens" (or "phytotestosterone") for transition; these are not plant sources of hormones—plants use different hormones than we do. A better name for herbs used to support transition is "phytosterols": these are herbs that act on the endocrine system, but are not hormones themselves.

In short, herbs classified or discussed as "phytoestrogens" act as estrogen blockers—their molecules are received by estrogen receptors in the body but have 1/200 of the strength of estrogen in our bodies; therefore, they block the feminizing effects of endogenous estrogen and may be used by trans men or other folks looking to masculinize their appearance. Some of these herbs are soy, red clover, wild yam, alfalfa, American ginseng, and anise. Similarly, "phytoandrogens" occupy testosterone receptors and may be used by trans women or people looking to feminize. Some sources of "phytoandrogen" are yohimbe, saw palmetto, salmon, zinc, and vitamin A.

Protecting the Liver in Hormone Therapy

Hormones are processed in the liver, so taking exogenous hormones makes our livers process twice as many hormones. As we are often warned, one of the "side effects" of taking hormones is a risk of liver disease, but there are many ways to protect our livers! For anyone taking hormones, I recommend milk thistle in a tincture form or ground up in food—a liver-protectant and nourishing tonic for the liver

Photo by Amos Mac

> *"Herbs classified or discussed as 'phytoestrogens' act as estrogen blockers—their molecules are received by estrogen receptors in the body but have 1/200 of the strength of estrogen in our bodies; therefore, they block the feminizing effects of endogenous estrogen."*

that promotes its longevity and vitality. Milk thistle is not soluble in water and should not be taken as a tea. As a tincture, take 1 dropperful 2 times per day; ground up, take 1 handful of the seeds, grind them in a coffee grinder or mortar and pestle, and sprinkle into food (best uncooked).

Treating Depression and Anxiety from a Transphobic World

Herbs are a great way to address some of the effects of harassment, assault, trauma, and internalized transphobia. One classification of herbs is nervines, which nourish and restore the nervous system, allowing us to act from a more settled place.

Some herbs that do this are skullcap, oatstraw, and passion flower. All three herbs combined make a great tea (1 Tbsp tea to 1 cup water; 1 cup per day), and passion flower and skullcap may be used as tinctures (1 dropperful 2x/day). Another classification of herbs is adaptogens—they help the body adapt to stress, and can elevate one out of the lows of depression or put to rest one's anxiety or hyperactive mind. Some adaptogens I use are American ginseng, ashwagandha, and schizandra. All of these herbs are best as a decocted tea (1 Tbsp herb to 2 cups water; bring to boil, then turn down and let simmer for 20–40 minutes).

"In San Francisco overall we have great access to hormones and primary care. Most guys aren't in SF, so some of their main health concerns may be access to competent primary care and getting on **T**. I really do think a primary issue for us is mental health, and I see access to hormones and surgery as mental health issues because you can feel so crazy when you need those things and can't get them. Then there is the isolation a lot of us feel and body image stuff, depression, anxiety, and a lack of family support. Also harassment when you aren't passing and you're living somewhere not all that hip to the queers, the harassment on a daily basis can sure give you some mental health issues if you didn't have them already! I say that from experience. Poverty and lack of access to jobs and education and housing prevent a lot of trans guys from being able to be healthy too, and of course those issues disproportionately impact trans people of color."

Luke

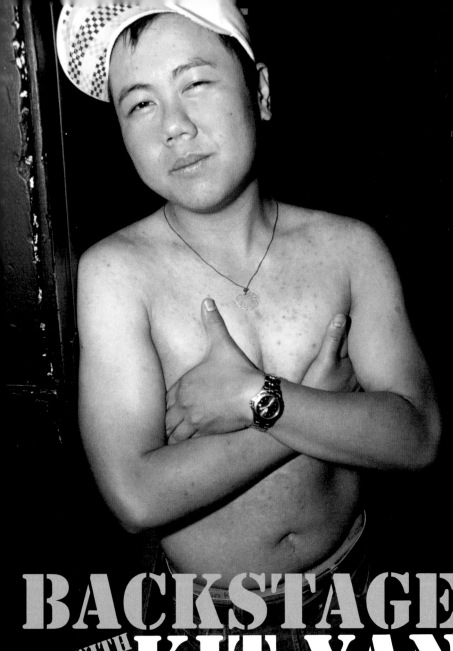

BACKSTAGE
WITH KIT YAN

Interview by Rocco Kayiatos Photo by Amos Mac

Rocco: Introduce yourself!

Kit: Aloha, my name is Kit Yan and I'm a 25-year-old trans slam poet from Hawaii, currently based in New York. I tour solo and also with *Good Asian Drivers*, a poetry folk rock band.

How did you get your start performing?

The first time I performed spoken word was in the 3rd grade, covering the "Peanut-Butter Sandwich" poem by Shel Silverstein and when I discovered slam in college I fell in love with the form. After that, I started competing and was on the Lizard Lounge team repping for Boston. I've been competitive and performing professionally for the past 8 years.

How does your identity influence your work and your audience?

I'm very out in my work because my poems come from a personal place and that includes the identities that I have rooted in the queer, trans, Asian, Asian American, and POC communities. Because those identities drive my content, the audiences tend to be people that come with open ears, people that like stories, connections, and hot queers and people of color looking for a voice that they can see a reflection in.

You tour quite a bit, how do you take care of yourself on the road?

It's really hard on the road, but I try to set small goals to eat regularly, sleep, drink tea, and do something relaxing each day. Since I'm a vegan, I take some vitamins, mangosteen juice, and protein shakes. If I'm sick or feeling low energy, the show suffers and then no one's having a good time.

What three things are crucial for you to feel comfortable in your body?

1. Being surrounded by friends that are great trans allies.

2. Dressing up, because when I'm wearing clothes I like, clothes I have spent so many years wanting to fit, it makes all the difference.

3. I don't always like to bind, but some days I like the feeling of a tight chest.

What is one thing you wish you could go back and tell yourself when you started your transition?

I would tell myself to buy some damn Rogaine in bulk for the future and to take a smaller dose each week rather than taking the full 2-week dose. The peaks and valleys of the T's effect on my mood made it difficult to ease into my physical transition.

Do you see yourself as an educator as well as an entertainer?

Absolutely. The content of my poetry fosters conversation, so what's great is that people have things to think and talk about when they leave. I also try to connect with people after the shows, answer questions, and be a resource for young folks struggling with some of the questions and issues I deal with in my poetry.

What is the coolest thing that has happened as a result of you taking your work on the road?

I love being able to experience queer culture all over the country and as a result, I am inspired by the stories and channel them into my work. The diversity of the queer/trans community is amazing and I've become a better writer, performer, and person just by being surrounded by other people's talent, love, and energy.

Do you have any particularly interesting (negative or positive) stories about being trans at the Dr.'s office?

I did my psychotherapy at my school's recommended mental health office and I took two years to get through it with my doctor. At the time I was unhappy, but it was what I needed and since I was her first trans client, she became more educated in the field and can now help others in that town from all the schools there.

Is safe sex something that is important to you?

Yes. I get tested regularly, use protection, and communicate/negotiate with partners.

LESSONS FROM THE LOCKER ROOM

Cooper Lee Bombardier

Prior to transition, I was as active as I could have been given that I had no relationship to my body at all. I remember this crazy, instant sense of being in my body after my very first shot of T, perhaps psychosomatic, but I didn't care. After chest surgery, I developed adult-onset athleticism. Having a new relationship with my body, I felt eager to see what it could do. My body and I were like a brand new couple, marveling at how even the mundane bits of life could feel so thrilling. I lifted weights three times a week, learned how to do handstands, began to train for a Century race (a 100-mile road bike ride), I hiked more often with my dogs, and joined a soccer team. I quit smoking, ate better, drank infrequently, and slept more. I became more athletic in my late thirties than I had ever been before in my life because exercise made me feel better mentally and emotionally.

Early in transition, no place evoked internal contention and palm-moistening anxiety like the locker room. Out in the world, I mostly enjoyed the blissful nobody-ness of being seen as a guy. After years of being freaked-out-on in women's restrooms and having security called on me, it was a relief to be suddenly nondescript and virtually invisible. But all bets are off in the locker room.

At first, I changed at home whenever possible and showed up at the gym ready to go. Eventually I had to sack up, and deal. Changing at the gym caused time to slow to a cold and glacial movement. I hurriedly fumbled and jammed myself close to my locker, staring at the floor. I found it difficult to make eye contact or engage with other guys in the weight room. The first time I entered the men's locker room at the local Japanese spa, I was bluntly stared at by the other men. I cringed under the scrutiny, and yet it was validating to my manhood to be cruised by gay men in the spa locker room. I stripped to my boxer briefs, put on my spa kimono, leaving it open, I moved in close to my locker, stripped off my boxers and packer, quickly stuffed them in a wad into my locker, and in the darkness slipped into the cloak of hot water.

I chuckled at myself when I observed guys with man boobs in the tub that rivaled my pre-surgery chest. Later, my good buddy reassured me: "Dude, you will never get looked at in another locker room the way you get looked at in the locker room at Ten Thousand Waves."

As I progressed in my transition, I began to see these locker room moments as valuable education into the myriad ways of being a man in the world. I learned that it is not okay to talk to other guys in the locker room, except when it is: generally the other guy has to start speaking first, no one knows how the guy who initiates conversation knows that it is okay to do so, but he does. Once, while getting dressed, I was approached by a completely naked septuagenarian (save for flip-flops). In a thick New York accent, unabashed in his nudity, he said, "You have more keys on your belt than a Manhattan building superintendent!" Being a guy means not caring (nor showing you care) what anyone may think about you strutting your stuff—beer bellies, back hair, dickie-dos, muffin tops, man boobs, droopy ball sacks—across a locker room, or weight room, or the deck of an Olympic pool.

With time, my confidence has increased. Now I change right next to other guys in the locker room without a flinch. My new challenge: I enrolled in a swimming class at the local community college and brought the locker room issue up a level. Now the challenge is to change into swim trunks, no briefs, no packer/jockstrap configuration, and walk out into the pool area. I am self-conscious of not packing, of my chest scars being scrutinized. Good thing I am covered in tattoos. I consider it my dazzle camouflage, deflecting notice from my scars to the bright colors tracing all over my arms and torso. The thing I have to remember is that in most situations, everyone is so absorbed with thinking about themselves that they likely are not paying much attention to me, or you. And even if someone notices my scars? So what. If they realize I am trans? Well, there are many ways to be a man.

OP

TRANS MALE QUARTERLY

ISSUE 04 $8 US

WORKIN' STIFF

LETTER FROM THE EDITOR

Welcome to WORKIN' STIFF, *Original Plumbing*'s 4th issue!

Being a person of trans experience can sometimes make the process of going for that well-deserved job a bit more daunting than it should be. The anxiety many of us go through when transitioning at the workplace can be overwhelming! It was the hardest time in my life, mentally. In this issue, you'll meet trans men with diverse jobs—a baker, a stunt man, a businessman, a drag queen, an activist, and a prolific writer with dozens of entry-level jobs under his belt who is now retired—and they'll share with you how they've made ends meet.

For your enjoyment, I'll cut out early and leave you with a special treat: a combined list, in no particular order, of all the jobs titles that co-editor Rocco and I have held so far in our lives. Can you relate?

House painter, on-air radio DJ, pizza delivery boy, drug store cashier, laundromat attendant, camp counselor, Youth Speaks outreach coordinator, movie theater ticket taker, file clerk, faux finisher and venetian plasterer, babysitter, dildo factory worker, doggy day care worker, SPCA cat caregiver, barback, bartender, UPS dude, coat checker, organic vegetable delivery, flower delivery, bar supply delivery, light construction worker, American Apparel stockroom clerk, nightclub guest list checker, website editor, camera store clerk, club promoter, postproduction film editor, LGBT bookstore cashier, and customer support for a streaming gay porn website. Not to mention that when combined together we have worked at 2 video stores, 5 telemarketing firms, and 11 different coffee shops.

Amos Mac
Editor in Chief / Photographer / Workaholic

xo
Amos

COVER MODEL: Matteo Montone; photo by Amos Mac

STUNT MAN

GETS SET ON FIRE AND GETS PAID FOR IT. MAY HE BE SO BOLD?

Interview and photos by Amos Mac

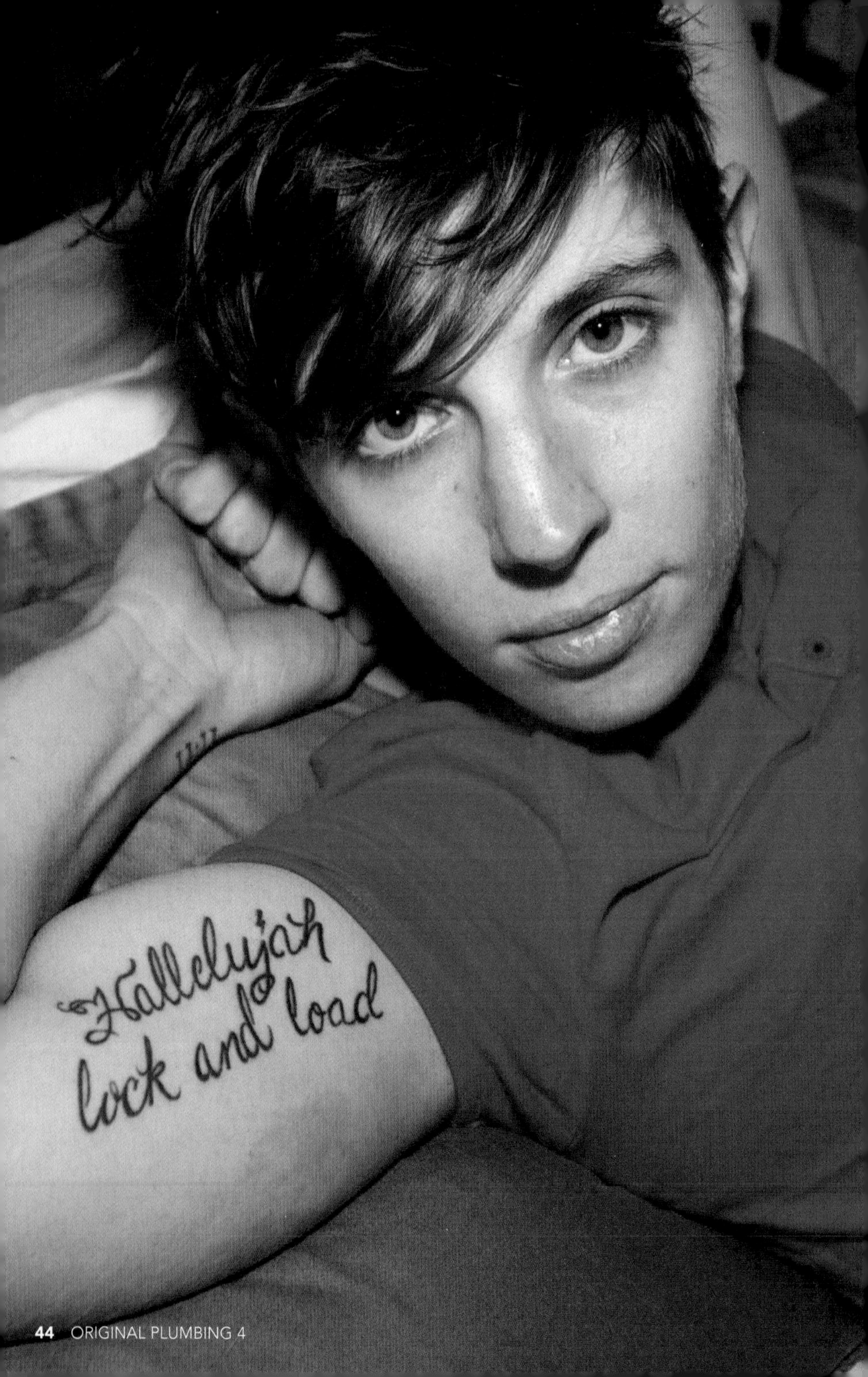
Hallelujah
lock and load

Amos: How long have you been working as a stunt man? And how did you get into that line of work?

Sawyer: I've been working at it for about two years. It's all about meeting people and building relationships with them so they trust you. It can be really dangerous, and no one is just gonna trust you right off the bat.

I remember seeing some sort of behind-the-scenes footage of *Honey, I Shrunk The Kids* and all of the teenage boy actors were having their stunts done by very small women! That was in the 80s though.

That's crazy! Well, kids are a different story altogether. But in general, stunt coordinators will try to find someone of the "appropriate gender" for that actor. I actually doubled for Andie MacDowell, doing some glass breaking and a fire burn. I had to wear a wig, of course. Dress suit, heels, the whole nine, and I'd never worn heels before. I was more nervous about the heels than I was about being set on fire with broken glass everywhere!

Are people in both of your work- spaces respectful of your trans identity?

Definitely. I am who I am. I wasted enough time lying to people and myself about who I was. There are a few younger guys who are respectful of me, but I've heard them talking to each other about gay workers. They won't be getting a raise for a while.

EnTRANSed

Junior Brainard is a college English professor and a trans man. Tina Montgomery is a drag performer and a trans woman. They met at one of Tina's performances. He was instantly smitten. She was more reluctant but encouraged by her friends to try something different. She did, and they have been together ever since.

Junior: When did you first start performing in drag?

Tina: When I was younger, wearing women's clothes was drag. At age 12, I started playing in women's clothes at home in the basement. I did my first show when I was around 17. My next-door neighbor wanted to do a talent show at our block party, so I impersonated Diana Ross. From that day on, you could never get me off stage.

What's one of your favorite performances?

When I can share it with you, either by performing for you, or when you perform a song for me on my birthday.

You've dated a few people in your life. How would you describe your sexuality?

I think I'm bisexual now. If a person comes on to me that I'm attracted to, we take it from there.

Is there anything challenging about being with a white trans man 15 years younger than you?

I don't want to grow old on you. Sometimes it bothers me, but I also like a young man. And if we had met when I was younger, I would have been too busy.

And I would have been too young...

Yes, I met you at the right time in my life. Sometimes other people say, "You're with him? You've got to be kidding." I don't worry about what other people think. I think people were surprised when I started dating you. They didn't think you had swagger—and I didn't either. But you did, and you got game, too.

What do you enjoy the most about our relationship?

There's always something different and new happening and I can always count on you—it's hard to say one thing. I like the fact that you know what you want and you want to be in this relationship with me and what I have to offer. And you are my best friend.

Given your experience, what do you think makes a strong relationship?

Two people really knowing what they want, not guessing. Communication. Not trying to make a person into who you want them to be and loving them for who they are.

ALL BUSINESS
WITH SETH LIST

"We're all different, with different skills, different passions, and different definitions of success. Do what makes you happy and don't let your parents, peers, or society tell you what you need to be. Leverage your network—whether queer-identified or otherwise—to get your foot in the door. Don't be afraid to talk to strangers in the trans community and certainly don't be afraid to ask for help. The worst thing that happens is they tell you to take a hike, and you find someone else who may be more willing to give you the advice you need. But I promise you'll learn a lot about yourself and the working world along the way."

RUBIN

RED
JORDAN ARGBATOU

Photos by Amos Mac

Simone
theBaker

Adrian

ULTIMATE CREATIVE OUTLET
MATTEO MONTONE

When I think back about my life, it's a sweet surprise to realize where I am now. I was born into a Catholic Italian American family, and was raised in a middle-class suburb right outside Boston. Where I come from, people adhere to a strict set of social rituals. Few question these rituals, leaving little room for people like myself to thrive happily in their odd fashion. You were born, baptized, schooled, received communion, and were confirmed. Let's stop right here for a minute and think about this. I am 15 years old and now it is time for the church to confirm me? As if my breathing flesh and blood born of 15 years wasn't evidence enough? Now I have this priest who probably diddled the altar boy telling me that I am a confirmed human being in the eyes of the Vatican Church? Point being, I come from a very suffocating and judgmental upbringing. Once I hit 18, the last thing I wanted to do was perpetuate this insanity. I vowed never to work for someone who would not allow me to express myself in all my hedonistic glory.

Which brings me to my line of work. I am a body piercer, and it's more than just a job for me—it's a way of life. It goes beyond vanity and the latest trends. For me, it is my religion. It is my confirmation. My body is my vessel, and what I wish to do with this vessel and this being that inhabits this vessel is completely in my control. In conjunction with those ideals, I feel very blessed to be surrounded by like-minded individuals, each one of us socially unique yet the same. At long last, I've found social comfort.

I transitioned on the job. Literally I had my first shot at work. It was late October 2007. Half of San Diego County was on fire. Frantic news reports jammed the airwaves and an ominous cloud of thick smoke loomed on the horizon. The atmosphere was ripe with buzzing energy. We are a mystical bunch. We live for this kind of symbolism.

"Dude, fuck this shit. No one's coming in." I stood there in the doorway at Apogee, staring off, my mind wandering through a thousand "what ifs."

"Okay, I'll set up." Ronnie and I disappeared in the back piercing room. He laid out a sterile field and went through the ritual of "setting up." I pulled down my pants to expose my tight, hairless butt cheek.

"You want it in your ass?"

"That's where all the cool kids do it," I joked. As he prepped my plump posterior, I wondered aloud, "Were you nervous when you tattooed your face?" We had never talked about his face, but seeing as I was on the verge of a major physical transition, I found relevance. There was a pause. Ronnie always pauses when he answers me. "No." Pause. "There was this one point when I was half-way through it and for a second I was like *Fuuuuuck* but I got over it."

Most of the time he gets asked what his mother thinks about his tattooed face. "My mother is dead." It's true. He has no family that I know of. His friends are his family, and we love his tattooed face.

Any drastic changes to one's self can be hard for a family to stomach. My grandmother couldn't stand my tattoos, and she let me know it. My parents were more forgiving, but being Italian, I found it difficult to avoid getting

tangled up in the judgment of all our uncles, aunts, cousins, and great aunts. Can you imagine how scary it was to come out to those Santa Claus–fearing Red Sox fans?

My chosen family, the family I work with at the shop, they are my strength. My loudest advocates. After all, we are in the business of body modification. To me, top surgery is no different than a nose piercing, except one has a direct correlation to your gender and the other doesn't.

My job has taught me a lot about myself. About accepting and honoring myself and my desire to be myself despite harsh social criticism. It's something I didn't grow up with. I always thought there was something counterproductive about who I was. My teachers frequently said I never lived up to my potential. Quite a bothersome remark when you take into consideration that I wasn't presented with many options and the idea of "my" potential didn't exist in their world. Body piercing has given me the outlet and the means to be a productive and creatively unique individual. I have found a rewarding, reaffirming place in a society that I once believed had no love for me. It's a very empowering place to be.

OP

ORIGINAL PLUMBING

TRANS MALE QUARTERLY, Nº5
USA $8.00

FASHION
ISSUE

FASHION ISSUE

The other day I saw a commercial for J.C. Penney's back-to-school sale and felt something in my body tighten. I hated shopping for a new school year because it signified the end of summer, and the beginning of a new long year filled with homework and people I was forced to spend time with. As a kid who never felt like my gender fit right, it was almost impossible to find clothes that suited me. My parents were progressive and let me wear whatever I wanted, but still I dreaded the idea of stripping down in the women's dressing room and trying on gender-ambiguous sweaters and button-down shirts with culottes.
At the onset of puberty, I discovered extremely baggy skate pants, flannels, oversized hooded sweatshirts, and grunge rock. This was perfect because then I never had to try anything on and no one could see the outlines of my body. So began my love of counterculture, thrifting, and fashion.

—Rocco

I remember clothes shopping with my mother when I was a little kid. These department store excursions were always emotionally and physically exhausting for both of us. Like clockwork, I'd feign illness if we were in a store for longer than five minutes. Lying on the ground dramatically I'd say that I felt dizzy, or that I couldn't bear the smell of the department store carpet. Sometimes I'd blame my sickness on the neon overhead lighting, or the Muzak being pumped in from the ceiling. Often I'd just hide in the center of the circular racks amongst the dresses and gauzy blouses. At the age of 7, I didn't have the language or understanding that my uneasiness around shopping in girl-specific sections stemmed from feeling totally misrepresented as the kid I saw myself as.
My parents learned quickly that I preferred collared shirts with dinosaur print, suspenders, and hightops over the other stuff, so except for the holidays and celebratory events, I was spared from wearing the type of clothing that turned me inside out. Whew!

—Amos

LETTER FROM THE EDITORS

A lot of us end up having a strained relationship to clothing because we had to wear dresses we never should have had to wear. Nothing accurately represented the way we imagined our bodies should look. Whatever the reason, we all find ourselves trying to feel at home in our skin, while struggling to outwardly show the world who we really are and who we are not.

What we wanted to showcase in OP's first fashion issue goes beyond up-to-the-minute trends or people who dress ahead of the curve. We felt it was also important to concentrate more on specific stories and explore individuals' unique fashion styles, comfort levels, and backgrounds. While many of us find what feels best to wear and stick with it, some of us push the boundries of gender in fashion, constantly playing and blurring the lines of self-expression.

In this issue of OP, you'll find guys talking about how fashion is not just the act of frivolously adorning yourself in the latest trends, but rather, a proclamation of newfound confidence and comfort.

—Amos and Rocco, Editors

COVER MODELS: Christian and Gavin; photo by Amos Mac

JESS CUEVAS

"I feel like I make all my style choices based on comfort. Do I feel good? Am I comfortable in this? Not comfortable like 'I am in my pajamas' but comfortable in the world. Then moving forward in your look feels good, builds confidence, and voila, you somehow start dressing for you, not everyone else."

GLENN MARLA
BROOKLYN, NY

Whats your favorite clothing item this week?
A white denim jacket with pearls and rhinestones on the shoulders. Made by Quacker Factory bought at the QVC outlet at Rehoboth Beach.

Favorite place to shop for garments:
Re/dress NYC, QVC Outlet, or custom-made by Bertha Pearl, Garo Sparo, or Machine Dazzle.

How would you describe your personal fashion?
Deep color embrace, Old Queen, Dan Conner or Butch in the 90s, Fierce and Dapper Dandy.

Has any particular person/place/thing inspired your fashion?
My mother not only inspired my bold fashion choices on a fat body, but more importantly taught me how to shop. I would also say the place that inspires my fashion most is New York City in particular, downtown performance communities, small grimy dressing rooms shared with the most beautiful showgirls (of all genders), and Coney Island, sideshow colors, when amusement lights hit the beach, water and dark alleys, watching people negotiate between functional and fierce and some finding the balance.

SANYU
BROOKLYN, NY

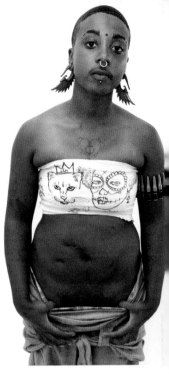

How would you describe your personal style?
Tank Girl as a boi meets the Mursi tribe of Ethiopia.

What inspires your fashion?
My fashion has always been inspired by a lot of the pain that I've experienced from having Lupus. From the surgeries to the long hospital stays, my style is a reflection of a lot of my chaotic experiences associated with a chronic illness.

Do you have a collection of binders that you've drawn on or is this the only one?
The concept of putting art on my binders came when I realized that I had gone through so many surgeries already that I didn't think that top surgery was going to be an option for me anymore. I was also at a point where I had stopped taking testosterone and was questioning my health and not only my mental gender identity, but the physical one that I desired to reflect. I knew that maybe I would never have the physical attributes of a bio-male chest. But, I told myself that I had to find something, something beyond the mundaneness of my binder that could make it almost as personal as my flesh. I created a series of personalized binders that I've entitled "second skin" and I have a few up on my website at www.phantom.echoz.com.

Tell me the story behind the binder you have on right now.
Well, the cat on the binder represents the myth of the black cat. It also ties into issues of race and semantics surrounding the word black and its many pejorative meanings in the English language. I also love cats.

DARRELLE
BROOKLYN, NY
LOS ANGELES, CA

My personal style is an ever-evolving entity that revolves around taking looks that are WAY out of my price range and turning them into something affordable. I'm really inspired by high street, as well as runway, and live for the ways those looks are shaped and styled by queers, club kids, and different cities. As long as it's androgynous and not too preppy I'm willing to give it a try. Some of my favorite looks are from stores like OAK or the online retailer Oki-Ni.

TIQ
BROOKLYN, NY

How would you describe your personal style?
I like to keep it simple. Classic shit that won't ever go out of style. I don't do trends. I'm not a label whore.

What inspires your fashion?
I don't know what inspires my personal fashion. I just want to look half decent without having to do a lot. I like when a look can come together rather effortlessly. I don't like a whole lot of fuss.

Do you draw on anything specifically for your personal fashion?
Nah. If it fits good and feels good, I'm running with it.

CHRISTIAN
PHILADELPHIA, PA

My personal style is a fusion of vintage and high fashion with a splash of hip hop. My style is inspired mostly my own creativity. As an artist I like to think that I also am art and so are my stylings. And I don't draw on anything specific for my personal fashion, just an awesome queer eye.

GAVIN
PHILADELPHIA, PA

How would you describe your personal style?
Hmmm...Queermosexual!

What inspires your fashion?
I just work around my sexy. I'll wear anything that looks good with a Converse.

Do you draw on anything specifically for your personal fashion?
I can't really say. I just enjoy looking good and choose things that look good on me.

GRIFFEN
SYDNEY, AUSTRALIA

How would you describe your personal style?
Perhaps the description mid-90s/vintage-
70s faggot fits? I guess I like to think that my
fashion exists at the intersection of an early 90s
faggot, River Phoenix (especially his character
in *My Own Private Idaho*), Prince, Morrissey,
Querelle, and *The Lost Boys*. Actually, perhaps
my style spans the 70s, 80s, and 90s. My staples
are definitely white socks and a fabulous shirt
(tucked in of course) and my faithful TBJs (tight
black jeans).

What inspires your fashion?
I like to think that I take a wee bit of fashion
from a number of sources, some of which I
mentioned already, but if I had to add to that
list I'd say Wham! and Johnny Depp in the film
Cry Baby. It's as though I throw all these things
into a fashion blender to to make somewhat
of a faggotista-blenda! Although, some days I
definitely feel as though I'm channelling some
kind of River and Corey Haim combination.

KALE
KOREATOWN, LOS ANGELES, CA

My style is like skipping in a field full of synthetic flowers.
Some are tall metallic wire twigs with neon tulle sprouting
out the tops; others are knitted true purples and turquoise
draped around pompous lame pillars.

I am inspired by things around me: the modern world. The
sickening gleam of an advertisement, an armature from
a fence, glitter in the sidewalk, and hot steaming freshly
laid smoky black asphalt. Of course fashion of the past,
especially the 80s and 20s and timeless couture. But also
music, specifically opera, bosom-busting out the top of that
velvet corset opera—not the fashion, but the sets and the
music. I've pretty much been obsessed with opera since
I was a wee pee-pee in the pants ragtag stick of kindling.
The sets are THE BEST. The textures manufactured by
layering painted wood to look like anything under the tragic
moon that sings down from the ropes and pulleys above.

WORN OUT

E-J SCOTT

I know a guy who is one of those people who wears the same thing every, single day. Every, single day. I wonder if in reality, he secretly has a couple of each of the same things he wears, inconspicuously rotating them like a black clad ninja locked in a tumble drier. Maybe he just gets naked once a week in the local laundrette while he washes his only outfit. It must be a very comforting thing to do—to wear the same thing over and over (as opposed to standing naked in the laundrette). Comforting like the sturdy, reliable taste of Builder's tea, or the crunchiness of clean bed linen stiffly dried in the sun.

Another friend I know never wears the same thing twice. Ever. She hunts through thrift shops like a little bespectacled mole, touching and smelling and stroking, composing textures and colours and lines in which to house her etch-a-sketch personality.

I myself flit between both these worlds. I have worn my favourite shirt at least once a week for eleven years—it has been stitched back together so many times it is almost a new shirt entirely. I like how softly it sits on my skin, how well it knows my shoulders. Other days, most days actually, I'm simply running late getting out the door, and a few clashing layers and a neckerchief suffice. It's a standard repertoire. But I often forget it's not up to everyone else's standards, and that our clothes talk volumes about who we are, even when we're entirely

shut up in our own little worlds and are in no mood to communicate anything to anyone, in any way whatsoever.

Like the time I went to check out Dizzee Rascal at the Concorde (a wicked renovated warehouse space on Brighton's pebbly beach). I'd unexpectedly been given the night off work and swung a free ticket, and was killing time waiting for my friend to finish his shift.

I was wearing not-so-skinny-anymore black jeans, very well-loved; an orange, red, yellow, and black cotton cowboy-esque shirt I've also had for years; a deliberately clashing, oversized red hoodie that's got a somewhat remarkable lemon background which contrasts with an overprint of differently sized floating manga bubbles (the hood is lined in lemon too, the cord you use to pull it tighter has those little clear plastic bits that are wrapped around the ends of shoelaces, red on one end and black on the other); my trainers were a well-loved pair of limited edition Rubik's Cube Converse (c. 2008 & seen better days); accessories included my rain-dimpled, black, pork pie hat; heavy black frames with flush matte metal studs that match on both the front of the hinges and on the arms; my truly beloved handmade, glazed Pac-Man ring from a terrific little lane in Singapore that sells all kinds of stuff made by local fashion students; and cheap leather wristbands wrapped around twice and clipped on with forked clasps.

I remember that clearly, because of the "what next." The gig wasn't my scene, surprisingly I didn't recognise anyone there, and then I realised it was a Bank Holiday weekend, and this wasn't the usual local crowd at all, it was all touristy out-of-towners and not the geeky retro chic Brighton cliques one comes to take for granted. A group of guys with lingering eyes were sizing me up for sport. So I left.

On purpose, I headed off walking under the street lights on the opposite side of the road. Within thirty seconds a car started tailing me, then pulled up and drove alongside me, the accelerator physically breathing aggression in and out. It was overloaded with young lads, no doubt in town to gawk at Brighton's famous "gay" scene and to stir up a bit of trouble. They started turning it on—all the usual bullshit—"You from Brighton, then?" "What's that you got on, then?" "Is that what people wear in Brighton, then?" Everything was "then, then, then." Their language was doing my head in, quite literally. It turned nasty. They got out, circled me, pushed me between the lot of them, it was like being on the telly. I wasn't actually scared—but I was frightfully bored and unimpressed by their homophobia. "You gay, then?" Yawn. I felt like taking my clothes off and giving them something to really wrap their little heads

around. Being gay really is the least intriguing phenomenon I have on offer.

Next thing I know, a guy who'd caught the backend of the scene from across the road was shaking me and slapping me across the face to bring me back into consciousness. A cracked rib and a couple of black eyes later, I was home and taking off my hoody, my cowboy shirt, my Pac-Man ring. I would wear the bruises to bed.

Everyone has their own relationship with their favourite clothes. They all have stories to tell, and memories to hold onto and secrets; they live on top of us and touch us and tell us who we are, where we've been, where we belong. But they can only tell the world what the world wants to hear, inviting speculation from utter strangers, somehow giving these strangers the freedom to redress our coat hanger in life, somehow certain they know where we have hung ourselves out to dry, and why. Our favourite clothes simultaneously make us who we are and who we are not.

And now? Now I have to face another day by getting up out of bed and getting dressed all over again. Bugger it. Maybe I'll go to the warm laundrette instead, and get my kit off. £3.20 a load, innit? Seems a small price to pay for refreshed sanity, a sense of self, my identity, a notion of shared humanity, and a reality that's mine, smugly self-defined, and snuggly.

'dan·dē

Photos by Amos Mac

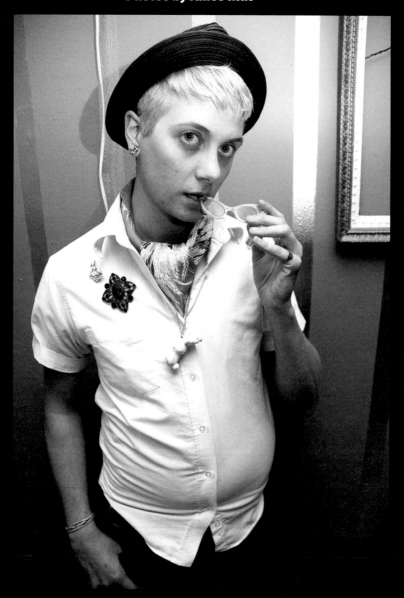

DANDY

A man who places particular importance upon physical appearance, refined language, and leisurely hobbies, pursued with the appearance of nonchalance in a cult of self.

◀ **KETCH**

"The story to my cravat, which I love almost too much to part with, is that it could be the final leg of my surgery savings (which is just one of those unending processes). It's an original Hermès scarf that I bought at a thrift store for $1.99. According to a more fashion-worldly friend, it's worth more than my rent."

DANNY

ELLIOT

SEBASTIAN

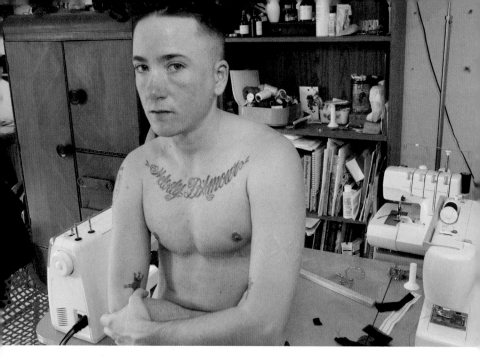

AUSTIN BJORKMAN

INTERVIEW BY ROCCO KAYIATOS
PHOTOS BY AMOS MAC

What was your initial interest in fashion and clothing design?
My initial interest came from vintage clothes shopping and trying to find clothes that fit me. So I started by altering my vintage finds. Then I got a job at Mr. S Leather making latex clothes and such. I taught myself how to use the industrial machines and started sewing bondage suits and deprivation hoods. Which led me to taking classes in design, pattern-making, and sewing in SF. I wanted to design menswear and the only design program in the country was in New York. So after having a small line of clothes and accessories and doing a lot of custom work in SF, I moved to New York to study menswear at Fashion Institute of Technology.

I think I remember hearing that you made leather pants for Joan Jett. Is that true?
Yes. I did.

How did that happen?

Well, she was dating a friend of mine and we became friends during that time. She liked my work and asked me to make a custom pair for her.

Have you outfitted many other celebrities?
Ha! Everyone wants to hear celebrity gossip. I made a pair of leather pants for Margaret Cho and Jane Wiedlen as customers for Mr. S. I used to sell my line at Villians Vault and the manager told me that David LaChapelle bought a hat of mine.

I dressed a lot of famous models when I worked with Thom Browne and Loden Dager. Does that count as celebrity gossip?

You dressed them?
For runway shows. They are sooo tall. I would style them and dress them.

What does that involve?
Getting them to take their clothes off and dressing them like you would a 5-year-old,

then send them to hair and makeup.

How tall are most male models?
They are like 6'6" on average.

Wow. That is a foot and two inches bigger than I am. There goes that dream.
Ha. Us shorties have a place in fashion, just not on the runway.

You are proving that right now. So after teaching yourself to use the industrial sewing machine and getting all kinds of real world experience, what was it like to move to NY to go to school? Did you keep making your own stuff or take a break?
In school I tried focusing on design to hone my skills. We had lots of sewing and pattern making so I definitely had a huge advantage. I really studied menswear from a historical perspective as well as what all the top Parisian, Italian, British, and American designers are doing currently. I immersed myself in New York High End Fashion.

I interned with Thom Browne, who is my favorite New York designer; he is known for his Pee-Wee Herman–type tight suits with short pants, cuffed above the ankle. His runway shows are extremely theatrical, which I love. His suits were all hand made here in NY and I got to experience that type of fine hand tailoring, but also to run around the garment district and learn where to source things and actually get things made here in New York. And to do major runway shows.

I interned for another menswear label called Loden Dager, young designers who were in the position I knew I would be in in a few years. Which was another amazing experience to work with and learn what it is like to be young designers getting started on your own in New York.

You are about to launch your new line, SIR, with Frederico Viseu. Can you tell us how you guys came together for this project?
We met at FIT. He is also a very gender nonconforming person born male but definitely a "lady." Freddy also started a line previous to FIT called SEXES and played with androgyny with that line. We started working on a couple of group assignment projects together and hatched the idea of SIR by the end of our first semester. We initially intended to use our Senior Collections to launch the line.

We kind of took some time off a little bit after school just because we sort of needed a mental and physical break. It was really an exhausting program.

So we took a little time and came back together to put this our first collection together.

How did you pick the name SIR?
We thought about something that sounded gentlemanly, but we wanted to make our own definition of it because we are making clothing for all genders in the tradition of menswear.

Can you tell me more about your collaboration? Who does what? And do you both share a vision?

We work extremely closely together on every decision. We have many of the same visions but then definitely have our own unique point of views on it. We have to believe in and trust each other and ourselves. There are times that we see things exactly the same and times when we want to go in slightly a different direction. We know when the other person is right sometimes. And we know when we have to compromise. It can be difficult at times with two really strong designers, but it can only work that way for me. I mean that I believe in my partner's work and they are very strong willed, because I am too.

It is more of a real partnership then, if you both have a strong vision. I think that comes across in your line. It is clear that there is a strong point of view and that you two work well together in the execution of it all. I had a chance to see a few of the pieces for the line and I love how tactile it all is. Can you tell me about your relationship to different fabrics? Why do you choose what you choose and how do you make patterns?

I am happy to hear you say that because you got it. For this collection it is all about texture. We wanted to create new prints and patterns using texture. In this season we use mesh. We use it layered over wovens and knits, like in the details of a button down shirt or layered over jersey on the tank tops. And in some places just mesh not layered over anything. Fabrics are already so tactile. How something feels on the skin is called the hand, and this is extremely important when selecting fabrics. We hunted for fabrics and collected swatches in the color story we chose, which was very simple; we knew that if we were introducing mesh in a new way we didn't want to hit you in the face with color. Menswear is really tricky and we wanted to make this line very relatable.

Can you tell me a bit about the history of mesh? When and how did it become something that people were wearing?

Mesh was originally produced for fishermen's netting. It only became a part of clothing in athletic wear. We drew inspiration from fencing, bee keeping, and basketball for SIR New York's Spring Summer '11 collection.

Well, you managed to do something new and different, and you clearly took risks but your use of minimal color made it incredibly wearable.

Exactly! That was our aim.

Perfectly executed. The tank top that I tried on hung better on my body than anything I have ever worn.

Yesss. Fit was also something we worked hard at.

How do you do that? Get something to hang right? Especially on someone like me, short and stocky.

That is an art really. We do multiple fittings to make sure we get everything right. Our sample sizes are smaller than most lines. We know who our customers are and wanted to fit smaller guys and women because all genders wear men's clothes but nobody caters to the smaller folks. We also didn't want anything to have a "skinny" fit. You might have noticed everything fits just the way you would want a slim fit with ease to fit.

You have had such a cool career and it is just beginning in some ways. Could you be the only trans guy that is a designer?

The only one in the universe on a major scale. I am sure there are lots of people making stuff and people who are aspiring designers but at this scale, yes.

What is your favorite part of design and clothing making?

I love clothes, not gonna lie. I think because as a kid I never got to wear what I wanted to wear, I developed a deep love for clothing. Maybe an obsession, really.

As a guy who is not as tall as a runway model, what are some tips to appear taller?

Stand up straight, keep your head up, walk proud and confident. Look people in the eye when you talk to them.

Scout Rose models SIR, photographed at International Playground in NYC's Lower East Side.

WELL-PRESSED ROOTS

BY BRANT MacDUFF

I know this is the Fashion Issue, but please allow me to pontificate momentarily on the subject of style. Style is timeless, where fashion changes with the seasons. I am a WASP (an atheist one), a trad, a prep. And there are a few things a right prepster is nary without: booze, leisure sports that involve boats or horses, and anything made in Maine or England. To quote *The Official Preppy Handbook*,[1] "Preppies wear clothes for 25 years and no one can tell the difference. The fabrics, the cuts, the colors are the same, year after year after year." I still have button-downs that I got when I was in the sixth grade; the sleeves are too short now, so I have to roll them up. I like to think of prepsters as the original eco-friendly people, since the longevity of our wardrobes make them inherently green. Our clothes come from quality purveyors, so they last forever and get handed down to us from parents and grandparents.

You might think growing up in (what you might view as) a conservatively attired environment would be difficult for a fellow such as myself, but on the contrary. The prep wardrobe is full of khakis, button-downs, topsiders, and sport coats. This is the uniform, and it doesn't matter if you are a man, woman, eight or eighty years old—everyone is in the uniform. For the first twelve years of my life, I only wore khakis and white polo shirts (collar up to protect my neck from sunburn if I was riding or sailing, of course). And a little girl in a blue blazer, even with a necktie, is nothing out of the ordinary. To quote the prepster bible once more, "Androgyny: Men and women dress as much alike as possible and clothes for either sex should deny specifics of gender." This was wonderfully convenient for me in my youth and allowed me to fully indulge in my penchant for boys' clothes. And because I was my father's only child, he took great care to pass down the fundamentals of menswear to me, from suiting cuts to riding breeches.

There's a lot of talk about identity these days, and I have to confess that when I hear it, I think: prep first, trans man second. The recent appropriation of prep style into the mainstream fashion world has had me positively seething for the past year. There are far too many NYC hipsters kidnapping my heritage in order to look cute on their bike rides through Williamsburg. But there is something terribly plastic about the way these phonies dress—like cartoon versions of the real thing, trying too hard. If your "go to hell" pants have little skull and crossbones on them, then you are part of the problem. Learn how to sail, then wear topsiders; learn how to play rugby, then put on that thick-striped jersey. You don't see me walking around in scrubs and a white lab coat pretending to be a doctor.

Perhaps you think I'm being rather exclusive? I'm just being protective of my people. They're not all great people—every nest has its bad eggs—but we are still a culture I belong to, and we do not appreciate being appropriated by the American hipster. But eventually it will be passé to dress like an old prep. Shrouding oneself in Mayan fertility ritual gowns will be the next big thing[2] and we will get back our bow ties, seersucker, and madras. Now if you will excuse me, I have shirts to monogram.

1. *The Official Preppy Handbook* was edited by Lisa Birnbach in 1980 and would be the one and only textbook needed were you to study the social/cultural anthropology of preppies.

2. I believe it was lumberjack chic actually, but I was right.

OP

ORIGINAL PLUMBING

OP ISSUE 6
TRANS MALE QUARTERLY
SCHOOLED

USA $8

the editors pass notes in class:

ROCCO: I hated almost everyone in my small town. Loud, outspoken, and the only out queer kid, I got a lot of attention—whether I wanted it or not. I established myself as a huge class clown—early on, I learned my best defense was humor and verbal acuity. I would seize any opportunity to make other kids laugh, whether it was in a classroom or at a school-wide assembly. I learned early on that the easiest way to get by was to out-bully the bullies. Constantly aware of my own weaknesses and vulnerabilities, I found myself equipped with the ability to determine almost anyone's Achilles' heel, and announce it to the rest of the student body.

AMOS: I was the biggest band geek in high school! I played alto sax in the marching band and clarinet in concert band. I still remember the uniform we had to wear to the football games—red and yellow with obscene plumes sticking out from the top of the hats. Hideous! I spent the first 2 years of my high school existence trying to find a community of friends where I could feel comfortable, but in the end, I was invisible. I wanted it that way. In class I was quiet and angry and spent my time dreaming about the day I'd leave my hometown. I felt no connection to any of my surroundings; I only felt a connection with the future. Amidst all the confusion I felt around where I fit in, I was never too depressed because I was inspired and excited by the fact that I knew from day one that there was life—REAL LIFE—outside of high school.

ROCCO: I was able to do spot-on impressions of our teachers, sending my classmates into uproarious laughter and me to detention, suspension, or a special and isolated seat my 7th grade teacher had created just for me. In class I was funny, entertaining, and distracting, and kids would vie for a seat next to me. But as soon as the bell rang, I was alone. No one

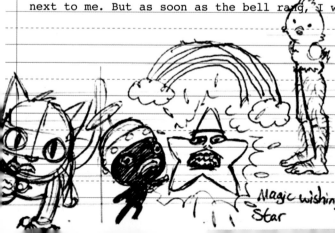

Magic wishing Star

wanted to hang out or eat lunch by me. Despite the fact that I didn't like these kids I shared space with, it killed me—I still wanted to be liked.

AMOS: I wasn't "out" as anything in high school. I didn't know what was going on with my gender, and I didn't have the understanding to confront what I felt, but I knew that it went beyond not "fitting in." I knew it was something I would never be able to learn inside the walls of any school.

ROCCO: Towards the end of my freshman year, my honors history teacher informed my mom that perhaps the lauded suburban public high school at which I was enrolled was not the right place for me because I did not "fit in socially." This was the same year a teacher used the word "fag" in class. I called him out on it, explained to him in front of the class that it was his job as an educator to not teach ignorance. He half-heartedly apologized directly to me and proceeded to "accidentally" use the word again less than a month later. His slur was indicative of the atmosphere—I knew in my gut that no one at school understood me, and my queerness was only a part of that. I was defiant and worked hard to prove that I no longer cared about fitting in. It must have shown, as I was voted "Rebel Without a Cause" in my high school yearbook.

AMOS: I was made fun of and rarely stood up for myself. I was kicked from behind in the hallway and had lots of cruel pranks played on me, mostly by boys. That stuff started in middle school. Even people I considered friends would make snide comments about my appearance and how I dressed. I never knew what to say, I never understood how me being myself was bothering them. I wasn't a fighter. Instead I would just shut down. In 9th grade I discovered our high school radio station and loved working there so much that I got a job at a major Philadelphia radio station after school and on weekends. I threw myself into my work. I spent more time at the radio station than at home, working around adults and pretending that my high school life didn't exist.

ROCCO: The thing is, I did have a cause, it just lived outside the asphyxiating walls of high school. My senior year, I got involved with Youth Speaks, a progressive organization dedicated to fostering a love of writing and performing in teens. I started competing and winning poetry slams and met other queer kids and allies. Instead of attending my high school graduation, I opted to perform at Luna Sea—an all queer woman performance space. My adventures and presence in the poetry slam community led me to Sini and Michelle, two ladies that created Sister Spit's Ramblin' Road Show, an all-girl spoken word troupe that toured the country. They invited me to go on tour the summer after I graduated. I was 18 and had to decide whether I wanted to go to junior college or go on tour. The decision was not a difficult one. I packed my bags, got in the van, and never looked back. A lot of the time it is hard for queer kids to know or trust that there is a larger world that exists. But there is and it does get better.

AMOS: In 10th grade I found a loophole in the system! You need 4 years of high school English to graduate, so I figured out

that if I took 2 English classes my junior year I would have the correct credits to graduate an entire year early. I was an average student, bored to death so I didn't study, but I had enough outside interests in the arts, lacked a troublemaking record, and had the ability to articulate myself quite well on paper. I wrote a letter to the principal telling him my future dreams and goals, all of which did not include my senior year. He was impressed and wished me the best. My friends freaked out, insisting that I would regret this, and questioned why I would want to leave and miss out on our senior year, where we would be "in charge" of the school. Other friends couldn't help but constantly remind me I would miss our senior prom and insisted that I would get nonstop rejection letters from colleges, which of course would send me on a fast-track to what they considered a tarnished life. But a year later, it happened. I was accepted into my first-choice school, a small liberal arts college in Vermont. I graduated at the end of 11th grade. I remember walking to receive my diploma surrounded by a bunch of strangers, realizing that this was barely the beginning.

Welcome to the Schooled Issue!

TWIZ

Gender variant artist Twiz Rimer
spends a lot of time talking about emotions.

Interview and photos by Amos Mac / Paintings by Twiz Rimer

I've always known you as a painter, not as an art therapist. Why did you start painting?
My mom was an artist and she was always pushing creativity in my early development stages and I did art in school with other kids and I was always really good at it. I felt good, I stuck with it, I was praised with it. With Tourette's, when I really concentrate on something that I am good at, it's a kind of release and it goes away.

When did you realize you had Tourette's syndrome?
I was 7, so 22 years now. I made art before Tourette's. I used to play the drums too when I was younger, and other things help control the Tourette's. Weightlifting, that helps, sports, and sex. You know, I was shy before Tourette's, then one day I got really angry and just started twitching.

Does your gender identity directly effect your art?
In the beginning, when I was getting my MFA at SF Arts Institute, I used my art to process who I was and tried to figure out if I wanted to start taking T, or whatever. I used art as a process because that was a time when I was not comfortable with where I was on the gender spectrum. As a kid I had no idea, I just painted pictures of horses. When a lot of friends starting taking T, a lot of people were on my nuts about it! I always passed before and I was lucky enough to get top surgery, but there was a lot of push-pull around hormones and if I was going on T. I wanted to make goddamn sure I did it for the right reasons.

Once I had surgery I felt pretty comfortable. Now, I can pass if I want, or I can pull out the dyke card or the straight card. I'm from Viking descent. I'm also a Russian Jew. That's probably where my moustache comes from. It's all genetics, baby.

Describe your relationship to your art.
My early MFA career I did in-your-face, sexual emo shit, almost too much. Now I play with metaphor and the commercial aspect of painting and drawing to sell and make images people will like. It's more about other people now as opposed to myself.

If you could go back in time and mentor your child self, what would you say?
I would tell me what my mother told me at 9. I was an early bloomer in puberty and I was humongous. My body started changing, I had been twitching for a year and a half. I couldn't stand developing breasts, especially being the first kid in the class to get them. I had a shaved head and a rat tail and suddenly I had breasts and I didn't know what I was supposed to do! My mom came to me and said, "You know you're gonna be made fun of. A lot. Kids are cruel and you're gonna be made fun of. You're going to have to deal with it." It changed my world. It made me own it instead of be insecure about all of it. With Tourette's and my body changing, it made me realize it was out of my control so I could get over my insecurities. Saved my life actually, the honesty and the validation.

CAYES

Cayes Domonick Jarda tells us why
he's teaching kids to read.

Interview by Rocco Kayiatos / Photo by Amos Mac

My name is Cayes and I live in the West Adams area of LA. I am a site coordinator for Reading Partners. I teach reading skills to students and train tutors to do the same.

Do you have any stories that stand out from your time with the kids you teach? Any personal triumphs or moments you're moved by?
I got a betta fish for my class, the kids named him Sgt. Kevin Newman. You can imagine how the kids want to feed him all the time. I don't believe in prizes for doing things you're supposed to be doing. That's how my parents raised me. I make the silliest things seem so amazing. The students have to read him 10 stories to feed him once! This girl came in and it was her 10th time reading to him. At first they weren't buying it, they'd be like, "Mr. Cayes, he can't hear us, he's not listening," and I'd tell them, "Well, slow down and make sure you're reading all the words right. Use expression!" It was funny because he'd actually sit still for a moment. While she was reading to him she goes, "Mr. Cayes! He's not listening and I'm reading really, really good!" Sooo cute, 2nd grade, had to take a picture.
I also have a couch they can't sit on until they've done 5 book reports. I have 6 students on the couch as of today!

That is such a smart way to motivate kids. So you work mostly with young ones?
2nd through 5th grade. Can I tell you how the fish got his name? A lot of our students lack vocab skills for all sorts of reasons. At Reading Partners defining words is part of the curriculum so I had a little raffle. Students wrote definitions to words and they put the suggested fish name on the back of the definition. I let them pick as many names as definitions they put in the box. I was going to

choose 1 name, but the kids convinced me to pick 3 so he'd have a first, middle, and last name! And that's seriously what came out! With the extra raffles, I've been putting up one a week on the board and giving the student credit for it. They love having their names on the board in a positive way.

If you are teaching younger kids, I imagine that you have to be pretty theatrical to keep them engaged (along with your excellent system of motivating them to feed the betta and sit on the special couch).
I'm constantly dancing around the room. My kids think I'm nuts I'm sure. But yes, I do feel satisfied and I'm constantly working on ways to reach my students personally every day. I just want them so badly to know how they can catch up to their friends. I can't lie, it feels really good having a rush of students to greet me every morning. I had a girl start bawling because she passed the assessment to be in the program. She begged me to be in Reading Partners. It's hard because we are totally volunteer tutor-driven. I wish I had 300 tutors, then every kid could have a reading partner. I have to tell the kids, "Guys, it's great to be with me, but it's also great to not need me."
I'm happy everyone thinks it's cool to be a Reading Partner. It makes it easier for my students to come to my room confidently and not feel ashamed for having to need extra help. I have to make it fun. Confidence is a killer and I want my kids to feel safe so they can actually do the work. I have a few kids who hate it, but they are my lowest. I know it's only because they are so frustrated and feel bad about. I can't imagine what it's like to be 5th grader reading at a 3rd or 2nd grade level. They know what they sound like next to their peers.

BAKING STUDENT IN BRIEFS

DENTO

"My specialty is cheesecake. It's one of those things I can do so easily I can do it in my sleep. I make 15 different kinds, or ask me what flavor of cheesecake you want and I can make it."

Photo by Amos Mac

SCHOOL BOYS

Concept by Rocco Kayiatos / Photographed by Amos Mac

Tuck

AGE: 29

What's in your locker? **Old candy wrappers, porn, cheat sheet.**

One sentence to describe your high school self:

Awkward man with long blond hair.

Give your high school self advice as the person you are today:

"High school will be long forgotten one day, so don't sweat it."

Scott

AGE: 23

What's in your locker? **Trash and sweaty clothes.**

Choose your book report topic: **Aerospace.**

Give your high-school self advice as the person you are today:

"You shoulda hit that."

Johnny Mission

AGE: 36

Favorite class in high school: **Art.**

Choose your book report topic: **Ozzy Osbourne.**

One sentence to describe your high school experience:

1980s skater boy angst with a Southern backdrop.

Jae
AGE: 23

What's in your locker? **Journal full of bad poetry.**

Reason for your last detention: **Stealing an ice cream sandwich.**

One word to describe your high school experience: **Trangst.**

Give your high school self some advice:

"It gets better! One day you will become a handsome man and escape to a land of beautiful and inspiring queers."

Aaron
AGE: 22

What's in your locker? **Old food and homework.**

Choose your book report topic: **Zombies.**

Reason for your last detention:

Yelling "FUCK" because I hurt myself.

Yelz + Alex
AGE: 23 / 26

Yelz–Favorite high school class:

Ceramics / calculus (calculus homework during ceramics class).

What's in your locker? **The P.E. clothes I "left at home."**

One sentence to describe your high school experience:

Me against the world.

Alex–One sentence to describe your high school self:

Class president who ran with the artists and fellow delinquents.

Give your high school self advice as the person you are today:

"Read more books, and don't worry about being trans–it's great."

Photo by Amos Mac

BENJI

**"I feel like every school needs to have a
Gay-Straight Alliance because just the presence
of one already makes the school a safer and
more inclusive place for everyone."**

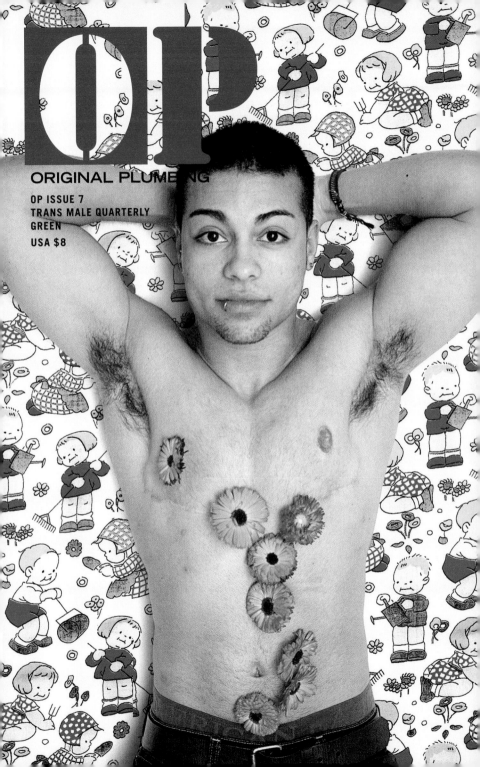

ROCCO

· When I was in high school, my sister informed me I was an agro-hippie, which basically meant that I didn't brush my hair, rarely bathed or washed my clothes, smoked too much weed, and angrily urged everyone around me to "be mellow." I spent a lot of time outdoors smoking pot and trying to commune with nature. I thought I was one with the earth; meanwhile I did little to consciously take care of the planet.

It wasn't until I passed the age of 25 that I finally realized I was not going to die young. After that I really started to think about how, as a species, humans keep getting farther and farther removed from the natural world. It was also right around that time that I read an article about how much fossil fuel and energy it takes to transport vegetables from other countries to ours. I decided that I should do more to help conserve and take care of the planet. I became really interested in where my food came from and how much energy I was using on a daily basis. I started doing small things to reduce my own carbon footprint. I did lots of little things: I plugged everything into a power strip, which I would shut off when I wasn't home or while I was sleeping. I started shutting the faucet off while I lathered my dishes or while I was brushing my teeth. I recycled and composted, I got rid of my car, and I even became a locavore.

AMOS

· My earliest green memories revolve around food. I remember at age 6 I visited my grandmother in Philadelphia and followed her into the "backyard" to check on her beloved tomato garden. Despite living in a constricting urban environment not meant for growing food, my grandmother had managed to locate a tiny square of green amongst the black tar cement and started her own garden that bloomed and exploded with colorful red and green fruits every year. She made an edible something out of nothing, even in a space where it seemed like such an idea would be completely unsupported by the earth.

In the years to come I remember going to local apple orchards where I'd climb trees and pick bundles of Red Delicious, Gala, and McIntosh apples for a season's worth of pies, even taking home the bruised ones for homemade apple butter. My mom would shop for breads, meat, vegetables, and fruits at the giant downtown Amish farmers market; it was more affordable than going to our local chain supermarket, which was important in my single parent household—not to mention healthier and supportive of local farmers. Even though I lived in a town that was far from rural, I realized where food came from at a young age, although I can honestly say it took me until I was living on my own and buying my own food to truly care.

COVER MODEL: Danny Bee; photo by Amos Mac

A BUTCHER WHO KNOWS HOW TO
HANDLE HIS MEAT

BERLIN REED

"When I asked [my friend] if we could use [her butcher shop] for the shoot, she started telling all these scary stories about it being haunted. Finding bloody boot prints . . . seeing a guy in the old-school freezer wearing a parka over knee boots . . . So yeah, during the shoot me and Amos got really West Coast Gay and smudged the entire place, telling the ghost we were cool and just wanted to take some photos."

DANNY BEE

"I feel like no matter where I am in my journey, I am in an ever constant state of growth in so many ways. Sometimes I feel like I am growing in a million different directions at once. With change comes growth. It doesn't just mean physical but emotional and mental.

Many guys put an emphasis on physical changes testosterone will bring when starting transition and rarely discuss any other changes. It's important to think about how thoughts, emotions, and how we sense the world around us may change as well.

This is an important part of how we move through the world. It can be challenging but can also be a wonderful experience to embrace. Sometimes part of making it through those changes is to accept the mystery and embrace the unknown."

APAULO
❦ HART ❦

"I am a sexual creature, I let it all hang out. It might not hang too low but it's out all right. I am the faun in the forest that whispers in your ear when you're hiking, 'You know you could totally jack off by that gorgeous tree and feel the wind on your ass. Go on, run around naked with your dog! Just watch out for poison ivy.'"

OP

ORIGINAL PLUMBING

TRANS MALE QUARTERLY
ISSUE 8 / FAMILY MATTERS
USA $8

THOMAS BEATIE
EXCLUSIVE!
TRANS DADS!

Your Mom

For *OP*'s Family Issue, instead of the usual Letters from the Editors, Amos and Rocco give their mothers the floor and they share the correspondence that forged a new friendship from 3,000 miles away.

HI DIANA!

Thrilled to have the opportunity to "chat" with you about our children! I hope we get to meet in person on one coast or the other.

I feel tremendous empathy and compassion for these children. Imagine knowing something wasn't quite right with yourself, with your "assignment," and not being able to articulate these feelings. Mix in the crazy soup of adolescence and imagine the challenges and hurdles these kids face. Did you ever feel something was "amiss" with Rocco growing up? Did you think he was a "tomboy" based on his preferences in sports, toys, and clothing? I sure did, but that was fine with me. I was comfortable with my child liking sports and rough and tumble stuff because I was such a "girly girl" growing up. It was kind of refreshing.

Were you relieved when Rocco told you he was transitioning? I was relieved and a little scared, just because anything to do with surgery and my child frightens me. I wanted it to be all about Amos. I knew Amos struggled for years, fearful of telling me the truth, because I would freak out or not want to see him again. Imagine what goes on in their minds: they want us to know who they are desperately because they love us, yet in sharing they risk losing their families or parent completely so they hide it, don't reveal it, remain distant.

In 2007 I read an article in the *New York Times*, something like "When Susan Becomes Steve," about a lesbian couple with kids. One partner wanted to transition. That Mother's Day, Amos came to my house to tell me about himself. I showed him the article before he told me. I wondered if that was what he was going through. He was happily surprised, relieved, I think.

I was okay with it because I want him to be happy and healthy. He asked if I wanted to name him, as I had when he was born, which I thought was so sweet. I said I think you've been through enough of what other people think you should be—you should choose your own name. Did Rocco give you any books to read about transitioning? Amos gave me several; one I recall was *Our True Selves*. I remember reading them alone and crying because I was mourning the loss of my daughter. I figured that was normal, and went with it. It's important to remember that time, because now it is as if I have always had a son. But when I talk with other parents of newly transitioning children, it's important to know that they are going through their mourning time now, and are not quite sure of anything, just as I was.

What do we do with the old photographs? Now I have such a huge collection of photographs of my handsome, beautiful son… I feel very proud and happy to frame them up and make wall groupings all over the house! Rocco is in quite a few of them as well! The other photos just stay where they are in the family albums or in the occasional frame. They are a part of history, after all.

What have you learned from being the parent of a transgender child? I know for me it was acceptance, tolerance, and love. Even though I grew up during hippies, the summer of love, and Woodstock, I could be judgmental about what I did not understand, and I know Amos hated that about me. I also learned how grateful I am to have such an amazing person in my life as Amos, and I wonder how I got to be so fortunate.

—*Carole*

     COVER MODEL: Ky and Sol; photo by Amos Mac

Photo by David Alfe

• AMOS AND HIS MOTHER CAROLE •

HI CAROLE!

I, too, hope that we can meet face to face someday soon. I would also like to thank you for watching out for Rocco; it makes me feel better about his move back east knowing there is a mom for him.

Our sons and all of their friends are my heroes, in that they have not taken the "life is unfair, so I won't do anything" attitude, but rather they have taken the ultimate responsibility for their lives and become who they felt they truly are. I am so proud of Amos and Rocco for what they are doing with OP, and being role models.

Speaking of role models, Rocco would hardly have been considered a role model in high school. You ask about Rocco and clothes, let me give you a brief history. As a small child, when we had ultimate control over clothing, the dresses were worn. By the time Rocco was in kindergarten he was sporting short hair. He liked to be called Perry or George. He was always dressed as a boy and preferred to play with the boys. However, his sister was much tougher than him. Junior High was a horror show for Rocco, as he developed he became so uncomfortable in his body. He felt gawky and awkward, and it showed in the way he related to fellow students. His voice was deep (already) and he hated his body. By high school, Rocco had found a way to circumvent the dress code; he was into the whole stoner unisex look—baggy jeans, over-sized T-shirt, and "I hate school" attitude. My husband and I really didn't try to enforce dress standards. During high school he also came out to us, and everyone else, as a lesbian, the only openly gay kid in high school. Who would have thought Rocco would be the shopaholic he is today, he is such a dandy, and fashion plate. I think it is because he loves his body now.

I love how Amos came to you to let you know he was transitioning. Rocco was on tour, and one night called us from a truck stop in Phoenix, Arizona, to let us know that he had made the decision to start transitioning. Very Rocco. He then asked us about family names. John's Grandfather was Rocco and that is how Rocco picked his name.

I don't remember being surprised since I knew Rocco had defined himself as butch. I guess it seemed a natural progression. I don't remember mourning for the loss of my daughter; I know that my husband was deeply affected by the change, and it was difficult for him. I think because Rocco had always seemed to be a boy that it did not seem such an upheaval. I had also worked for years with an FTM, and knew what the challenges and heartbreak were, so I had a different perspective.

I think the most difficult thing for me has been the surgeries. I can't even imagine it. I know going through them with Rocco was some of the worst experiences I have had, the one thing you never want to see is your child suffering. I told myself that his physical pain was to eliminate his mental/emotional pain. (But it still didn't help.)

You asked about the pictures. We are able to display so many pictures of Rocco when he was little because he looks like a little boy—he knew. Others are put away, which means putting away part of his sister's history as well.

The most difficult thing I have found is how to relate to people who knew you before your child transitioned. We have lost people who we thought were close friends. Or what do you say to the person who knew you before you became the mother of a full grown son, when they ask about your daughter, and you are with someone who has only known you with a son. You really don't want to get into the whole explanation/education of you and your child's experience. I have found that I have lost friends and found friends along the way. I have changed the way I explain my family history and the way I relate to the world around me.

My greatest hope, for both of my children, is that they are happy and healthy and are able to live their lives to achieve whatever they want. I would hope that they know that I think they are amazing!

Fondly, *Diana*

• ROCCO AND HIS MOTHER DIANA •

HI DIANA!

That was a rich introduction to your family and the "growing up" times. I feel like I know Rocco (and you!) so much better now. While Amos and Rocco certainly share a story and a personal journey, they followed very different paths to become themselves. The double mastectomy surgery frightened me, also. In the beginning, all I could think of was "self-mutilation" instead of "self-creating," but I knew it was necessary. Amos insisted on being alone with friends in San Francisco for the surgery and did not want me present. I was called immediately afterwards by both the doctor and his friends, which made me feel so much better. I even spoke to him right after surgery. Amos's decision to not have me present was his own and I had to respect it, even if I cannot totally understand why.

As the mom of a transgender child, your experiences with "friends" and other parents through the years have taught you much about prejudice, fear, and human frailty. Amos's aunt and adult cousins' first reaction when I told them about Amos transitioning was "That's ridiculous; she is a beautiful young woman." Later, they read up on the computer and seemed accepting. I was also told that I should "get therapy" by my adult niece, as if I was the one having difficulty accepting it! My husband, who is Amos's step-dad, felt sad for me. He started to get a little emotional around the time of the surgery. He thought it was making me sad. I had to reassure him that it was a good, important thing for Amos, and we would all be happier for it. He sees that is definitely the case today. I have to say that we are closer to being a "happy family" than we have ever been in our lifetimes.

You have become an "out" spokes-mom and that is so uplifting. I was so inspired by the children and adults at the Attic Youth Center in Philadelphia that I met at a Trans-Health conference with the boys that I volunteered to help them out, talking with other parents… if that would make a difference. I contacted a counselor there who was glad to have me as a resource. He said sometimes parents feel isolated and need someone to talk to, other than the therapist.

Yes, these children are my heroes, as well. I almost cried when I saw first-hand how much their magazine encouraged others in the FTM community when I tabled with them at the Trans-Health Conference for the past two years. People approach the table and these kids with reverence! They thank them for making the magazine. They ask to have their pictures taken with them. They try to tell them the influence it has had on their lives and self-esteem, without loosing their "cool" too much, of course. I thank them each day for making such a difference in the lives of others, and through simple words and photographs bringing hope, humor, and role models where there was none.

Thank you again for your letter and I look forward to meeting you in person soon!

—*East Coast Mom*

HI CAROLE / EAST COAST MOM,

What a joy it is talking with you. I really have not had much opportunity; actually I think that I have only spoken with one other mother of a transgender son. So this is a treat sharing our experiences and getting a sense of community. I am very proud of you for committing to act as a resource to other parents; you must be a great role model.

You mentioned the "T" in the LGBT. I have found that sometimes the least accepting members of society toward the "T"s are the rest of the LGBs. I think that even with groups like PFLAG, the parents of a transgender child are not addressed. After Rocco became Rocco, he experienced the loss of many of his lesbian friends who felt that he was a "traitor" to the cause. Even when trying to pass legislation, the "T" is frequently left out, with a "we can add you later." I have a number of gay friends that I have had to "educate" on what it means to be transsexual. Everyone always assumes that it means you are a drag queen or butch dyke. The attitude in the queer community seems to be changing and now there seems to be greater acceptance of the "T."

I had been leery telling my family about Rocco's decision. They really surprised me, in the best possible way. My mother, who had always favored my brother (it's a Greek thing, boys being the favorites), said, "Oh, good. Now I have a grandson," and proceeded to tell him and her four granddaughters that he was now her official favorite. And the sad thing is she means it. The rest of my family was great; they referred to Rocco as "him" and took down any pictures where he did not look like a boy—not that there were many.

When this journey, which is for all of us, began, I could not imagine it would take us where we are today. I am looking forward to what comes next. Carole, I know that the boys wanted us to do these letters for *OP*, but I would love to be able to talk with you on an on-going basis. It is really a joy to share experiences.

Hope to hear from you soon.

—*Left Coast Mom*

Beyond the Pregnant Man

THOMAS BEATIE

Interview and Photos by Elliot Foxprince

"This story is about so much more than just a man giving birth. This is a story about being true to oneself, following one's dreams despite the challenges and overcoming adversity."—Excerpt from Thomas's book, *Labor of Love*.

Thomas Beatie and his wife Nancy held a seminar during Pride Week in Stockholm, Sweden, to talk about their story and discuss their family's struggle. Thomas is internationally known as "the pregnant man," having legally transitioned from female to male and gone on to bear three children using his original plumbing. During the seminar, Thomas and Nancy spoke about the process they went through regarding the decision to have biological children, the hostility and adversity they faced from the medical community as well as the LGBT community, and the happy ending they've fought so hard for.

"Aligning myself with [Stockholm Pride 2011's] theme of 'openness,' I'm proud to show the world the beautiful children I've created with my wife Nancy, and I'm proud to be able to show the world our family. It's a mission that I'd like to continue, and I want to show them everything, different countries, different cultures, thoughts and philosophies, and all sides of humanity."

Throughout Thomas and Nancy's efforts to find medical support with conception, they were turned away by nine separate doctors, including a transgender doctor, who were unwilling to involve themselves with such a controversial issue. This transgender doctor told Thomas his child would be seen as an abomination in society. After finally finding support elsewhere, Thomas was able to conceive but had complications and lost the the embryos that had developed. They tried again with success, but had difficulty keeping the pregnancy private. After seeking legal consult and advice, Thomas was asked to write an article in LGBT news magazine *The Advocate* based on his struggles with the medical community as a pregnant trans man. The release of the article, along with a photograph of Thomas several months pregnant, sparked an unwanted media explosion, along with hate mail, death threats, and even letters of support. Their family now includes Susan (3 years old), Austin (2), and Jensen (1).

ELLIOT: Do you feel part of any specific community? Or do you feel pushed out of communities?

THOMAS: That's a good question. I've always felt strongly a part of the LGBT / GLBT / Q / QI / ABCDEFG… Yeah, I've always felt a part of that community for a really long time, until this happened, the "pregnant man" thing happened. I feel completely excluded, and it's really ironic because before we are used to the heterosexual society and the public at large discriminating against us and now it's been the reverse. It's like heterosexual, religious, conservative, Republican people are saying, "I support you," and meanwhile the GLBT community, especially in America, are like… I get emails that say, "I fucking hate you, I want you to die." And I get that first thing in the morning when I have a cup of coffee. And it's not just one day, I get at least—it depends on the week—but I may get one a day, I may get five a day. It's like, how can you take this kind of "Chinese torture" every single day, and this is within our community! I'm not just talking about the nut in Idaho, I'm talking about some transgender FTM who says, "I would never do what you did, and if I did I would kill myself." So I have to say part of me feels excluded although I still consider myself GLBT.

E: That's completely horrendous. I can't even believe that that happens inside the community.

T: Whenever I speak on TV I'm so PC and I don't like to offend anyone. But the trans issue and the GLBT in America really piss me off, and I have good reason to feel that

way. It is what it is, and I would like to be able to be part of Prides there, because I have a message and you know, I think a large part of it has to do with the fact that people think I got paid to do this, they think I want to be famous, and I don't know what the hell that's about. I just wanted a family, that's it.

E: And now you're here!

T: Yay, Sweden! Sweden's GLBT likes me! I'm gonna go and talk to people that like me, you know? People who want to hear a warm, fuzzy, positive message, because that's what it is. (*Susan walks up and tugs on her father's arm.*) And I got this!

E: And she's beautiful! All your children are! So, this is a pretty obvious question, but do you think that your newfound fame has altered your family life? For instance, if you hadn't had to be public about it, do you think it would've been a different sort of lifestyle?

T: Well, I think it was inescapable, it's like all destinies pointed to this because *National Enquirer* was—boom—there. And I was either going to let them tell my story, or I was going to go to Oprah and say it respectively, because I had that choice. I could've let the

tabloids have their way with me or say my peace, and that's what I did. And I feel like I made the right decision. So, I mean, is my life different? I liked obscurity. That's the whole reason we moved to Oregon, was to blend in. I wanted to assimilate. I didn't want to be recognized. I mean, I went from being a lesbian and the 'tweener thing and getting all those weird looks and then transitioning everybody rejects you, including your gay and lesbian and bisexual friends. So starting over in Oregon I just wanted to blend in. So, no. I mean, being public like this? Like I said, I don't like public speaking, I get nervous, it's one of my biggest fears. I can't believe I'm doing it, but I'm doing it because I feel like it's important for me to do.

E: What advice would you give to men of trans experience who wish to bear children but are worried about the experience?

T: Well, you know, barriers are crashing down, because stigma is dissolving. It's not such a shock now, you know? And people are getting it, because it's not just a national thing, people all over the world are talking about it, so it's not such a brain-buster anymore and I would say go for it.

WYATT & MAX

Two BFFs chat about
solo parenting & partnering up.

Photos by Amos Mac

"I became an adult and there she was. Zoe's at this point where I can have these really in-depth conversations with her, and she can really talk about things and it's this really great experience. . . . It's kind of phenomenal to talk to this little person who is becoming herself."
—Max

• MAX WITH HIS DAUGHTER ZOE AND BOYFRIEND MORGAN •

"Our entire adult lives have been defined by our children and spent with our children. Adrian was born four months before I turned 21, and I have been at home taking care of Lillie for the past year. Even though it's only been a year I feel as though I've known her forever, I can't imagine her not being there."
—Wyatt

• WYATT WITH HIS WIFE CHRISTINA AND THEIR KIDS ADRIAN AND LILLIE •

We Got Sol

KY & SOL

Words by Ky Platt / Photos by Amos Mac

I'm 38 and I'm a welder. Sol is 2 and a half. I always saw myself becoming a parent, as I have a huge family and family is extremely important to me. I never wanted to be pregnant and had always wanted to adopt a baby. I think I always had a phobia of pregnancy and was actually kind of repulsed by the concept of labor, but also I imagined I'd feel super trapped in my body if I was pregnant, sort of claustrophobic or something. Adoption can be very expensive, so there were times (in the beginning of our adoption process) that my partner and I considered getting pregnant, and I always reluctantly volunteered, but I have to admit that pregnancy was just really a means to an end for having a child, rather than something I actually wanted to do!

On the adoption process: It took so long to get Sol, from start to finish about 5 years. We started working with an NYC adoption agency that had a reputation of being very LGBT friendly, and after many failed attempts to match us with a birth mother, I got a call from the agency while I was at a conference in DC. I spoke to a coworker/friend hours before I was to meet our birth mother and she said something that has stuck with me to this day and I think reflects the kind of anxiety many trans male/butch women may feel in situations like these. She said, "No young African American woman is going to give her baby to a woman who looks like a man!" She told me that I needed to "femme it up." So… I femmed-it-up, which was a very dishonest thing to do, especially because my partner and I were adamant, even political, about having an open adoption, and I felt this was somehow in violation of that. I met our birth mother wearing a flouncy blouse and some dangly earrings, but I didn't hide any of my tattoos. We hit it off and later that night, around 2AM, our birth mother called our agency to tell them she wanted to choose us to be the parents of her then 6-month-old fetus!

A few weeks later, my partner and I drove down to DC to take our birth mother to her prenatal appointment. I was not dressed in femme-drag for this! We saw the sonogram and the most beautiful fetus in the history of fetuses!

We talked constantly to our birth mother during the last months of her pregnancy, and on January, 2, 2009, I was getting out of the shower to meet my friend for whisky and cigars, when I heard my partner screaming in the living room, "She's in labor and has been for 12 hours!" Thank god I didn't drink any whiskey beforehand, I was about to drive to DC from NYC to meet my daughter! There was no way she could hold off giving birth for our 4 to 5 hour drive, so our sister-in-law attended our birth mother in the labor room. At 1:17AM, we got a call, Sol had been born 5 lbs, 10 oz, perfect Apgar test, and she came out with nothing on her… the nurses didn't have to clean her off. I like to think Sol came out of the womb with her bags packed, ready for NYC!

There was plenty of drama during our stay in DC. We needed to stay in northern Virginia until we got court clearance to bring Sol home, thanks to the Interstate Compact Law on the Placement of Children. I won't focus on the negative events that occurred during those 10 days, but it takes a really strong person and a supportive group of friends and family to help you through, and thankfully, we had that! There are so many people to thank, but the two strongest women I know are my partner and Sol's birth mother.

In April of 2010, we finalized Sol's adoption in a Manhattan court.

On transitioning: I have always been trans. Always. My mom says she knew I was trans/queer at the age of 3. All of this knowing proved to be a pretty uneventful and underwhelming coming-out-as-trans experience. My family and friends have been like, "Umm… wait… you're not living as a guy now?" Or, "Yeah, I always considered you a white guy trapped inside a black girl's body." Nice. Anyway, when I moved to NYC from southern Ohio to live a more honest life, I also began to focus on creating a family. I guess in part, I'm just not good at multitasking major life changes, so I postponed transitioning to focus on the adoption process. I have to say, this was probably a good decision, at least for me. To start with, unless you change all of your ID papers, driver's license, birth certificate, Social Security card, etc., you are likely going to have to tell someone along the way during the adoption process that you are trans, and that could potentially derail an adoption or at least be very stressful to explain. We wanted an open adoption and that, in a basic sense, means that your child will know who their birth parents are and they have the option of meeting them at some point. So, with transitioning in an open adoption, I would have started out pre-T looking a certain way and post-T looking a certain way, and during the course of an adoption from birth to finalization I would have potentially looked like an entirely different person. So I chose to wait to begin T after finalization. The issue now is with changing my name on my birth certificate and then changing it on Sol's birth certificate. That would take more lawyer's fees and another trip to the courts, so I am choosing not to change my name, simply because it could cause so much disruption in our lives. That's my choice, but other trans folks may feel that's a process they can handle. I just keep reminding myself that what seems important right now in my experience as a trans parent, may not 5 years from now, so I'm taking it slow and enjoying my life with my beautiful child!

Describe Sol in 10 words or less:

That's impossible! Let's see… soulful, smart, confident, strong, loving, athletic, personable (she says hi to all the neighbors and random people on the street if they make eye-contact! Pretty much the opposite of me!), a mama's girl (she and my partner are absolutely obsessed with each other), musical, beautiful! I could really go on and on, I've never met a person quite like Sol.

On Names: She has an adult vocabulary! I call her a "bossy Capricorn" and a "little bossy black woman!" She calls me whatever she wants. I'm not particular about being called "dad" or "he" (at least for now), so I've never really attempted to persuade Sol to call me male names, but she's so smart, she'll say things like "good boy, mom mom!" if I do something she likes, or she'll call me "the handsome mama." Lately she's been calling me "Papa Ky" or just "Ky." The best advice I could give trans folks who want to be parents is to do it! I think if you know you want to be a parent, you'll regret it if you don't at least try. And, the opposite is true, if you know you don't want to be a parent, then don't! Not everyone needs to be a parent. The one thing I didn't know before I adopted a baby was just how strong I needed to be. I really needed to conjure up a reserve of courage and strength to complete a process that is currently very hostile to trans people and LGBT people in general. The most important thing to remember is that this is your process. If the lawyer you hired is even remotely transphobic, fire them! If your agency has questionable policies or is not as progressive as other agencies, fire them! There are resources out there for every type of family and you shouldn't settle for a situation that disrespects you in any way.

StoryTime

Me and My Teen Queen

By Charlie Stephens

James and I are an unlikely pair. Our daily, private joke is being in any public space and watching people try to figure out what is going on with us, our relationship to each other. People stare unabashedly at him in his tight pink leggings and assortment of scarves and bracelets, booty-popping in the line and singing way off-key while waiting to get a vanilla latte. Recently at his school, where all students entering in the morning get a quick pat down (how is this legal?) and their bags checked, the security guard called me "son" and held out his arm to block me from entering the grounds. It took him a few minutes to realize I was not a student, and his face paled about thirty shades when James said, "Um. That's my parent."

Actually James alternates between calling me his "foster mom" and "foster dad" and yes, I did get a different handwritten card for both mother's and father's day. While he occasionally goes by the name "Latoya" he mostly identifies as a boy. I enjoy the times I pass as a male, but it hasn't been my focus in recent years. We are both sort of "in the middle" in terms of gender at least these days. It's a rather amazing thing to be able to relate to each other about, given the vast distance between our generations and our histories.

The long story of how he came to be with me is not mine to tell, but transphobia and homophobia are two main reasons why he has been in the foster care system most intensively since approaching puberty and coming out. The ongoing violence he has experienced in neighborhoods, homes, and schools for identifying as gay, and sometimes transgender, is devastatingly disappointing and has definitely made me more skeptical of safety in general as he and I both navigate the so-called "gay mecca" of the Bay Area. Tonight he is home from the hospital, after getting an intensive surgery after being gay-bashed in San Francisco after a visit with his favorite cousin. Dressed in feminine clothes, mostly varying shades of pink, he is an easy target, and yet refuses to hide his true self. In conversations, I am constantly humbled by how true he is to the parts of himself that most people in his life have actively rejected: the parts of his gender that do not conform. On his wall hangs his "prom dress" that he convinced someone to buy for him a couple years ago, and then hid even from me, even after all our open talks, for half a year. When I've asked him about going back to the name "James" after asking to be called "Latoya" in the past, he answers very straightforwardly that he is afraid of being hurt or killed for "getting caught." "I'll just be a gay boy for now," he says, "it's easier, and maybe things will be better for us in a few years."

Social workers I meet with weekly give me regular praise for opening my home to a gay/trans child, because these children remain by far the most difficult young people to place in accepting homes and most often "age out" of the system without ever having experienced any familial acceptance for their whole selves. I'm typically uncomfortable with this praise, as I honestly can't think of anything more gorgeous, beautiful, heartbreaking, and worth it, than trying my hardest to be a positive and accepting human in the lives of James and his friends, all with their tiny, tight shorts, their sometimes girl names, their dangly earrings, and their regular weekend sleepovers that typically showcase amazingly incessant singing, as femininely high-pitched and soulful as they can muster, which is very much so, on both counts.

Carry an Eraser and Other Tips for Drawing Your Own Family Tree

By Nick Krieger

Some of us like the relatives we're given. Some of us prefer to select our own. If you're creating a chosen family, I recommend following these guidelines before you commit to a decade of Pride festivities, New Year's Eve drag shows, and vegan Thanksgivings.

Sleep with them first. In queer life, this is the opposite of incest. It is actually a prerequisite for family. Sex produces the intimacy that was missed in childhood from sharing bunk beds or learning to ride bicycles together. And, by getting sex out of the way, you won't be left wondering whether you do, in fact, want to sleep with each other. If sex has not happened, you should at least make sure you've slept with them by proxy, like through an ex of your ex. This way at holiday parties, instead of playing the Kevin Bacon game, you can play Six Degrees of Family Boning.

Recruit one functioning uterus in a body that desires to procreate. It may take a village to raise a child, but only one reproductive system (and a vial of sperm) to produce one. Of course, adopting, fostering, or existing children can fill the void if nobody is interested in pushing one out for the family. The point is, kids are a lovely addition because they encourage us to grow mustaches and call ourselves uncles.

Make sure they can give T shots. While you may want to take care of this yourself, there comes a time when everyone wants their mama, so make sure you have one in your family, regardless of their age or gender. If your mama is also your daddy, then you can either get kinky with it, or you can take turns shooting each other up. It's similar to bonding like blood brothers, except safer.

Develop a quiz for them called: "Will you still love me if?" This is especially important if you're estranged from your given family because they answered "no" when confronted with the real-life "Will you still love me if I'm trans?" question. Here are some suggestions for your quiz: "Will you still love me if I do fetish porn? Miss your top surgery anniversary? Call myself a straight man? Say 'bio' instead of 'cis' or make another mistake that sets back The Movement?"

Ask yourself, "Will this person represent the family well?" This is more than making sure your older brother, sister, or broster is attractive, fashionable, and cool. It means checking for quality. Because when they drop their drawers in the car and moon that elderly couple for no reason, you can't just shrug your shoulders and blame shared genes. You choose these people. So, you better choose wisely.

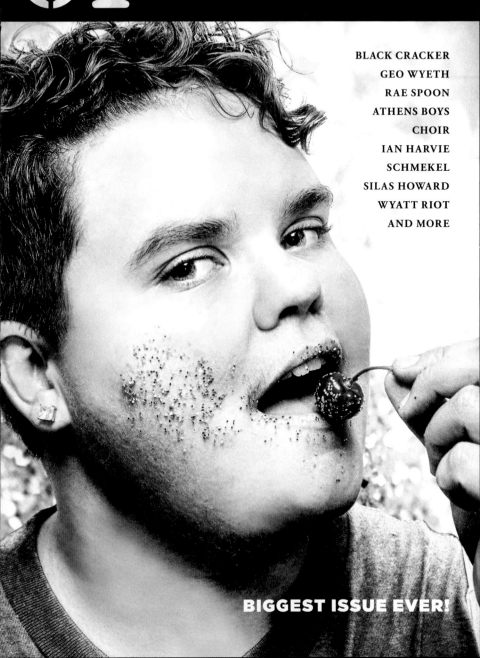

OP
ORIGINAL PLUMBING
TRANS MALE QUARTERLY
ISSUE 9 / **ENTERTAINMENT**
USA $8

BLACK CRACKER

GEO WYETH

RAE SPOON

ATHENS BOYS
CHOIR

IAN HARVIE

SCHMEKEL

SILAS HOWARD

WYATT RIOT

AND MORE

BIGGEST ISSUE EVER!

WELCOME TO OP's FIRST ENTERTAINMENT ISSUE

COVER MODEL: Wyatt Riot; photo by Amos Mac

When we first started *OP*, I knew immediately we had to do an entertainment issue at some point. Being a performer myself, with a trans identity, I have experienced the difficulty surrounding my identity and media outlets. All too often all that is asked of trans performers and artists is how far along they are in their transition and what the next physical step will be, with a side note about whatever it is they have created. We are seeking to change that.

I am so excited that *Original Plumbing* is a space where we can focus on the artists and their desire to create and share their work with the world. There are so many people in our community who are brilliant musicians, filmmakers, artists, actors, playwrights, and comedians, and we are thrilled to be able to spotlight a handful of them for you.

—Rocco

There is something special that happens when I photograph performers and artists—they either love it or hate it; feel incredibly constricted or feverishly alive in front of the lens— and flipping through the images, the end result is never what I assumed I'd get from them beforehand. It was a privilege to photograph every artist in this issue. I hope you enjoy the visuals as much as I did creating them.

I felt inspired by the old days of Andy Warhol's *Interview* magazine circa 1970–90 while working on this issue. The cover boy, Wyatt Riot, conveys a sexy vintage Hollywood look, while the Schmekel spread was my own take on the iconic "sock" photo shoot of the Red Hot Chili Peppers. Mixing it up a bit, we had artists interview each other: In Harvie On Harvey, comic Ian Harvie and Harvey Katz of Athens Boys Choir shoot questions at each other. We are honored to be a media outlet where these artists are able to let their guard down and share their work with the world.

—Amos

SILAS HOWARD

The 90s punk rock musician-turned-filmmaker remains legendary

INTERVIEW BY ROCCO KAYIATOS & AMOS MAC
PHOTOS BY AMOS MAC

Let's start from the beginning. How did Tribe 8 come together?
Lynnee [Breedlove] and I wanted to start a band but didn't have a
clue how to play, minor obstacle. It was the 90s, anyone could be in
a band. So we enlisted Kat our first drummer and played a friend's
birthday party where we met Leslie Mah, who was way cooler than
us. She gave Lynnee a first-rate punk sneer, and then joined us. We
started playing queer clubs and straight punk venues like Gilman
Street in Berkeley. Our third show ever was there with Bikini Kill,
Nation of Ulysses, and Fugazi.

***We've heard rumors about how you had to steal
musical instruments...***
Since I didn't play guitar before the band there was the pesky problem
of not actually owning a guitar. Back then we were very aggressive in
alternative funding and so I decided to steal a guitar. It was a major
sting operation. I went in dressed like a hippie, another friend was
planted outside to run into the store clerk once he chased me, another
friend out front on my motorcycle waited for me to hop on and drive
us to a fourth friend in a van where I was to hop in and drive off. All
should have gone well except that...

the clutch popped when my friend revved it to take off and we crashed right into the car in front of us. The bike went down in front of the shop. So we ran. I went one way and my friend, the other. I ended up taking off my wig and shirt and walking right by with mohawk and t-shirt trying to get my bike, as it would lead them right to me, but no luck. My friend got chased by the clerk and turned around to scare him, she was a badass passing butch, and as she did so the Guardian Angels came around the corner and grabbed her thinking she was a man, and a black man at that, coming toward a white man and grabbed her before asking any questions. Luckily we were rescued by Bo Brown, an ex political prisoner involved in the George Jackson Brigade who I worked with at the lesbian-owned organic vegetable distributor (oh-so San Francisco). Bo took us under their wing and into the arms of a liberal lawyer who got us off with minor charges and fees that I paid. Later I had to do a different scam to get the guitar but that's another story.

In 2002 you made the film By Hook or By Crook *with Harry Dodge, the first film I've ever seen where trans characters existed but where it wasn't the centerpiece of what the film was trying to tell you. Why did you decide to transition into filmmaking?*

Honestly? Pure ignorance. I had no idea how hard it was going to be, definitely a case of leap before you look. And I came out of this mid-90s SF mindset of "What you don't see, make," don't wait for someone to do it for you. Harry [Dodge] and I wanted to see a different story up on the screen, one that embraced those living on the outskirts of "normalcy" but dealt with universal struggles, like the frailty of dreams and search for home, and for it to be funny and risk-taking even if it failed. Rather than bear the burden of explaining ourselves (gender stuff, why Harry had a beard, etc.) we chose to focus on a tale of transformative friendship, on being the hero to the person next to you. Anyway, we went forth and

made a feature with no prior film experience. It nearly undid us, as we finally finished the first draft of *By Hook or By Crook*, the dot com craze had firmly gained hold of San Francisco and the few artists who hadn't been evicted were now making money. The community really came out to support us, investing whatever they could. Three years later it was done; the first screening was at the Castro Theater to a sold-out crowd and received a ten-minute standing ovation. It was one of the best moments. I remember after, this very young punk girl came up to me and said, "I've been waiting my whole life for a movie like this!" It touched me so profoundly, I felt like saying, "Thank you for telling me that, because it took us practically your whole life to make this movie."

Tell us about the Bearded Lady Cafe.
I had been to Europe with Tribe 8 and seen all these amazing squats and it emboldened me.

The cafe's full name was Red Dora's Bearded Lady Cafe and Truck stop. For real. It was meant to sound like part Bob's Big Boy Diner and part circus sideshow. It had a red door so that's where Red Dora came from. Harry had a cool beard but weirdly we weren't thinking of that when we named it. I just remembered someone's dad saying, "Who's gonna want to eat in a cafe called that?" Luckily he was wrong.

It was a tiny space, the size of an aspirin cap, bathroom so tiny you had to sit sideways on the toilet. We had food warmers for spot lights when the shows happened, we made steamed eggs on the espresso machine, it was amazing. You could walk in and see a rag-tag assemblage of neighborhood regulars, punks, fairies, and random indie celebrities—all in the mix drinking coffee out of these huge bowls we served it in. We thought it was very French to drink coffee out of bowls. The shows held there were amazing. It felt like anything could happen, good or bad. Kris Kovick would book a 20s style street musician, a first time reader, Jewell Gomez, films by Greta Snider and Kate Bornstein all in one show. It was a place you could

he co-wrote. At the screening a white critic complained about representation of Asians in this film, then Roger Ebert stood up and said if this was a white director with a film about white teenagers, they would never be asked such a question and perhaps likely praised for being "edgy." Then there's the flipped version of this scenario that I experienced with a project of mine, where the studio found it "not edgy enough" to tell a story that deals with matters of the spirit but isn't focused on explaining transgender or address it as the central obstacle to the story. Too edgy, not edgy enough—they screw you coming and going. I say this not to complain. Hell, I owe a lot to the obstacles in my life, they're the fuel behind almost everything I've made, but if I don't acknowledge the unspoken rules of the mainstream narrative, and how powerful it is, then I start to feel a little crazy.

We decided to return to our roots but with years of experience under our belts and make "professional film," a whimsical story with a subtle subversity, in a punk rock production style. That's how *Sunset Stories* came about. It still took goddamn years to finish and we're gleeful that its premiere is so soon on the horizon.

Sunset Stories will have its premiere at SXSW 2012, which I'm excited as hell about! It has cameos by Justin Vivian Bond, Sandy Martin (amazing butch dyke in her 50s who plays a man on *Big Love*), Nao Bustamante, Jim Parsons (from *Big Bang Theory*), and Lee Meriwether (original Catwoman!), and those are just the cameos. It's a sweet story of letting go. I'm also editing my chapter of *Valencia* (the Movies) Chapter 9, part of a very innovative approach to adapting Michelle Tea's novel into a feature film and I'm working with an NYC producer to make Michelle Tea's novel *Chelsea Whistle* into a film. In the wings still, the script Nina Landey and I wrote based on the Billy Tipton story. **OP**

start out reading your first story and evolve that into a show or a band or a book. It was, as Kovick put it, like we took turns being the important person in the room.

How did your new film Sunset Stories come about?

A group of us had dinner at my house, lamenting the games Hollywood studios play. We all worked professionally in that world for a few years, waiting, waiting to get financed and make our work. My co-director Ernesto Foronda had been to Sundance with a film

TRANS ON FILM

1919–1999

FILMS NOTABLE FOR THEIR REFRESHING, INTRIGUING, OR JUST PLAIN FUCKED-UP VIEW OF LIFE OUTSIDE THE BINARY.

BY HENRY GIARDINA

First off, forgive me if these all seem like incredibly negative depictions of trans folks (especially trans women, who got the shittiest end of the stick up until about, oh, 2010). So much of mainstream cinema is about dealing with concepts people didn't even know they were dealing with, which explains the misguidedness with which they usually went about dealing with them. Case in point: **Boys Don't Cry, Transamerica,** *Milton Berle's compulsory cross-dressing, all 200 versions of* **Charley's Aunt.** *I find myself extremely forgiving of certain developments in film (i.e., the trans-female psycho-killer) than I probably should be. But there you are...*

I DON'T WANT TO BE A MAN · 1919

A woman (played by the excellently named Ossi Oswalda) decides that boys have more fun. They get to wear top hats and smoke cigars, and—as it happens—drunkenly make out with their male friends riding home after a night at the club. Her rugged foray into alternative lifestyles only lasts a night, after which she decides she probably doesn't want to be a man, however fun it may have been.

TRANS HAMLET · 1921

Asta Nielsen's *Hamlet*, affectionately termed "Trans Hamlet" by the students of my Film and Psychology class, is possibly the first film to take on the notion of a trans character (albeit, weirdly forced into trans-ness) seriously. The great Danish actor Asta Nielsen plays Hamlet as a "secret girl." They even added some lines for context (i.e., "now thy secret is revealed.") Nice to believe that there was an innocent time, not so long ago, in which people believed that Shakespeare needed a little help, plot-wise. The boost is intriguing, if not much else. And it's believable—at least it was for me. While we were being forced to read *Hamlet* in high school, everyone else was trying to figure out what the hell his problem was. I felt like I already knew—if subjectively. At least, I had an easier time putting myself into the melancholy Dane, screaming at mom, driving the girlfriend to suicide, hating on uncle.

THE PASSION OF JOAN OF ARC · 1929

The usually boring fable of Joan of Arc is told through the lens of her trial, and becomes, like the Wilde trials and the McCarthy period, about a crime of personality.

Why do you wear men's clothes they ask? Joan says it's because she needs to lead her country to freedom, and that once she does she'll return to wearing dresses. The trial that follows is more to do with her unorthodox appearance than the fact that England is at war with France. They tell her that if she'll wear a dress, she'll be permitted to attend mass. It's one of the rare films, books, or really anything I can think of that regards faith and gender nonconformity as not being mutually exclusive.

FIRST A GIRL · 1931

An early version of *Victor/Victoria*, wherein English music hall sensation Jessie Matthews impersonates a man impersonating a woman so well that suspicions arise. The awkward title is perhaps the most appreciable part, which begs for a sequel to be titled *Secondly, a Boy*.

HOMICIDAL · 1961

Homicidal was a colorful, cold-war response to *Psycho*, which even a year after its release no one could stop talking about. A biological woman is made to present as male for her entire life in order not to be fucked out of an inheritance—or actually, it's possibly the other way around (so convoluted). In any case it fucks with her quite a bit, and she becomes: homicidal. She goes on a coldly calculated killing spree, trying to wipe out anyone who knew of her gender-identity mix-up at birth, including the nurse she had as a child who inexplicably accompanied her to Denmark at one point for gender reassignment surgery (don't ask). The denouement takes place in an abandoned mansion, where viewers get to see the shadow of the killer's last victim—the nurse, wheelchair bound—a silhouette of her detached head falling off and bouncing down the stairs. It's the revenge film to end all revenge films—but very unconstructive as therapy. Though a scene at the very beginning, when the killer is a child, is something that has become almost irritatingly recognizable by now: a little boy goes up to his sister, who is playing with a doll. He tries to take it from her, because he doesn't want to play with his own "masculine" toys. When he finally wrests it from her, we know he'll probably have to answer for it in more ways than one. Depressing, but for so many, a succinct summing-up of childhood.

DRESSED TO KILL · 1980

I love Michael Caine in this more than I love most things in life. I love his wig, the fact that his name is Bobbi with an *i*. I love the white hospital shoes he wears in the last scene, and the desperate message he leaves on his own message machine (even if they do make recourse to the "I'm trapped in a man's body" causology). Where trans imagery in the media is concerned, it's not the most diplomatic film in the world. But I can't help getting a thrill every time I watch Bobbi come out of the elevator in his cat-eye shades and blonde wig, looking sexier than Michael Caine in the raw—in the cis, if you will—ever could. Slash away, baby. Slash away.

BOYS DON'T CRY · 1999

The fictionalized story of Brandon Teena needs no introduction. I'm surprised it even snuck its way in here, but you can't very well not talk about it. The film that "broke the dam," so to speak, reads false and obnoxious to some and a groundbreaking and honest to others. What can't be argued is that it's one of the first films to show the risk of transgender life, and not try to link it to science, biology, or make any kind of "condition" out of it. That said, the protagonist dies at the end. But where Hollywood is concerned, we're always taking the wins with the losses.

BLACK CRACKER

INTERVIEW BY ROCCO KAYIATOS
PHOTOS BY AMOS MAC

You were a poet first. Did you always know you were going to eventually make music?
I actually wanted to make music all along. All my original writing was for music, but I could not afford any gear. Making beats with two cassette tape recorders got old very quick and a friend suggested I check out the Nuyorican Poets Cafe and then that was the start of my accidental poetry "career." Totally random considering I failed English in high school, preventing me from graduating on time.

Is it different for you to perform poetry than it is to perform hip hop? How?
Well, I don't so much consider what I do musically to be hip hop. I feel for me the main difference is with poetry I tend to be less able to go into a sorta character or character of the ideas. So for me my poetry was never a "performance," was always super real and was difficult to live that vivid. Music is more enjoyable for my spirit but I think I am a more powerful poet. So I am really working hard to let the two play together.

Tell us about how you started Bunny Rabbit, your old band with your ex girlfriend.
It's a long story. I had the idea one night then told her the next day. She had never made music before. She was an actress but not so much a writer. It took a lot of work and a lot of time. The second record was gonna be Bunny Rabbit and Black Cracker but we broke up before I could really get the "credit" I "deserved," ha ha this is clearly a soft spot. But yeah, Bianca from CocoRosie wanted to put out my record but I convinced her to put out the Bunny Rabbit's album. Wish I had had the self-esteem then that I have now but life is a lil journey I suppose.

What has it been like doing your solo project?
It's really just beginning. My debut record is coming out April Fools' Day on a small Swiss label called Hinterhaus. I am nervous and ex-

cited cause I have developed a lil bit of a "name" collaborating with other projects, so many people don't realize I am just getting started as a solo musician. I think some times it's hard to get the sorta support of being "new" cause I am not. But the best part of being solo is that I can be myself and be seen as myself. I like making friends and being human. Some artists can be so removed or uppity and that shit breaks my heart. So the time is just of a higher quality when I represent myself and my worldview.

What is your favorite part of being a performer?
Seeing people or, rather, being responsible for people, going from flat feet and inhibition to carefree and sweaty by the end of the night. My goal is to engage and access that piece of all of us made dim by the repetition of the mundane.

Do you have any good tour stories?
Well the "Tour of Tears" was quite an experience, with CocoRosie in 2005, I think. They wanted to do like 43 shows in 45 days, which is insane. Add to that a mom in the tour bus, numerous ex-lover dynamics, and me performing two shows with two broken bones before having to have surgery on Thanksgiving. I could go on but really the name says it all. Was cray for real.

What is the biggest benefit to having the career you have and what is the biggest drawback?
The drawbacks are as follows: lonely nights watching CNN, lonely nights watching German overdubs of *Law & Order*. Lonely nights in general, more or less broke as all living hell. The benefits: being able to see the world for free, making friends in small towns, free alcohol, this list can go on and on. I do at the end feel more than blessed and just try and give my all as a thank you towards what has been given to me.

"The best part of being solo is that I can be myself"

SCHMEKEL

DEEP INSIDE 100% TRANS JEWS.

INTERVIEW BY ROCCO KAYIATOS
PHOTO BY AMOS MAC

OP: *How does it feel to be, in our opinion, the most important, relevant Jewish "boy band" in the entire world?*

ITAI (FORMERLY RICKY RIOT): I'm loving it. I love my bandmates, and our fans are so fuckin' cool. I hope that this band will make more voices of queer and trans people heard in the Jewish community and, G-d willing, will make Jewish life more accessible to people who experience gender differently.

NOGGA SCHWARTZ: The entire world? That's a lot. It is super cool. It feels great to get to share this project with folks and hang out and have great conversations about issues that affect many people, and draw from that to find humor and lightheartedness in things that can be difficult to deal with. I have to say I also like the improvement in my dating life.

LUCIAN KAHN: I'm still kind of hovering in denial that anybody other than my roommate cares about our bonkers project. It makes me really happy, though. My biggest goal with this band is to cheer up some queers who don't have enough cheerful music that relates to their experience.

SIMCHA HALPERT-HANSON: Having had pursued and given up on the rock star dream earlier in life, I'm still unable to comprehend that the dream is now in fact happening. Once I stopped looking, my dream showed up.

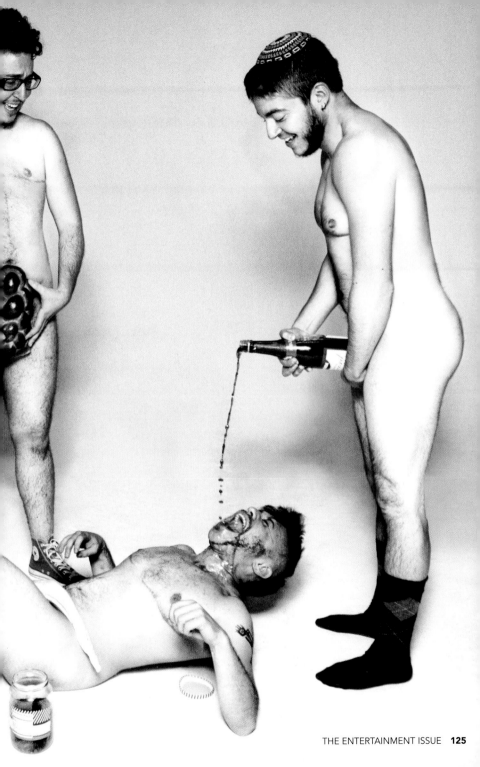

Photo by Amos Mac

IAN
HARVIE

HARVIE ON HARVEY

Ian Harvie

BY HARVEY KATZ

How has medical transition affected your Butch identity?

That's a good question. Internally and spiritually my Butch identity is completely intact and as solid as ever. I still identify as such, along with trans, and that's not only my history but my present. I didn't give up one to be another. I'm more of a collector of identities and words that feel right to me. To me this is an inarguable point. I am who I say I am and that's not up for debate. However, I do miss being visually Butch within my own queer community. Sometimes I look at Butch/Femme couples a little too long for their liking, maybe making them feel a little uncomfortable. I want to reach out and say, "Hey, I know that you are, and I am, and we are." I know in that situation, if I were to give the ole Butch nod, that shit wouldn't fly as easy as it did before.

I found a link to FTMLover.com on your website. Can you tell me more about it?

I started a dating site for people who adore FTMs. I know people get really bent about people who objectify trans folks or are considered tranny chasers. But there *are* people who absolutely, genuinely love us and want to fuck us. I wanted to create a space where people can find us and make friends or meet up and make sweeeeet looooove. It's a cool site and a lot of sweat and tears went into it. We have a zero tolerance for hate of any kind on there. We also have a video dating module for those who'd like to chat/play online. I'm always working on making it better, but we have about 2,000 members right now and it's growing fast. I'm really proud of it.

Who are your comic idols?

Some are my friends and some are long gone. Richard Pryor, Flip Wilson, Bill Hicks, Carol Burnett, Paula Poundstone, and of course, my gal pal Margaret Cho.

How did comedy become your performance of choice?

I tried all kinds of other shit that I was mediocre or just plain sucked at. This is the one thing that I felt connected to and wanted to do every waking moment and not half-ass it. Comedy is the best drug I've ever done.

Tell me about your first time doing stand up.

Angry all day before the performance, I don't handle stress well. Then diarrhea for 3 hours preceding the show, and then 5 minutes on stage in a comedy blackout. People clapped a lot and I was high and couldn't wait to do it again, and again.

Harvey Katz

BY IAN HARVIE

Define yourself. Who are you, how many parts of you are there?

As far as I know there is just one of me but with my sun sign in Pisces and many other planets in Virgo, I'm not sure it comes across that way. Today, I'm just a dude with too much to do and no focus. Today, Pisces wins.

How did you get started writing/performing?

Damn! This is the time when I have to thank my ex. I had a *really* bad breakup in 2003 and she had "mentioned" to me that she thought my writing sucked. I had started writing spoken word style poetry in 2001 just as I came out as trans. I was living in Athens, GA, where there was absolutely no resources or support for trans folks, so I wrote spoken word that was identity based because I was too broke for therapy and people tend to listen more when your journal entry rhymes. I had no intention of making this my career. I had some serious stage fright but when you have a broken heart, the crazy takes you to crazy places and I thought, "I'll show you! You may not like my poetry but there are people out there who will." It became my main goal in life then to prove her wrong so I hit the road with Rocket, who was formally the other half of Athens Boys Choir, got signed by Daemon Records, and inevitably had to thank her in the end. Such is life.

What are your feelings about your biological past/present/future?

I often think it was my hand in life to end up a trans person. I think if I was born a male assigned person, I would have ended up a trans woman. I'm okay with it. I can't imagine not being a trans person. I feel lucky to have this journey. Being socialized female and spending my life "othered" by this world gives me a unique perspective. In the past, this has felt like shit. In the present, it feels pretty good. In the future, I hope somebody loves me enough to watch me age ungracefully.

Are you a role model or a public figure?

I'm not sure if I'm both or neither. I know my figure is public. I medically transitioned on a stage and, for better or worse, my second puberty was witnessed over many years under unflattering lighting. I have also modeled many roles but that's another interview altogether. But seriously, I don't know. I think my words and music have helped some folks and that feels damn good.

What is your life's biggest struggle and gift?

Whew, that's a deep question. I don't think about the struggles too much because I still can't afford therapy. Hell, we all struggle. I struggle with worry and self-doubt. I struggle to say the right things and do the wrong things with gusto. The biggest gift in my life is that people give a shit what I say. I'm a guy with a career in the arts. That's a gift given to you by others.

What do you do when you retreat?

Make coffee and take my pants off, not necessarily in that order.

What does it take to be a poet/writer/performer?

A pen and paper, good luck, irrational thoughts, and blind faith.

You're a wordsmith. Any words you love/hate?

I love the words: irresistible, peninsula, grandma, serpentine, and debauchery. I dislike the words: moist (join the club), thee, and fortuitous.

Are you an optimist/realist/or...?

Optimist! No, realist. No, optimist. I think.

Tell me about your sexual history in relation to your identity?

I came out as bisexual as a 13-year-old to some folks and just about everybody else by the time I was 17. Nobody was surprised. My mom even made my dad see a psychiatrist about me being queer years before I came out to her. I have been so many different people in my own life but I've always been queer. For a long time I could only identify myself by what I wasn't. Queer was the only thing I knew I was. It's been the one identity I can always count on.

Photo by Amos Mac

GEO

How did you get your start making music?

I was extremely lucky and was given piano lessons starting at the age of 5 from a woman in our building in Hell's Kitchen. She was also Alicia Keys's piano teacher (Alicia lived in my building). But I have to say my first real experience with creating my own music was with my parents, particularly my mother. My mother used to sing throughout the day, without even noticing it—while she was writing books in her room (she's a writer), while she was buying ravi-oli at Bruno's on 9th Avenue (much to the confusion of the shopkeeper), while walking down the street, washing dishes, cooking furiously in the kitchen. She has a beautiful voice. I used to sing with her, random melodies, or songs from the Cole Porter songbook (her favorite), or just "talk singing," which is just a sing-songy way of saying anything. I think it helped her get through her day. She is a deeply theatrical and wacky lady, my mom, and I inherited this from her. My father also plays the guitar and writes

WYETH

INTERVIEW AND PHOTO BY AMOS MAC

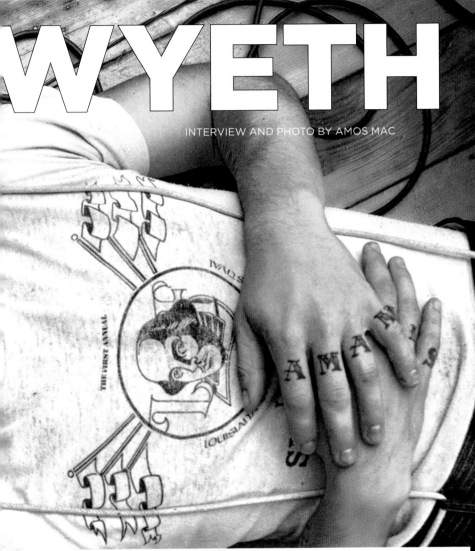

folk songs, so there was also a lot of that in our home. He bought me my first guitar. There was an amazing jazz program at our church and that's where I learned how to play the bass, which I played more and more in punk bands throughout high school.

Do you like performing as much as you like making the songs?

I consider these things to be very similar. When I am making the songs, I am performing. I am embodying and enacting emotion, usually through improvisation. I like to think that my performances carry the same energy as my rehearsals. I am very interested in the power of the moment to carry an idea, even if the outcome is not totally planned. Anyone who has played with me can attest that I often will have "sneak attack" moments at the show, where everyone is forced to think on their feet or make something up on the spot. Not everybody likes this... but that is when we are the most awake!

TYRA MALE

BY JOSHUA KLIPP

When people hear I went on *The Tyra Banks Show*, their first question is usually "What's Tyra like?" I say, "The first time she was all business. The second time pretty nice."

The story of how I came to be on *The Tyra Banks Show* is not glamorous. I'd like to say it's because I'm a big deal, but actually they wanted my 40-something-year-old roommate and he said, "No thanks, but talk to my friend Josh." He also told them I was a musician and they should let me play on the show. When they said they only have "high caliber" artists perform like Beyoncé, his response was "I don't know who Beyoncé is but Josh is great." (He really didn't know who she was—I love that guy.)

So they called me because they were doing a show on trans people in relationships and needed a trans man. I was in a relationship, but wasn't interested in splaying myself all over national TV if it did nothing for my aspirations of music superstardom. When they asked about my girlfriend, I knew they'd faint if I told them she was a former NBA cheerleader (true). Then when they invited me on I said only if you also talk about my music. Yeah, I played hardball with Tyra. I mean, not really, but when you're nobody in the music

industry with a chance to go on national TV, it felt like a big gamble. They agreed to do it.

The days leading up to the show were non-stop. The producers called constantly and wanted to know everything about my life: my past, my names, my old photos. All the ways trans people are traditionally exploited on TV, that's the direction it felt headed. But let me keep the record straight. The show's producer of this segment was a woman named Brooke. When she first called, I could tell she'd done her homework on how to talk to trans people —appropriate pronouns, terms, etc. I was impressed, though I couldn't tell if this was for real, or if she was just trying to gain my trust. In the end I trusted her, but set boundaries. No old names. No old photographs. No talk about bottom surgery.

We flew down to LA the night before taping and I remember taking a long shower at the hotel, rehearsing responses to the worst possible questions Tyra could ask. That turned out to be a good exercise. The next morning a limo took us to the studio and my girlfriend freaked out about what to wear right up until the time we went on. We were the third of three couples, the two ahead of us were trans women and their cisgendered male partners. It was an exploitive bloodbath. There were typical questions about how they met, how long they'd been together, etc. But then came the shitshow: surgeries, genitals, blow jobs, and doing it "with a towel" or some disgusting shit like that. Standing backstage, I wanted to simultaneously cry and vomit. Our turn came and we went on stage. Tyra barely made eye contact and read from cards. On breaks she talked to producers and reviewed notes. Once she told me what she was going to ask next to prompt my answer, something I said in one of those pre-interviews about having "Tom Cruise Syndrome" because I'm short—she liked the pop culture reference.

Finally, the producers kept their word and Tyra plugged my music. She had to re-do it 3 times because she kept calling me "Jason." I was stoked and figured that if even 1/10 of 1% of her viewership downloaded 1 of my songs, I'd be able to make albums for me and my friends the rest of my life. Later on I found out a Croatian website posted my album and let it be illegally downloaded for free tens of thousands of times. That. Sucked.

Oh, and despite assurances Tyra wouldn't ask inappropriate questions, she asked about bottom surgery. The rehearsed response was, verbatim, "You know, a lot of guys like to talk about what's in their pants, and I'm just not one of them." The audience cheered loudly in support, but this ultimately hit the edit room floor. Personally, I wasn't sad because my line got cut. I just wish trans people watching could've seen another trans person telling a major media personality "I don't have to answer that question."

When all was said and done, I felt I'd done nothing for my music career. But I stayed in touch with the producer, Brooke. When the show moved to New York a year later, I met her for lunch. She invited me back on, and this time they played my music video with Margaret Cho, and actually brought Margaret on. That was dope. The other guest was a 14-year-old trans kid going to his first school dance. That kid was amazing. So was his mom. They named the show "Transgender Triumphs." Eh, cute. My girlfriend had another wardrobe breakdown, this one less severe that resulted in her wearing almost the exact same purple dress as Tyra. Awkward. But hey at least this time Tyra got my name right.

Two years after the show I was performing at a rinky-dink Pride fest on the East Coast. After the gig, this kid came up to me and said, "If I hadn't seen you on Tyra, I'd be 6 feet in the ground right now." It changed my life. Sometimes Brooke and I email about having me on 20/20 (the show she works on now). I told her if I do it, this time it's not for me.

HEY READERS, you have Tyra Mail!
Dear lovers, Your bodies and lives are beautiful and resilient and no one has the right to take that away from you with dehumanizing questions. Thank you for having the courage to live your authentic lives!
Love, Tyra

RAE SPOON

Interview + Photos by Amos Mac

RAE SPOON HAS BEEN STEADILY TOURING FOR OVER A DECADE AND HAS SIX FULL-LENGTH ALBUMS UNDER THEIR BELT. DUDE IS PROLIFIC AND BUSY. WITH THEIR ROOTS IN THE INDIE FOLK SCENE, SPOON'S LAST RELEASE **I CAN'T KEEP ALL OF OUR SECRETS** IS THEIR MOST ELECTRONIC ALBUM YET. RAE'S MUSIC TRANSCENDS GENRE, DEFINITION, AND IDENTITY. SPOON CRAFTS A BEAUTIFUL SOUNDTRACK FOR ALL OF OUR LIVES.

How did you get started as a songwriter?
I started writing songs when I was about twelve. My family is Pentecostal, so I wrote some Christian contemporary music. I still think about selling those songs, but I'm not sure that market would like me too much. When I was in high school I started listening to Bob Dylan and got really into folk music.

Do you like performing as much as you like writing?
I like them both equally. I see them as two parts of the same thing. I never feel like a song's finished until I perform it because the way people react is part of my editing process.

What song are you most proud of and why?
I'm the most proud of the song "Come On Forest Fire Burn the Disco Down." My goal was to write an indie rock song about young people taking responsibility for the colonial history of Canada. I am proud of the song because it ended up getting played a lot in spite of the fact that it's a political song.

Has your identity helped or hindered your ability to get fans of your music?
When I came out as trans over ten years ago it was easy to see how it hurt my career. The trans community didn't exist then as it does now and the mainstream media didn't have much of a clue. I was constantly answering the question "What is a transgender person?" It didn't leave much room for my music.

Now, with the collapse of the big money music industry, I see it as an asset. Being trans is something that helps my music stand out among all of the indie music available to people. It might close me off from a larger audience, but I have come to terms with that. I wouldn't want trans- or homophobic people to like me, anyway.

How did you make the switch from acoustic to electronic?

The switch to electronic/more experimental music was fairly organic. I was living in Canada and playing country music and then I moved to Germany for a couple of years. I wasn't seeing many cowboys there and started to feel a bit false taking inspiration from them. A friend of mine was heavily involved in programming music and started to teach me to use my computer as an instrument.

What was a standout show for you?

I just played with one of the singers from one of my favorite bands Electrelane in London. It was so cool to see her perform. She was making some weird noises on the saxophone and loop-ing synths. I really look up to innovation and people who don't care about the music industry at all.

What is the best part of touring?

Touring is an amazing thing. On top of being paid, most of the time, to do what I love, it's af-forded me a way to see so many places and meet so many people. It's a certain kind of education meeting people and finding out about how they live. I wouldn't trade the fact that I spent most of my twenties on tour for anything.

What inspires you to write?

I like to write albums on broader themes. I usu-ally write half of the album, pull out the themes I see, and write the second half around them. I write from personal experiences mostly.

What is your writing process?

Since I started to make music on the com-puter my writing process has changed a bit. I used to sit down with a guitar, but these days I might start out with a beat or synth line. Finding new ways to write songs is great be-cause I write different things.

TRANS MALE QUARTERLY
USA $8.00

10 ★ THE JOCK ISSUE ★ 10
ORIGINAL PLUMBING

LETTERS FROM THE EDITORS

As a kid I was very active. I played sports, ran around, and loved being athletic. However, it was right after puberty that I gradually started quitting team sports. First basketball, then volleyball, and finally track. Uncomfortable with my physical self, I retreated from most physical activity. I didn't want to do anything that rooted me in my body nor did I want anyone looking at me, especially in a locker room. After I started medically transitioning, I regained my interest in physical activity. I returned to loving the feeling of moving my body and straining my muscles.

As I've grown older and shared my story, I've found that these feelings are not uncommon for many men of trans experience. In this issue of *OP*, you will hear from other men with similar stories, speaking about how as their relationship to their bodies changed, so did their relationship to being athletic.

—*Rocco Kayiatos*

While I know that the title of this issue, "Jock," is used loosely and fits on a case by case basis in terms of personal identity, it got your attention, didn't it? Do we all have some percentage of "jock" within us? As a young kid, I grew up on street basketball. I was an aggressive player for my age and good at it. Before I got super into boy bands and teen magazines with celebrity crush posters inside, I collected baseball cards. I had never even watched a game and I can't remember why this past-time started, other than the fact that I wanted something to collect and I liked the portraits of the players on each card. From my baseball card collection grew an interest in the game itself, which led me to play on the worst softball team in our district though my middle school years. Those were the most unfavorable years of my life in terms of how I felt within my body and my last time playing on a team, although I do wish I still had that uniform.

In this, our tenth (10th!) issue of *Original Plumbing* magazine, we'll hear from a basketball star and a triathlete. From gym dudes and a PE teacher, to guys who are breaking the mold of how gender collides with sportsmanship and team playing, this was our most collaborative issue yet!

—*Amos Mac*

COVER MODEL: Jesse; photo by Amos Mac

PERSONAL
BEST

BY T COOPER
PHOTOS BY AMOS MAC

Kye Allums is a twenty-two-year-old athlete who twisted everybody's panties into a bunch in 2010 when he came out publicly as a transgender male while playing on an NCAA Division I Women's Basketball team (George Washington University). He graduated last December and is currently taking a year off before graduate school to tour the country speaking about trans issues at high schools and universities.

T COOPER: From where you sit now, are you pretty good with how everything went down last year?

KYE ALLUMS: Yeah, I'm glad I came out. People shouldn't have to hide.

TC: What about all of the drama and media frenzy?

KA: All I said was, my mental state is, I'm a man. It's just how I feel, it's just a word. I never said I had a penis. I never had any advantage. Of course I shouldn't have been able to play on the women's team if I had been taking testosterone. But that came after I decided not to play [on the women's team] anymore.

TC: A lot of people were asking, "Well, if he's a guy, then why does he want to play on a women's basketball team?"

KA: That's a stupid question. I mean, why do I feel like going to chemistry class today? Because I signed up. Why am I on a women's team? Because I have been since I was a kid, and I can't play on a men's team.

TC: And you weren't on testosterone at that point, everything was the same as it was the day before the NCAA and ESPN and everyone found out that you consider yourself a man…

KA: Yeah, and my teammates had already known for two years, and they were like, "Why does it matter now?" When I was traveling with the team, we never had a problem, but when the whole world wanted to focus on it, then it became a "distraction."

Thirty-two-year-old Chris Mosier has been a triathlete for four years. His first race as a male was the 2010 Florida Ironman. In August of the next year, he competed in the Olympic-distance New York City Triathlon, which was the first race he completed as female, and then again as male.

T COOPER: I'm assuming you felt a marked increase in overall strength and endurance after starting T. As an extreme athlete, do you notice things in more specific detail? Or was it just a gradual matter of minutes getting shaved off races?

CHRIS MOSIER: I definitely felt an increase in strength over time, but not really endurance. I was an endurance athlete before transition. I ran ultra marathons and did 100-plus mile bike rides. The changes took time. I wasn't noticing that I was able to run longer or faster during training, but I noticed a big difference this year in races compared to previous times. Since starting testosterone, I've consistently set personal bests in all of my races.

TC: What are your thoughts on transgender athletes competing in the Olympics and in professional sports in general? Is it different for FTMs and MTFs?

CM: For FTMs, there are no sports I can think of where there would be an advantage over some biological men. The rule is: any time a female would be taking testosterone, they would need to compete as male, or else they would be considered to be doping. This means that after my very first shot, I had to compete as male—which I was happy about personally, but it certainly didn't give me any advantage over anyone, male or female, at that point. There's a two-year rule that applies to MTFs, to allow time for the estrogen to take over and some of the testosterone levels to go down.

Trans people should be able to compete, and it would be up to the Olympic committee and organizations like the NCAA to think of ways to include these athletes—not only in categories of competition, but also in facilities and access.

QUARTERBACKING

BY JOSH KLIPP

Photo courtesy of Josh Klipp

When my little brother Luke was born, it was more jealousy than my tiny 4-year-old, gender mis-assigned body could bear. When he grew to be broad shouldered and 6 feet tall with no interest in sports whatsoever, I seethed in silent envy. "What a waste!" I thought. I would've killed for his Romanesque physique, ruggedly handsome face, and panoply of sports options. Instead, however, he pursued musical theater, and my stubborn 5'4 ½" frame resigned to an athletic existence of ostracism and second class citizenry. I spent a youth imagining how things might've been if my brother's and my body were switched at birth, and here's a brief list:

1. In 3rd grade, I could've changed into my basketball gear with my teammates in the locker room, instead of with the cheerleaders in the bathroom. (Maybe this sounds awesome now, but at the time I received no shortage of "eww!" directed via makeup mirrors toward my short hair and tube socks). Also, I could've walked right into the locker room for coach's post-game analysis, rather than knocking first to ensure my teammates were "decent." (And by "decent" I mean in their underwear, because god knows they weren't kind.)

2. In 4th grade I could've worn the track shirts with the cool side vents instead of unfortunate shoulder vents, and winning the soccer camp juggling contest might've been chalked up to skill rather than luck.

3. In 6th grade, I would have been celebrated instead of mocked when I bench-pressed more than my classmate Eric Anderson, who, until then, had a crush on me.

4. In high school I could've been captain of

the varsity football team instead of the varsity softball team.

5. And these days, I wouldn't get funny looks when I mention playing volleyball in high school. (Note: Despite a killer overhand serve, I warmed the bench most of my senior season due to a repressed gender dysphoric self-hating coach who couldn't bear in herself what she saw in me. So she pretended I didn't exist. I made up a song about it that went like this: "I'll be back on the sideline again. It don't matter how much practice I attend. When it comes to game time, I'll be on the sideline. Oh I'm back on the sideline again." Note: unmanaged business affects others.)

The list could go on.

As a child, I dreamed of being the star quarterback. Every year I looked forward to Halloween because it was the one day I could dress up like a football player and no one questioned it. I was the only non-football player in high school to use the weight room. And since I couldn't play on the team, I landed the enviable position of team trainer. This meant I taped a bunch of high school boys' stinky ankles before every game and stood on the sidelines at kickoff. (Note: Ironically, I twisted my ankle falling off a bench at a game. Also note: All of this led to studying sports medicine for 3 years in college, until I realized how much I hate taping stinky ankles).

Fast forward to 2012. My brother is engaged to the man of his dreams, and I write OP blogs on "How to Get 6-Pack Abs." I subscribe to *Men's Health Magazine*, teach hip hop dance class, study yoga, use a TRX on my back porch, and lift at Gold's Gym. Once, I even became a certified personal trainer for about 4 months (until I realized that I am not a morning person).

Sometimes I wonder how I'd be different if I'd been a successful cis-dude athlete. I'd probably be a major d-bag. Or if I sucked, I probably would have gone on to become a sad government lawyer. Sometimes I have this conversation aloud on my therapist's couch, and after the pity party, my therapist inevitably asks me this question: "So Josh, if you could go back in time right now and say anything to your younger self, what would you say?" He knows this gets me every time. Because to answer this question, I have to close my eyes and face that quivering little four-year-old, holding in all that hurt and fear, so aware of how unfair the world is at such a tender age. So if I went back to that kid, with tears in my eyes, I'd probably say this:

1. Hey kid, you are not alone.

2. Sweat and dirt make you awesome.

3. Your muscles are big and strong and that's beautiful!

4. Be courageous. What you're doing right now, at this very moment, is changing the world. Try it sometime.

Go find your little kid who felt out of place no matter which locker room they walked into. Track down that little one inside you who was jealous of your brother, the neighborhood boys, the football players walking the hallways in their jerseys on game day. Find that little spirit who wanted so bad to be on the field instead of the sideline. Find that tiny, strong being who played through the pain, and tell that kid everything you wish someone had told you. Give yourself this gift, right now, no matter how much it hurts to say the words. And when you're done, please do two more things. First, go for a walk. Exercise, take care of your beautifully gendered body because it deserves your love. Second, go find a kid who needs to hear the words no one told you at their age. And tell them: they look great in tube socks, dirt, and sweat; they are strong; and they are not alone. You won't just change their lives, you'll change yours, too.

Photo by Amos Mac

JESSE

OP

OP

LEE

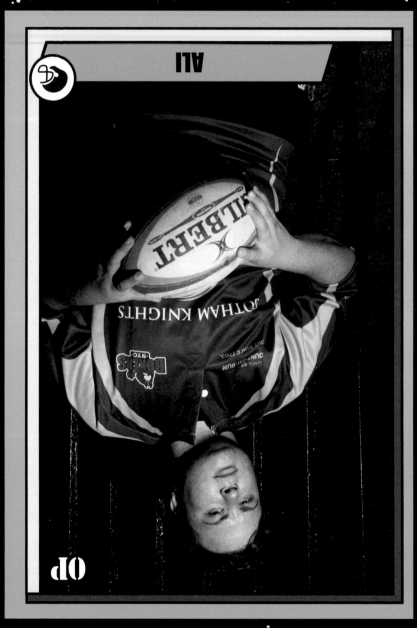

ALI

OP

MY PULLUPS PARABLE

BY COOPER LEE BOMBARDIER

In the beginner's mind there are many possibilities, but in the expert's there are few.
—*Shunryu Suzuki*

I banged out five pullups on the bar I'd just installed in the doorjamb of my kitchen.

"Must be nice to be on testosterone," my housemate's visiting butch-dyke friend Jan drawled from the couch.

My cheeks flushed with irritation. I wanted to volley back with the fact that when I first decided I wanted to do pullups, my then-girlfriend could whip out countless reps. She's the one who coached me from zero to hero—she wasn't on T. I wanted to point out all of Jan's trans guy friends who couldn't do pullups or chinups, never mind the male-born-men we all knew who couldn't eek out a single chinup. I thought about all the muscle-heads and gym-rats at my gym who avoided the pullup bar with a wide berth. I wanted to educate—maybe if she wanted to be able to do pullups, she should get herself to the gym, take better care of herself, stop self-medicating with weed and beer. I wanted to shake off her negative projections flung at me like manure. But I bit my tongue. Something that I have learned in my new life as an adult male, which only started ten years ago—it is better to offer advice only when solicited.

It was a hard, humiliating place to be, hanging red-faced, aching, and panting from the pullup bar at the local community center gym. My core muscles felt like they'd rip apart. My fingers screamed with effort. I'd hurtle myself up to the bar however I could, hands burning from the sticky, blackened athletic tape wound around the bar, and lower myself as slowly as I could. Negative repetitions. It was not comfortable. Not being any good at something is uncomfortable. Trying to do it anyway is uncomfortable. When I'd be about to reach the bottom extension, my then-girlfriend or our workout buddy Drey would place a palm between my shoulderblades and shove me back up to the bar. Just two or three reps of this were enough to cause full-body pain at first. My hands would be red and raw, stuck in a half-curl. But eventually I could slow my descending body, stretching each rep to thirty seconds or more. Callouses replaced the raw red spots on my palms. Finally, after weeks of this, one day I hauled myself up to the bar, chin clearing the top. I did it—I did a pullup. High-fives all around. I thought of the humiliation of the Presidential Fitness test in middle school, the commercials with Arnold in his robo-fascist accent, the standing broad-jumps, sit-ups, and for girls—hanging from the chinup bar. They didn't even expect girls to try, nor did our gym teachers want to help you work it out. This was the first pullup of my life and I was in my mid-to-late thirties.

Why did Jan's comment chap my caboose so hard? It had to do with the pullups, but I realized that pullups were just a symbol. Jan saw testosterone as a magic wand waved over my life, something that gave me special powers and strength. She saw testosterone as the lucky rabbit's foot that fixed my life, and since she was never going to transition (even though there was some intense jealousy-feelings there) maybe that was her out, and now she didn't have to fix her own life. If only

my life was "fixed," my problems vanquished, my self-work done. Far from it.

It was only after choosing to transition that I wanted anything from this life, that I was able to choose anything, to commit, to achieve. I was adrift before that, a ghost ship floating on a dark sea. In choosing to transition, I was choosing to live, and choosing to be the captain of my ship, to inhabit it. In choosing to transition, I made a powerful discovery: I am the only person responsible for my life. Despite where I come from, how I grew up, what I've been through, what has happened to me—what happens next is my responsibility. Being able to do pullups was just one small task on my list of things I wanted to accomplish, now that my life had actually begun. Having a list of goals was new to me, having lived for so long in a state of survival, where all my energy went to meeting my day-to-day needs. My new list ranged from learning pullups and benching 225 to doing some major healing work to getting an MFA and making writing and art my career.

My irritation fizzled as quickly as it had flared, replaced by a pang of compassion. I could see something of my stuck former self in Jan, and I could see that she wasn't ready yet to take responsibility for her own life and happiness. It wasn't for me to teach her either, just to be a silent witness.

"Naw," I shrugged, wiping my palms on my jeans. "I can do pullups because I've worked hard at pullups."

OP

ORIGINAL PLUMBING

Trans Male Quarterly
$9 US

THE
HERO
ISSUE

Lou Sullivan

HONORING TRANS HEROES OF THE PAST AND PRESENT

THE NEW
ORIGINALPLUMBING
.COM

In January, we launched an Indiegogo campaign to raise funds for a complete overhaul and redesign of our website, originalplumbing.com.

It felt like a 30-day rollercoaster between the all-or-nothing fixed funding, our own anxieties around asking our readers for financial help, and humbling feelings from the outpouring of love and support we received daily.

With your help, *Original Plumbing* raised over $20,000 in one month to go towards the relaunch and sustainability of Original Plumbing Online. We were, and are still, blown away! Words can't describe the gratitude we feel. Thank you.

Before launching the campaign, we spent many months discussing the feedback we've received about the website over the past few years. We thought long and hard about where we wanted to go with this project, which has expanded so far beyond just a physical magazine. During this "vision quest" we realized that OP Online is much more than just an online space for "spillover" articles that we can't fit into the print zine. It has turned into an online home for various communities within the trans community.

With the relaunch of Original Plumbing Online coming soon, it's official. Starting in 2013, OriginalPlumbing.com will feature exclusive writing by trans men, trans women, people of genderqueer

THIS IS ROCCO KAYIATOS

THIS IS AMOS MAC

Illustrations by Erin Nations

experience, allies, family members, and partners. This relaunch will include not only a broader space for commentary on trans experiences, but also a heightened aesthetic and organization! You can look forward to an organized way of finding the thousands of past posts by specific categories, different editors for certain topics, a worldwide calendar listing trans events that anyone can submit their event to (free of charge), and exclusive video content.

While *Original Plumbing* magazine will remain the same and dedicated to "trans male culture" (whatever that is), Original Plumbing Online seeks to share the vast experiences of trans people from across the gender spectrum. Join us. If you or a friend fancies themselves a writer or an artist, consider this an open call.

HI, WE ARE THE EDITORS AND WE WROTE YOU A LETTER

I know, I know! It's been a minute since our last issue. We took our time with *OP*'s Hero issue. Compiling a portfolio of trailblazers and focusing so much on trans history left me feeling both heavy-hearted and inspired. To learn the backstories on so many trans people who paved the way, whose visible lives alerted me to where I could go or who I could become, was an intense experience. Many of these people have made it possible for Rocco and I to do the work that we do, creating a magazine that focuses on the lives of trans people.

We all have our own definition of what makes a hero, and this issue includes just the tip of the iceberg regarding who has made a mark on the trans community. It's my hope that after you flip through the pages, you'll muse on your own list of people who first shaped your moment of trans clarity.

After this issue it's obvious to me how important it is for us to archive our own history. The responsibility lies with us to document our truth.

—Amos Mac

Just twelve years ago when I began my own medical transition, the world was a different place. There were no YouTube channels with other guys explaining to me when I could expect to grow sideburns, when my voice would change, when I would lose the ability to multitask, or where I could find a community of men like me. There were very few books and even fewer pictures featuring trans dudes. I had to search for role models and dig to discover the relatively young documented history of trans men.

What you will see in this issue of *OP* are some of the men that I have looked up to, been inspired by, and are forever grateful to for making the world an easier place for us. In one of our first brainstorming sessions about making *OP*, Amos and I discussed the day when we could make this issue. I have been looking forward to it for awhile. When I was younger, for the most part, history did not interest me. But now I love learning about queer history, because then I know exactly who to thank. We are pleased to pay homage to some of the brilliant men and women who came before us and are emerging now with shovels and picks in hand to dig the road we walk upon and carve the space we occupy. Brave enough to be exactly who they are and fearless enough to take a stand for what they believe in, all of the people in this issue are my heroes.

—Rocco Kayiatos

COVER MODEL: Lou Sullivan; courtesy of GLBT Historical Society

AUNTIE KATE, TELL ME A STORY

People have done this before, people will do this long after you

text by **Kate Bornstein** as told to *OP*
photography by **Amos Mac**

Rocco and Amos had the pleasure of sitting down with Kate Bornstein surrounded by a pug, a puggle, three cats, and a turtle named Bruce to chat about some of this trailblazer's favorite moments. Here we have it, straight from the mouth of Auntie Kate!

FREEDOM

I've been hidden and guarded most of my life. I think most trans people go through a phase, or some of us the majority of our lives, hidden and guarded and "I've got a secret," and that just comes with the territory. Me, I've also got, what the hell is it called... borderline personality disorder! Which makes me particularly fond of lying. I've lied a lot in my life and I lie a lot now. I have to remind myself not to. After I got out of Scientology in 1982ish, it was like, there's nothing left to lose, because they come after you. They would expose all my secrets and at that point I made a decision to listen to the Kris Kristofferson song made famous by Janis Joplin, "Freedom's just another word for nothing left to lose." And I said, let's try it out. Freedom. I'd never really experienced it. But pre-transition, did you feel free?

STAY ALIVE

I have so many thoughts now about life and death. In September 2012 I was diagnosed with early stage lung cancer. In October they took out the top third of my lung. Before I went in for [lung] surgery I had to decide, do I want to go on living? And a large part of the reason I decided yes was because of our community and because of my place in it. I like being Auntie Kate. I love my nieces and nephews, I love my family, I love my tribe. So that weighed a lot into the decision of "I want to live." That was a big breakthrough for me.

DRAMA

The first thing I staged was a play called *Hidden: A Gender*. San Francisco, 1989. I wrote it on 5x7 cards, there were no computers at the time. The show opened in the downstairs theater of Theatre Rhinoceros. We got rotten tomatoes thrown at us. One guy sat outside giving them to audience members as they came in because in the early days of Theatre Rhino there were 6 shows—3 for gay men and 3 for gay women. And then there was us. They had to take one show away from someone. They took it away from the gay men because it was a dyke who was running the theater at that time. The gay men were incensed

One day you're gonna become old. And I don't mean age-wise. The identities you've claimed are gonna go out of fashion at some point. That's gonna be an awesome moment for you.

and one guy gave away rotten fruit and veggies and they threw it at us at curtain call.

OLD FRIENDS

Lou Sullivan lived right around the corner from me! Literally, we were half a block from each other in the Mission and that was impossible! It was kind of like the East Harlem of San Francisco in those days where we could afford to live. Lou and I didn't hang out, but we laughed as soon as we met each other. And Jamison Green! So fun and awesome. You talk about FTMi, you go, "Wow!" There was no FTM community at the time and there was no real blending of MTF and FTM, so there were scattered guys and gathering gals. I didn't want to gather with the gals that were gathering. So who did I have to hang out with were the drag queens and the boys! I hung out with the most outlawed; the S/M community, the artists, the theater folks. There was a community.

GENDER OUTLAW

I wrote [books] ahead of where my head was. [My writing process] was like, "This makes sense, this makes sense," and then I saw people living and I was like, "WHOA!" I was making it up, you know? I worked by logic I guess. I still do. I've got an update to the Gender Workbook coming out in a few months, it is so hot. I just had a marketing meeting yesterday, it's gonna be a lot of fun. More fucking. Chapter six is "Chapter sex," and the title is *Sex Sex Sex Sex Sex Sex*. No mistaking it. It's taught in over 250 colleges and universities and high schools around the world. And all I can think about is how dated it is! For example, I used the term transgendered. I didn't know! And then it came out and all these activists were like, "You shouldn't say that, it isn't something that's done to you." Okay, you're right. But "transgendered" caught on because it's in that book! So in the new workbook I changed all the transgendereds to transgender.

FROM THE PAST

So many people came before me. Holly Hughes, Spilt Britches, Candy Darling, Billy Tipton, Renée Richards, they all came before me. Every drag queen that ever fucking walked a stage. I still admire them. They're still my heroes. All the ladies of the balls up here in Harlem who are dead now. All the drag queens from the eighties who are dead now. They gave me the strength. Doris Fish. Miss Tippy. X. Those were the three reigning drag queens of San Francisco when I was there. International Chrysis. She passed from AIDS some time ago but you can still find her on YouTube. She was the most gorgeous boy and that's who I wanted to be. She was a boy and she was a drag queen and she walked around the world and everyone thought she was a girl. That's what I wanted. We all find folks like that.

TO THE NEXT GENERATION

Those kids are gonna have to find people the way we found people. They're gonna have to lurk around until they find someone and say, "I wanna be like that!" The trans movement is a wave. It's an overused metaphor, I know. And right now we're sitting at the cutting edge. I wouldn't want people to feel like Kate Bornstein is the "right way" to be a tranny or a trans person. I would send wishes, I would light candles. I would say "Brave, brave you, my darling." People have done this before, people will do this long after you. Welcome to the world. Find your tribe. Be well.

FRIENDS, LOVERS, AND MUSES

photographs and memories
by Catherine Opie

ARTIST CATHERINE OPIE TELLS STORIES
BEHIND THE PORTRAITS OF SOME OF HER FAVORITE
TRANS MEN THROUGH THE YEARS.

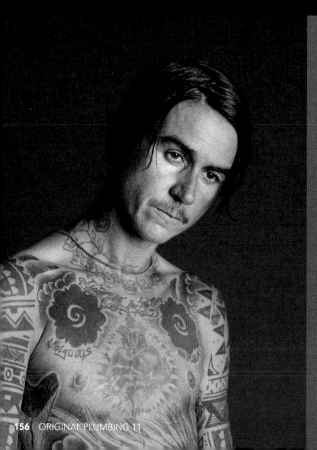

One of the things about Pig Pen that I love is that there's unbelievable possibility within his body and in terms of his identity; it never went to this hypermasculine place. Pig Pen is beautiful.

PIG PEN (TATTOOS)
2009 / C-print / 32 x 24 in.
Courtesy of Catherine Opie
and Regen Projects,
Los Angeles

Hans was from Austria. Everybody looked at Hans, everybody desired Hans, and I ended up with Hans as my lover after a really horrible breakup. Hans and I continued to be long-distance lovers whenever we would see each other and just fall into absolute love for each other and he was also really fantastic to photograph. When Hans transitioned it was really interesting because it was at his 40th birthday party and Del LaGrace (Volcano) did a shot of testosterone in his ass for a birthday present. Then Hans decided that was exactly what was needed in his life; to transition.

Hans is utterly a dandy and remains a dandy. There were years where Hans only wore turquoise; even the white shoes that Hans picked were painted turquoise so the whole outfit was always turquoise.

HANS
1994 / C-print / 60 x 30 in.
Courtesy of Catherine Opie
and Regen Projects,
Los Angeles

They were my best friends and one of the things happening in the community at that time is most or all of my butch friends were transitioning to men; it was kind of the first wave. . . . There was a lot of presumption . . . with me having my identity as butch, that I would transition as well. It was part of the body of work of portraits because that's just what was going on within my community.

MIKE AND SKY 2
1994 / C-print / 20 x 16 in.
Courtesy of Catherine
Opie and Regen Projects,
Los Angeles

Mitch was just a friend in San Francisco who I would have coffee with; not super close, never a lover, but I loved Mitch's being in terms of his tattoos on his arms and the statement he was making on his body and I felt like he had such a kind of fantastical look that it was really important for me to include him in the body of work.

MITCH
1994 / C-print / 60 x 30 in.
Courtesy of Catherine Opie
and Regen Projects,
Los Angeles

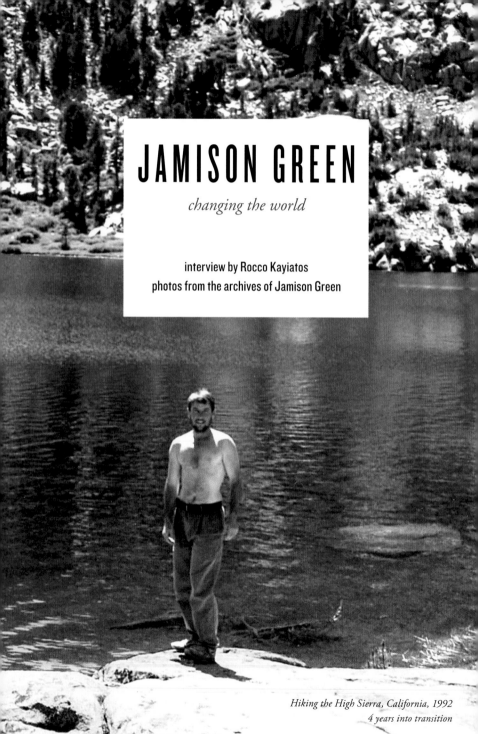

JAMISON GREEN

changing the world

interview by Rocco Kayiatos
photos from the archives of Jamison Green

Hiking the High Sierra, California, 1992
4 years into transition

To say Jamison Green is an activist is an incredibly reductive way of putting it. Mr. Green has devoted over half of his life to changing the world for trans people. He has chaired boards, written law, edited a newsletter, held conferences, written a book, earned multiple degrees, advocated tirelessly, raised kids, answered personal phone calls and emails from thousands of guys like him, and helped lead the transgender rights movement. We owe him a debt of gratitude for paving the way for our generation to have access to health care, rights on the job, visibility and respect. I sat down to talk to him about all he has done and seen, how he did it, and what he sees and hopes for the future of this movement.

How did you first come to know about trans people and transitioning?

I suspect I had an awareness of trans people in my late teens early twenties, but had never seen a trans man until I saw Steve Dain on TV in 1976.

Do you remember how you felt when you saw him?

I just was like, "Oh my god...this is entirely possible." Because he was really good looking, articulate, poised, and confident, and not ashamed of himself. And that was what I wanted to be like. Shortly after I saw Steve on TV I got this letter from my friend saying he had seen a flyer in the backstage area of a theater where his partner was performing. He had found this flyer, with tear-off number things, for sex reassignment. And it was a program which turned out to be in Oregon, where I was living. University of Oregon's medical school was looking for twelve people to transition from female to male. Basically female-to-male people were invisible at that time. So he applied to this program.

He writes me this letter and tells me he is in this program and he thinks I would like it too and he is coming back to Oregon to start his treatment and have surgery. And I'm like, "Whoa, this is intriguing."

Did you transition at that time in that program?

No. In the mid-1980s, I started working on a novel in which a character was changing their sex from female to male and was observed by the main character. The main character is processing all of this...basically the main character is me and the person changing their sex is my friend. I wrote all this fictional stuff about all kinds of events in their lives and their friendship, where this person is hashing all of this out. By the time I finished writing this, although the character didn't change sex, I realized that I needed to.

I transitioned using what was called the Stanford Program, one of the University programs that was around in the 1970s. I had my top surgery on the Stanford campus, and shortly after that the University asked Dr. Donald Laub to take his program off campus, because some wealthy donors got upset about it. He later did my genital reconstruction. He is the surgeon that invented metoidioplasty, and what he called the Cadillac phalloplasty.

What led you to have the path of activism that you have and continue to have?

I got involved in FTMI which was just FTM then, when Lou Sullivan died. He died in March of 1991 from complications of HIV. He started the group and the FTM newsletter. A week before he died, he asked if I would take over the newsletter. The newsletter was really important because we only had a few people coming to the monthly meetings, between 12–20, but the newsletter went out to 230 subscribers and I suspect an even larger readership.

It was 1992 when I was invited by a local therapist

who had been reached out to by someone on the SF HRC to find trans men who'd be interested in coming to the HRC meetings to educate them about trans men. So I went to the HRC and kept going back month after month while we were trying to get the LGB HIV advisory committee to the HRC to include trans. In 1994 we held a public hearing in front of the board of supervisors. Later I wrote the report that on that hearing, which lead to the nondiscrimination ordinance. I was asked to draft the language of the nondiscrimination ordinance. All of this I found exciting and interesting and fascinating and meaningful... So I kept doing it.

At what point did you start to see a shift in the numbers of guys in the trans male community?
In 1995 we held the first FTM conference ever. I called it the FTM Conference of the Americas. People came from Japan, Germany, all over the place. We had to change the venue at the last minute and we even had to turn people away at the door because the attendance was so big. I remember Susan Stryker was there and she and another trans woman were talking at the opening ceremony, and the other woman says to her, "Wow, I don't think I have ever seen this many trans men all in one place." Susan said, "There have never been so many trans men all in one place before. Ever. In the world."

The big moment for me was at the beginning. I gave an opening speech and I talked about how difficult it is to build community, especially since we were not all united by space. So we were forging new ground in many dimensions. And so in the speech I said, "We have always let other people drive our lives." Because we always let other people take control, we give control to doctors, to legal systems, all these things. And I

Did you know

In 1973 Jamison became the first woman cable splicer for the phone company.
"I went there asking if they needed writers or photographers and they said, *No, but how do you feel about climbing poles and do you think you can lift a manhole cover?* I said, *I can do anything.*"

urged people to think about what it takes to take control of our own lives and what it would mean. On the closing day I wasn't expecting to give any kind of speech. The conference coordinator invited me up to give a few words and I went up and looked at everyone and was so blown away, I just started to cry and said, "So, who's driving?" and everybody shouted, "We are!"

That conference spewed out a bunch of energy and people went back to their homes and started organizing support groups and started communicating with each other and building websites which back then were just listservs.

I know the world is still a very imperfect place for trans people. So having lived through and helped build a space for this community to exist, what are the major changes that have yet to happen that you hope you get to see? One thing I have been working on since 1994 is access to health care. It was basically my work that got the city of San Francisco to have health insurance benefits for their employees. It has been a lot of assertion and convincing that we do, in fact, have medical needs. That is one of the reasons that in 1997 I got involved with what

Cape of Good Hope, South Africa, 2011
23 years into transition

later became WPATH. I got myself elected to be the next president of WPATH, which is a 6-year volunteer commitment and the equivalent of an unpaid full-time job.

It's nice that you are still fighting for us to have our basic needs met.
Yeah, we need to be safe when we can't take care of ourselves and we also need to have our autonomy recognized. Those are the two overarching categories that I am working on, and I am working on them in a lot of ways and through a lot of different avenues, through a lot of different kinds of policy and efforts. Having our autonomy recognized and being able to drive our own lives and to be safe doing it are the major things. People asked me back in the early 1990s about safety, civil rights, and health care. Those big issues have not gone away. We have made outstanding and tremendous progress. This is probably one of the fastest growing civil rights movements in history of the world, but we still have so far to go. That is what gives me the drive to keep going, because I know that this is not a short time effort. People expect results instantly, and they don't get them and they give up, or they burn themselves out, because they don't know how to pace themselves. I think that is something I want to get across to people, that it is a lifelong battle and we can only make things better by stepping in and taking that on.

Sherwood, Oregon, 1972

LOU SULLIVAN

you are the beauty that you create

text by **Sean Dorsey**
photos courtesy of San Francisco **GLBT** Historical Society

I never met Lou Sullivan—he died years before I moved just down the street from his Albion Street home.

Lou Sullivan was a pioneering gay FTM community organizer, writer, researcher, educator, and historian who dedicated his life to advancing knowledge about FTM identity and creating FTM community.

Before his death from AIDS in 1991, Lou bequeathed 30 years of his diaries to the San Francisco GLBT Historical Society—which he himself helped found.

In 2008, I spent a year reading these diaries. I came to know Lou's private thoughts, fears, dreams, fantasies, sexcapades, friendships, activism, illness, and acceptance of his own death. I wrote and choreographed a show based on Lou's remarkable life. *Uncovered: The Diary Project* continues to tour the US, keeping Lou's words and legacy alive.

> **"While many men go through life wishing they weren't gay,**
> **I spent years wishing that I were."**

Louis Graydon Sullivan was born in Milwaukee, Wisconsin on June 16, 1951. In his early child-

hood, Lou began his intense identification with men and passion for male same-sex relationships. Lou wanted to become a gay man. At the time, there was no information anywhere about transsexuality or transgender identity—and Lou struggled in isolation. As he entered adulthood, he was compelled by early gay rights organizing and launched his activist career in Wisconsin.

> **"I want to look like what I am ... but I don't**
> **know what someone like me looks like."**

Lou moved to San Francisco—and starting in 1976, he sought out hormones in order to begin his physical transition. His applications for hormone therapy were rejected over and over again by the Stanford Gender Clinic, however, since Lou openly identified as homosexual.

At the time, medical "experts" deemed it untenable to be both homosexual and transsexual. In order to be approved for hormone therapy, an FTM had to profess heterosexual desire and identity.

An out, proud gay man, Lou began a lifetime of education of medical and psychological professionals about the distinction between gender identity and sexual orientation, and the need for culturally competent and sensitive services for transpeople.

"Limitless joy... just joy"

Lou triumphed when he connected with Dr. Lin Fraser, who became his therapist and advocate. Lou began hormone therapy in 1979. In 1980, Lou had chest surgery and in 1986, genital surgery (his testicular implants had many resulting complications).

"I never knew how fine it felt to feel attractive and worthy, to feel sexual, and self-aware. My body tingles all day long."

After years of physical self-consciousness, Lou blossomed into a voraciously sexually active gay man. Throughout the 1980s, many of Lou's diary entries are rollicking odes to the joys of the flesh. These entries follow Lou through the San Francisco gay men's scene—in bath houses, sex parties, nightclubs, dark movie theaters, and back alleys. These were years of profound excitement and adventure—full of cocksucking and wonder and joy.

"Take the next step. You are the beauty that you create."

Lou Sullivan was a visionary who was deeply concerned about other struggling transsexuals. Lou founded FTMI—the world's first FTM organization, authored an international FTM newsletter, and conducted groundbreaking research and publishing (including *Information for the Female-to-Male Crossdresser and Transsexual* and *From Female to Male: The Life of Jack Bee Garland*). Lou was a tireless correspondent, personally answering letters from transgender people around the world. Trans people lived in profound isolation and often loneliness: Lou was determined to create community and connection for FTMs.

"It all kind of proves that I was successful, doesn't it, that I really did live as a gay man..."

In December 1986, Lou was diagnosed with HIV. In his journals from that time, Lou articulated very clearly that becoming HIV positive was ultimately an affirmation of his identity as a gay man. Dr. Lin Fraser, Lou's therapist, told me that Lou talked a lot about this in their sessions together.

"On Sunday they came over to discuss transferring over the duties of the meetings and the newsletter, and that everything I'm bequeathing will be kept together under my name."

"I really feel good about that.... At peace now, and not afraid."

As soon as he was diagnosed with HIV, Lou set energetically onto the task of organizing and bequeathing all of his research, writing, diaries, letters, medical records and other papers—in order to leave behind a companion for other struggling transsexuals, to educate, and to ensure the progress he had fought a lifetime for would not be lost.

As an historian, Lou understood the critical importance of records and documentation. He devoted countless hours during the last months of his life to creating the collection that today continues to change lives and inspire countless people.

"Every day is a blessing. How lucky I am to be Lou Sullivan."

Louis Graydon Sullivan died of AIDS complications on March 2, 1991, at his Albion Street home. He was 39 years old.

Lou will be remembered as a trailblazer who dedicated his life to educating and organizing for his community. Lou was an authentic giver, a brave spirit, and a sexual pioneer. He befriended hundreds of people and influenced thousands more—staying true to himself, against enormous odds.

Lou would urge us to document our lives and our community. Let's continue his work.

JANET MOCK

hashtag hero

text by Janet Mock as told to OP   photo by Amos Mac

Making media waves with the #girlslikeus campaign for trans women visibility, Janet Mock is an inspiration, using the limelight to focus on important issues that the media glazes over, specifically around trans women of color.

Amos and Rocco caught up with Janet while she was in the final rounds of edits for her first memoir, and asked her to share stories around three hashtag topics.

#GIRLSLIKEUS

It was March 2012 after Jenna Talackova was in the news and I was irritated in hearing the headlines of "Trans women are not real women." So I wrote, "Sign this petition for Jenna Talackova and for all Girls Like Us," and I tweeted #GIRLSLIKEUS.

[Trans women] deal with a lot of struggles and a lot of being statistics, being reduced to our bodies, but at the same time we are amazing, excited, happy, beautiful, and diverse. I think just because I'm a woman of color and a trans woman there is already a sense of agency and activism and being radical and revolutionary, but people wanted to reduce it and say that, "Well she speaks for trans women of color, she doesn't speak for all of us because she's not like us." So I had to write about my intention of what this space was to me and where it came from. Some women were just like, "I'm not a girl, I'm a woman." I'm like, "Well then maybe it's not a space for you. Go create something that speaks more closely to you." We should occupy more spaces! Let's create more spaces. Create something that speaks to you.

#TRAILBLAZERS

My best friend Wendy from childhood who does my makeup now. To have met someone at 12 years old who was exactly like me, who I didn't have to explain anything to about who I was, was incredibly empowering. To know that she had known women who were older and who were able to go through hormones. . . . They instilled in me a sense of possibility.

Sylvia Rivera and Marsha P. Johnson! I think about how it was for them to grow up as street queens, hustling and trying to make money and supporting people who were younger than them, trying to teach them the way, trying to infiltrate these Gay spaces that didn't want them there. I think about their struggle. We have the mindset that they had, and we have the avenues to push that legacy forward.

#COMINGOUTx2

I was so "out" in middle and high school, living in Hawaii. Every place I went people knew who I was. When I left for graduate school in NYC, it was the first time in my life that I could just be another girl in the crowd. No one was whispering about me or misgendering me.

I started working at *People* magazine. I felt that no one was speaking to trans kids specifically about what they go through with despair and isolation, but everyone was talking about gay kids. I was starting to feel conflicted. Then the *Marie Claire* opportunity came up and that's when I came out. I knew there would be criticism. But the way I handled it was to educate myself about people who had already done this so that I wouldn't be replicating the exact same story, and try to advance the conversation. Not just what it means to transition, but what it means to actually live in this world as a person who had already transitioned and what that world looks like now.

KYLAR BROADUS

running towards it

interview by Josh Klipp
photo courtesy of Kylar Broadus

Kylar Broadus answers his phone, and from the minute our interview begins, I can tell from the sound of his voice that the man is tired. Exhausted. And not at a superficial level, but down to his bones.

I caught Kylar on his cell as he drove to see his mother, his only remaining parent (and she's not doing so well these days). And although he's been a national civil rights activist for nearly two decades, has testified in front of the United States Senate on behalf of gender inclusivity in the Employment Non-Discrimination Act (ENDA), is a lawyer and business law professor, and has his own law practice, inter alia, he's never left Missouri. It's where he was born, raised, where his father died, and where his mother still lives. And in a persevering lineage one generation away from slavery, nothing means more to Kylar than family.

But clearly, the man is tired. The National Gay and Lesbian Task Force doesn't give its "Longevity in the Movement" award to the unweary, and Kylar received it in 2011. (The award is akin to a Lifetime Achievement Award—for those who have shifted the horizon of hope millimeter by millimeter, yet managed to elude acknowledgment. I suspect it's the LGBT movement's late way of saying

thank you once it realizes where it wouldn't be without him and desperately hopes he'll stay a little longer. Just a guess.)

Kylar's list of achievements is lengthy, but as we talk, I'm struck by the width of his shoulders and the weight they bear. And his carrying of this weight didn't start when he began transitioning more than 20 years ago—virtual eons before the dawn of the internet, social media, or widely accessible information on how to go about that process (let alone legal protections which are still largely nonexistent). Kylar's burdens were wrought the moment he was brought into the world as black, and later as a (visible) black man.

As he drives and we talk, he tells me stories: experiences that this new generation of trans may not comprehend from a 2013 queer perspective, let alone anyone who knows anything other than white privilege. "People react to me more based on my race, than my transness," he explains. "Little old ladies still hit the wall at high noon." I try to imagine this, but I can't. It doesn't happen to me. Sure, I know the experience of people assuming (wrong) things because of how they visually perceive me. But I have no idea what it would feel like for those assumptions to be based on my being black because I'm not. So we talk about this, and as this man who has fought for all of his people's rights for two decades speaks and drives, I hear his heavy heart. "[Some queer people] think that because they're queer and not of color that they get what it's like to be of color. And they just don't. Unless you've walked a mile in my shoes, you can't tell me what it's like to be me. I don't believe in comparing oppressions, but I do believe that we suffer differently because we're of color."

You'd think it'd be enough for him to leave the movement altogether, hole up and go about his practice in family, business, and criminal law. But this son of a truck-driving, World War II–veteran, whose GI benefits were denied based on race, doesn't run from a fight. He runs toward it, founding the Trans People of Color Coalition (TPOCC)—the only national social justice organization that promotes the interest of Trans People of Color.

Kylar Broadus's life reads like biographies of many activists combined, and he acknowledges that story is nowhere near its end. He subscribes to what he calls the "Pebble Theory"—that a pebble in the massive shoe of oppression can create such spectacular discomfort it eventually grinds the machine to a halt. And in his long fight for social justice, Kylar Broadus has been that pebble.

Kylar tells me that he's arrived at his mother's home, but we talk for a few more minutes. I ask where he finds his seeming endless energy and the answer is simple. "When someone says 'I saw a picture of you and knew I could make it,' that puts me in tears." I ask him how we address the complex issues facing Trans People of Color, and he responds, "First, we acknowledge our own internalized racism…Second, we [talk]

> I don't believe in comparing oppressions, but I do believe that we suffer differently because we're of color.

about self-empowerment…And third, we take this conversation [about racism] into the greater community." When I ask how to make the queer community aware of its own racism, his laugh belies exhaustion. "That's the million dollar question. If we knew that we'd both be on a yacht smoking cigars. But really, it starts with being honest."

Kylar's trip to his mother's home to give her care and support has ended. But his journey caring and fighting for our community marches on. He admits, "I'd like a chance in my life to do my thing. Everyone knows that I'm about doing this work but one day I want to play, to do things that I enjoy. Do you know I'm a closet musician? I was a (brass) music major and have a recording in the Library of Congress?! No one knows that!" It was the moment in our interview that he sounded least weary.

We hung up the phone as Kylar headed inside, and I regret not saying a few things before we ended. So Kylar, if you're reading this, here goes. First, thank you. A longevity award is nice, but I want to thank you for every morning that you got up, put on your suit and tie, and did one thing that makes my life more awesome. Second, you're right. People who are not of color do not understand what it means to have that experience. And while the President's inaugural speech beautifully wove the legacies of Seneca Falls, Selma, and Stonewall, that doesn't mean we understand each other's oppression. I promise to do my best to be honest about this, and to speak truth to our community. And third, how about you make that jazz album now? You've done the work of a pebble for so long. So how about that horn, and your singing voice, playing out and changing the world in new ways. I think we're ready for you.

OP

FALL 2013 / ISSUE 12
ORIGINAL PLUMBING
TRANS MALE QUARTERLY
$9 US

PARTY

OP
PIX
TO
PROVE
IT

PHOTOGRAPHY BY AMOS MAC

COVER MODEL: Berlin Reed/El Ozito; photo by Amos Mac

From OP's first party, an event our friend Josh Klipp threw at The Stud that raised funds for us to print our inaugural issue, it was evident that our community didn't just want a magazine to see their lives reflected in a positive way but also craved a physical space to celebrate. Since then we've thrown release parties across North America every chance we get. It's important to create spaces for ourselves however we see fit - rallies, protests, pick-up games and especially parties. Please enjoy this 12th issue, our homage to nightlife. Even on our darkest days, we always work hard to find something that's worth celebrating!   Amos Mac   Rocco Kayiatos

LAST NIGHT A DJ SAVED MY LIFE

OP'S RESIDENT DJ D'HANA PERRY

INTERVIEW BY ROCCO KAYIATOS

PHOTO BY AMOS MAC

Have you always loved parties?
That's an interesting question. I think I've always liked the idea of parties, but I was a fairly reserved person as a teen and young adult, so I really didn't start going out until my 20s. The reserved side of me thrives as a DJ because I get to be behind the scenes and the center of attention at the same time.

What is your favorite memory from a childhood party?
Well the first thing that comes to mind is my 5th birthday party. My parents hired a magician to perform and he was using a live rabbit to do his magic tricks. The final part of his act was when the magician performed hypnosis on the rabbit, which totally freaked me out! But right when he ended that trick, the rabbit came back to life and he gave it to me as a birthday gift. It made me feel pretty special.

How did you get into throwing parties?
There was a documentary about the band Tribe 8 that was screened at the Boston LGBT Film Festival in either 2003 or 2004. My friend Aliza Shapiro (Truth Serum Productions) was organizing an after-party for the screening and asked me to DJ the party after taking a look at my collection of punk & electroclash CDs. The party was a success and things just snowballed from there.

After playing house parties and one-offs for a couple years I decided to produce my own night, so I partnered with Gunner Scott to start a queer and trans focused night in Jamaica Plain at the Midway Cafe. We decided to call it The Neighborhood (2006–2009), because it primarily featured music based on what JP queers were listening to at the time: a lot of synth pop, indie dance, riot grrl, blog house, 80s, 90s rap and R&B. The party also featured guest DJs, bands and performers like The Shondes, DJ Dirty Jean, and Nicky Click. We even threw an official PBR sponsored "Queers Who Look like Justin Bieber" contest, around the time that "Lesbians Who Look Like Justin Bieber" Tumblr popped off. Let's just say the contest was equal parts amazing and awkward. We also made sure that we gave back to the community by donating a portion of our proceeds each month to local nonprofits that were doing important work in the queer and transgender community.

I think nightlife is integral to community building if that's your goal with the space you intend to create. A lot of people assume club nights are solely intended for hedonistic pursuits, but that's not always the case. Personally, I love a dance night that successfully brings sexy together with the politically and socially astute; that's probably my number one goal with the spaces I create.

BKLYN

INTERVIEW BY ROCCO KAYIATOS / EDITED BY LAYNE GIANAKOS
PHOTOGRAPHY BY ZAHRA SIDDIQUI

BOIHOOD

How did Bklyn Boihood come to be?

Ryann: We came to be in 2009 by starting our first project (the calendar) in order to address the lack of visibility and some real ill messages about masculinity that we saw Queer and trans* bois of color were living by. It was a project meant to empower us. Our parties were also a huge part of our reach. Not only did the parties fund our projects, they became a staple on the queer scene.

What roles do the parties have in creating community?

Zahyr: We all play a role in creating community by building interpersonal relationships within the collective and supporting each other to the fullest... we strive to love and build that way in the broader community as well.

Chino: I think BBH creates a kind of space for all Queer bois and trans* folks to gather and celebrate and be harmonious even if only for four hours. We don't just throw parties, we spread love.

Ryann: It's really important for, especially, black and brown folks to have space. Then, on top of that, to be Queer and trans* and living across so many spectrums, to be able to go somewhere where people not only look like you but they feel you.

Jackie: Shit is real on these streets. Feeling unsupported and unsafe can bring about high levels of stress. The role of these parties is to do exactly the opposite. Have a good time in a safe space with people that go through similar bullshit.

What is your favorite moment from a party?

Chino: I love every moment from every party. I'm sorry my answer's bland, but it's true! We've done parties in lofts, in clubs and different venues. The best parties, to me, are always the house parties... it just feels awesome to have those kinds of parties in the heart of Bed-Stuy with no police showing up to harass the fuck out of folks all day, and rejoicing in that. It's really dope; I

love those parties.

Mo: One of my favorite moments happened when this person from Singapore came in to volunteer. It's really mind-blowing that they came from Singapore and were like, "One of the reasons I wanted to come to New York was because of Bklyn Boihood."

What were your hopes when you joined the Bklyn Boihood collective and where do you want it to go?

Mo: It was a beautiful experience to see parts of myself represented in a way that didn't feel whitewashed and didn't feel limited in its design. My biggest hopes and dreams for BBH are coming to pass. That would be becoming one of the major platforms for representing masculine of center Queer and trans* folks of color around the world.

Zahyr: I realized that in BBH, there was an opportunity and a family that was already established to tell our stories. I wanted to be a part of that because before that I felt so deeply silenced around the gravity of being black and queer. I would like to hear folks' stories that identify with BBH; I would live to see those stories collected in an archive accessible to future generations.

Ryann: My hopes are being realized every single time we show up, every single time we put a message out, every single time we meet or throw a party. I feel like everything that I hoped for is happening because I came from experiences where I didn't feel affirmed or like there was a sense of community... The ways that we are creating community among ourselves is spreading out from all these different points of departure.

Chino: It's an interesting question: our hopes as opposed to what our vision is. So, I hope a lot of things, but my vision for BBH is a lot of things that we're already doing. The part I think about the most is making sure that it lives beyond the individuals that are here right now... I hope that I would look back at BBH in twenty years and see young, masculine of center individuals run-

ning it, taking it to new heights that we probably couldn't have thought of, addressing things that we didn't get to address, or things that came up for these other generations to address. I want BBH to continue living forever.

Jackie: I guess I'd say... BAM! We out here! A beautiful rainbow of brown-skinned queers... and I want that idea (through our individual talents and avenues as a collective) to infect the world.

Bklyn Boihood is a broad spectrum of identities and it seems that there's a lot of talk about how masculine-identified females and trans* guys don't get along or don't create space or cohabitate, etc. But Bklyn Boihood doesn't seem to have this problem. How important is it to create a supportive space for butches, studs, AGs, etc. to cross-pollinate and commune with trans* men? Has there been any difficulty in doing this?

Mo: To keep it real, I think it's a journey for all of us. I don't think that we have a perfect formula. I don't think that we have the ideal spectrum of representation. I think at various points, each of us or many of us, in some capacities, demonstrated or indicated the desire to have more of our particular identity repre-

sented for whichever individual is making that statement. It's about understanding the concept of abundance rather than the concept of scarcity that demands we choose one avenue. I also think it's about understanding the ways in which our identities, no matter how unique or different from one another, certainly carry a lot of similar qualities. It's really a work in progress, but the important part is that we're committed because we're a brotherhood. It goes beyond just representation of groups and it becomes very important for us to represent each other and, hopefully, to represent ourselves. I don't think Bklyn Boihood is done changing or evolving in terms of whom it primarily seeks to represent. I think right now we're just trying to make sure that we're affirming each other and ourselves.

Chino: I agree there's no perfect formula. What is perfect is our willingness to struggle through that, be open to that growth, be challenged, and be accountable to each other and the larger community without sacrificing what we believe or downplaying what we see as our vision. That's a pretty great way to go about things and things will constantly evolve and grow as we constantly evolve and grow.

op cupid
with topher

PHOTOGRAPHY BY AMOS MAC

Self Summary:

A born and bred Brooklynite, I was raised on coffee egg creams, Manhattan Special soda, and an obsession with all things dairy and schmaltz! I'm part Brawny Man, part Mister Clean, and part Bette Midler. 100% trans fat, loyal as fuck, genuine, easy-going, and generous. A sneaker whore. Lover of lowercase letters, soft pillows, drop crotch pants, extreme deeeeeep V-neck shirts, tank tops, side boob, eyebrows, and best-of food lists. I rock Molecule 01 cologne and Old Spice deodorant. I love old people, talk in high-pitched voices to animals on the street, and search for shooting stars in the sky. I believe in life after love, taking deep breaths, and value long kisses.

I'm not afraid, apologetic, or ashamed of who I am and how I live my life. Nothing surprises me! I'm an ethical slut who has no time for haters, judgments, or mediocrity. I believe that anything that is worth doing is worth overdoing!

What I'm doing with my life:

I spend my days making people look and feel fabulous as a Top Stylist at Arrojo Studio. Touching someone's head is a really intimate thing and in some ways I'm a therapist too. It's amazing how much hair means to some people. Honestly, I'm really trying to live life to the fullest with love and truth, by following the four agreements and becoming the master of love!

I'm really good at:

Making love out of nothin' at all. Keeping secrets. Giving a mean head massage with my small but mighty hands (I'm ambidextrous which is better for you, better for me!). Getting standing ovations at straight bars by singing "Private Dancer" and "My Humps" at karaoke nights. Being a cat and dog whisperer. Confusing small children with my cartoon voice. Doing impressions of my Jewish family. Wearing my heart on my sleeve.

The first thing people notice about me:

My hirsute pelt of exposed chest hair and prevalent beard. Then, my killer smile and big personality. Oh, and if one views me from behind, some would say my ass. I also shine like a diamond.

Teddie B. Glaze

"I was fairly community oriented before I was crowned, but since winning Mr. Transman, I have felt a greater responsibility to positively represent trans people in life and in media. I try to support the community by being present at as many queer and trans-related events as possible."

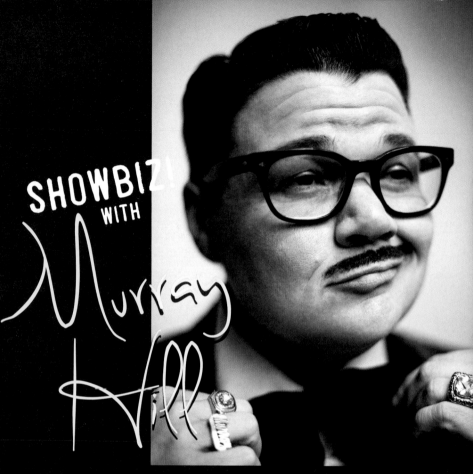

SHOWBIZ!
WITH
Murray Hill

INTERVIEW BY ROCCO KAYIATOS
PHOTOGRAPHY BY ALLISON MICHAEL ORENSTEIN

NYC nightlife legend, comedian, and renowned entertainer Murray Hill, "the hardest working middle-aged man in show business," is a relentless retro-shtick slinger, larger-than-life personality, and freewheeling ad-libber. Murray's razor-sharp wit and frenetic showman antics have delighted folks worldwide for over a decade. On any given night you can see him at a comedy club, calling Bingo numbers, hosting nightclub events, doing his one man show, making cameos on TV—you name it, he's all Showbiz, all the time. He took a minute out of his jam-packed schedule to answer a few questions for *OP*.

How long have you been performing?
My whole life! More consciously, however, almost twenty years now. I hit the YMCA regularly to keep in shape for the biz.

You bring all types of people together through throwing parties and nightlife events, is this what you dreamed you'd be doing as a kid?
Ha! No... had no idea. I wanted to be a

photographer, but soon realized it was too quiet for me. I never dreamed my life as it is now could even be possible! However, my experiences as a kid—growing up different and not accepted—set the groundwork for my career.

How'd you come up with the event Mr. Transman?

Pageants and contests have been a huge part of gay and straight culture forever. Big histories... especially in the gay male, drag queen, and transsexual communities. Not surprisingly, there has been little information about lesbian beauty pageants. So more than ten years ago now, I decided to start one and try to level the visibility playing field. To give lesbians a super fun, campy outlet to express their sexuality, and take up some space. As the queer scene has grown over the years, I felt the same need to bring more visibility and opportunity to the trans men community. The two Mr. Transman's we've had were so inspiring and amazing. I'll be working with you guys soon for the third installment!

How do you identify and how did you come to your identity?

I'm a bit old-school in this area. Back in my day, we didn't have language about gender identities like transgender, qenderqueer, gendervariance...none of that. There was zero visibility, no choices, and no access to information. If you can imagine, there was no internet when I was young! So I grew up feeling different and in the margins.

I personally don't believe in identifying myself by my sexuality or sexual orientation. For me, it's too narrow and reductive. Heternormative (a new term!) people don't have to identify themselves, answer questions about their sexuality, or have a label in front of their

names...they can just be. And that's how I've felt about myself and politically, I want all u. to be equal. I'm not one or the other gender As the song goes, "I am what I am." Now, I'm not pulling a Queen Latifah line like my private life is private. I'm certainly out and public as who I am. If had to choose a word tha most likely corresponds with my identity, it' transgender.

What is a nightlife moment that really stands ou for you?

A special moment for me was filming a "I Gets Better" video at one of my MISS LEZ Pageants. It was important to me to not jus show me talking to the camera, but to show the audience, to see the diversity in the quee community, and to hear and feel the energy o the crowd. When the camera panned out to the audience and everyone was screaming... I go goose bumps. That's what it's about it... creat ing those kind of spaces and moments where we all feel accepted for who we are.

Tell us about the exciting things you are involvee in currently.

I've got a new man-on-the-street show ti tled SHOWBIZ on MTV's new networl MTV Other. We've shot four episodes sc far and it's been a blast. I go around late a night and talk to the young kids on the stree about pop culture. You can see the shows a MTVother.com

Also, I'm continuing to tour the country witl burlesque star Dita Von Teese. We're hit ting NYC early October for a week then the East Coast. The show is out of this world and really a dream gig for me. I've been able to trav el all over the US and do my comedy with thi show and more importantly, I'm surroundec by showgirls!

Nightlife Legend, Host, DJ, Artist and Member of NY's Collective House of Ladosha, *Juliana Huxtable* finally answers our texts....

.... Text Message ....

> What's the craziest thing you've ever been a part of in an after-hours situation?

A sex party that was an after-party to a daytime sex party in deep Bushwick somewhere off of Flushing - a guy who I used to sub for invited me. I wore a mesh shirt and boxing shorts with a blue lip. I ended up having a public orgasm at the hands, mouths and otherwise of 5 people (boys and girls) and everyone clapped when I came and told me how amazing it looked with the lip. Not sure ill ever top that. Oh. And I went to Tandem after because my friend who was bar tending let certain locals stay and hang till early morning.

> What time do u wake up?

It depends - I'm a natural insomniac or at least a sleep minimalist because I love to take full advantage of the day but am clearly a night person. For two years I trained myself to wake up at 8:50 to be at work at nine and then would attend several parties during the week that would have me out till at least 4am. My natural time is somewhere between 10 and 11, assuming I'm in bed by 5-5:30am. Sometimes earlier sometimes later - I should probably get into naps more.

Husbands

TEXT BY SPENCER AND KELLY
AS TOLD TO *OP*

PHOTO BY AMOS MAC

"NIGHTLIFE HAD EVERYTHING TO DO WITH BRINGING US TOGETHER"

Spencer: Nightlife had everything to do with bringing us together. San Francisco nightlife is where our whirlwind romance took place. I mean, except for the night we went camping on a queer ranch. But I guess that was a party, and it happened at night!

Kelly: I've been working in the nightlife as a promoter/producer/dancer for the past three years. I met Spence working a party at Underground SF while he was visiting from Australia. We had a cute and awkward interaction. He offered to buy me a drink, and proceeded to run off after handing me the drink. I later found out he was really shy, hence the mad dash. I guess I owe my relationship with Spence to the nightlife.

Spencer: We work together on different nightlife events. Kelly books me to DJ his parties, or he attends parties that I'm DJing and looks cute behind the DJ booth. I also help him with designing flyers for parties he's throwing. I will let him tell you all the things he does. I don't have the time or energy for all that…

Kelly: Yeah, all of the above is basically it. I continue to throw a monthly queer hip hop performance party called Swagger Like Us. I also help produce large scale events with a crew of legendary SF promoters under the production title The House of Babes. We threw an epic 2000+ person event this past Pride. I'm still recovering.

Spencer: Nightlife will eventually become a business I think. Kelly is very driven and talented, and I can see him turning what he does into a business that will make us rich. And then he can buy me an island in the Pacific so I can swim in the ocean every day.

Kelly: Oh baby, I'll buy you two islands.

Spencer: There is a big difference between the nightlife scene in Australia versus SF. I think it mostly has to do with the population. Australia has a small population, therefore the LGBTQ community is a lot smaller. I mean, especially when compared to San Francisco, which has a large LGBTQ community relative to its population. There just isn't the same volume of parties in Australian cities. You can party every night in SF. It's not that way in Australia. Don't get me wrong, Australia is fun! Just different.

Kelly: Totes. Australia was super cute when Spence and I lived there. We didn't go out nearly as much as we do in SF. I mean, not that I'm going out tons in SF these days. I'm kind of nesting with Spence and our new cat Rihanna. But I felt similar when I was in Australia. The queer scene in Australia is way smaller than it is in the Bay. It makes running into your ex so much more likely.

Spencer: I feel like we have the most amazing community a person could ask for. SF is a really easy place to build community because there are so many people just like you. That sounds cheesy but it's kinda true. I also build community online. Being trans I used YouTube and Facebook to build particular community around that stuff. Now most of my community building exists IRL.

Kelly: I'm super fortunate in that I have an amazing preexisting community prior to my nightlife experience. I have the same best friend I went to elementary school with, and several BFFs that I went to undergrad with. I'm also fortunate to have Spence's amazing community now too.

OP

ORIGINAL PLUMBING

TRANS MALE QUARTERLY / ISSUE 13 / USA $9

JAMES DARLING
AND THE GEORGIA PEACH

THE REAL TRANS MEN
OF ATLANTA

The Wren's Nest

Riverboat, Hen

Greetings *from* ATLANTA

Cyclorama

Governo

Atlanta Stadium

World Cong

WELCOME
TO
ATLANTA

Stone Mt.

The General

Swan House

Memorial Arts C

LETTER FROM THE EDITORS

Last summer we had the pleasure of traveling to the Dirty South to table at the Southern Comfort Conference, a three-day event for trans* people that's been around for 24 years strong. In our time there, we met so many handsome and charming guys (Southern hospitality is a real thing) that really defined community in a way we had never experienced in our cities. If only *OP* was 1,000 pages long, you'd be able to see the vast love and respect they have for each other and the authentic, diverse community that exists in ATL.

In this issue you will see gentlemen that currently reside in the Atlanta area, and James Darling, who was born and bred on sweet tea and cornbread, right outside of Atlanta. Most of the guys featured in this issue spend their time really trying to build community and brotherhood in a way that speaks to a desire for real connectedness and support. Please enjoy our first city-specific issue of *OP*!

Y'all come back now, y'hear?

Amos and Rocco

HIT US UP!

- 🔊 originalplumbing.com
- 🐦 twitter.com/opmag
- f facebook.com/originalplumbing
- 📷 instagram.com/originalplumbing
- t originalplumbing.tumblr.com

COVER MODEL: James Darling; photo by Amos Mac

THE MEN

OF

ONYX

PHOTOS BY AMOS MAC

ONYX Southeast is a leather club for men of color, and the largest and longest existing fraternity of its kind. We met up with three members during our time Down South.

OPTIMUS

Name: Optimus / Raymond Walker III

Age: 31

Current Location: Decatur, Georgia

Career: Configuration Management Engineer (think IT Professional)

Favorite thing about living in the South: My favorite thing about living in the South is providing the Southern hospitality that people from elsewhere are always hearing about. It's just the way we are—we recognize and speak to each other on the street and can hold entire conversations in line at the grocery store. We're just downright friendly!

What was the first thing you said this morning: "My good boy." Pretty much no matter what my dog Chill does, by the time we get back in from our morning walk he is "my good boy."

Most annoying thing about living in the South: Mosquitoes... but the capacity for close-mindedness comes in close second. Mosquitoes you can't quite walk away from.

Define "Community": I define Community as a group of entities with similar and overlapping interests, principles, and/or desires that live out their interdependence in positive and supportive ways. I say entities because Community can be made of more than just individuals, there are businesses, support groups, and clubs that I believe can be part of community.

Favorite article of clothing: My favorite article of clothing is a burgundy thermal shirt—it's just so comfortable and can pretty much be worn anywhere.

Favorite body part: My favorite body part on me would have to be my eyes—they get a lot of my "talking" accomplished for me. My favorite body part on someone else is based on the person.

DR. STRANGE

Age: 37

Current Location: Atlanta, GA

Career: Human Rights Defender

Favorite thing about living in the South: I love Southern charm, Southern vernacular, and the resilience of People of Color throughout the South.

What was the first thing you said this morning: "Thank G-d for another day!"

Most annoying thing about living in the South: Hearing people outside the South describe the South in a way that dismisses the history, culture, progress, and people that keep pushing and sustaining change.

Define "Community": A beautiful meshing of diverse principled people who have shared values, respectful exchanges, and uplift and support the transformation of each other collectively and individually with love, grace, and style.

Favorite article of clothing: Clothing???

Favorite body part: Eyes.

BOY DANA
INTERVIEWED BY JAMES DARLING

How long have you been in Atlanta? 13 years, however it's been my home since around 1997. my Master at the time lived in Atlanta, so i'd travel from South Carolina weekly to visit. But finally moved here in 2001.

Is your use of the lowercase "i" intentional? Yes, intentional!

What's it like to be a trans man in the South? As a trans man, not bad. Now as a black man, that's a different story. i can't hide the fact that i'm black. Living in Atlanta makes it easier to be trans in the South. There is an amazing community here and i have access to great health care providers who are cool to the trans* community.

What communities are you a part of? Queer, leather, trans*, biker.

Do you feel accepted in your communities? Yes, i do. i make it a point not to waste my energy where i'm not wanted.

How has kink or leather influenced your experience of community? i've been very involved in the leather community since the mid-90s and it has completely shaped who i am today. It was a space where i could be referred to in male pronouns and be female bodied and no one blinked an eye. A space where i first met other trans folks, people with fluid genders and sexualities. No boxes. A space where i felt myself . . . my own normal. A space where people helped each other out in hard times.

What do you enjoy about kink/leather? i enjoy the freedom. The freedom to live out my deep dark fantasies . . . every day.

How'd you get involved in modeling? A sexy guy from Toronto thought i'd look hot wearing his gear and/or him! LOL! Before transitioning, i never thought about modeling or walking around half naked or less. But now, i love how i look. i finally feel sexy!

What other interests or hobbies do you have? i LOVE yoga! i first started in 2008 when my late partner gave me a gift card to a local studio. After my first class, i was hooked! Hot yoga is my favorite practice. Mmmm...sweat! i also ride motorcycles! i own a Custom Kawasaki Vulcan 900.

What is your favorite part about living in the South? The slow and lazy summers, rich history, and cuisine. i'm pretty good in the kitchen and enjoy re-creating recipes from my childhood. Atlanta has so much amazing history, you'd be a fool to pass up exploring it. And a lot of it is free to the public!

What has been the most challenging part of living in the South? Being a black man. Which is a reason i still have not changed my gender marker. Out of fear of getting thrown into jail, no questions asked because you matched description, with cisgender men. Ummm, i still have a pussy. Not quite the consensual gang bang scene i might fantasize about.

Do you find it's more difficult to be a trans man of color in the South than in other areas of the country? i think if i'd stayed in South Carolina, my experience as a trans man of color would be pretty bad. It was bad enough being queer, kinky, and black there. But, i think i'm spoiled by living in Atlanta, granted i do live inside the perimeter. So, i'm able to hang in areas that cater to queer folks.

Do you ever travel to fulfill your desires? i travel often and my Dominant is from Canada. i met Her in San Francisco at Internatonal Ms. Leather. If you are able, i think it's good to travel to other events and support each other. You never know who you might meet! Found my best friends and playmates at events around the country.

What about being trans brings you joy? Loving the man staring back at me in the mirror every day.

JAMES DARLING AND THE GEORGIA PEACH

By Courtney Trouble Photo by Amos Mac

James Darling is a trans man, a feminist pornographer, and a Southern boy at heart. Here's what he learned by growing up in the South, and what he's learned about leaving.

JAMES: I spent most of my life in Georgia before moving to the Bay Area. I grew up in Marietta, about an hour north of Atlanta. It's known for the Big Chicken, a restaurant with a giant robotic chicken on top of it that has eyes that circle and a beak that moves. That's how everybody tells directions in that town, it's always "a mile east of the Big Chicken."

COURTNEY: When did you move to the big city?
As soon as I turned 18 I hightailed it to Atlanta to live and find community. The first thing I ever went to where I was able to see other queer people was Atlanta Pride, when I was 16. It was such a phenomenal feeling to be surrounded by other gay people even if we were coming from such different places. Just to have access to other people who have experienced similar struggles and discrimination and harassment that I did in high school. That was my first access.

Who was one of the first trans men you met?
The first trans man I met was Sir Jesse who ran Trans & Friends and if it wasn't for him I don't know where I would be today. Through him I also heard about Sister's Room, a lesbian bar in Decatur. It's the best lesbian bar I've ever been to. I snuck through the back, climbed up a fence, jumped on a tree, and climbed down into the back. That was the first time I saw people who identify as femme, first time I saw stripping or burlesque, and the first time I saw a trans man. PeeWee Hyman, he was performing that night. He was an influence for the kind of masculinity that I aspire to. Incredibly dapper, a gentlemen. He always sang old soul and R&B songs, always wore the best three-piece suits. I wanted to look like that.

How did you start the technical aspects of your transition in the South?

I found out about everything through message boards. There was a doctor who would prescribe testosterone without a referral. I didn't have insurance, so it was incredibly expensive. He said no, that I was 18 and too young to know what I wanted and worried he would get sued. This happened several times, with therapists and other doctors. Thinking they might understand why I would need access to hormones, I decided to go to an abortion clinic, where I had heard a trans-identified person was working. I'm really grateful they were able to help me. A lot of guys have stories like mine, and many have gone unmonitored or under the radar.

Robert Eads, who lived in a small town in Georgia like you, died in 1999 after dozens of doctors refused him treatment for ovarian cancer, because of stigma around his trans status and a lack of trans health education at that time and in that state. Have things gotten any better?

Eads was a stealth guy who lived in a small North Georgia town, though in the 90s resources weren't much better anywhere else. The clinic I went to (the Feminist Women's Health Center) now offers the Trans Health Initiative, which was launched in his honor as part of the Southern Comfort Conference. They offer gyno care and cancer screenings to trans men, among other support.

Southern Comfort is a conference that happens in Atlanta every year. It's a very different kind of conference than the Philly Trans Health Conference or Gender Odyssey. It's very old school. I went, and it was a lot for my little punk rock genderqueer pink-haired self, they did not know what to do with me. But it was my first exposure to a lot of trans people.

What was good about being queer in the South?

The South is a place where people take community and family very seriously. People really stand up for each other and really follow through in a way that I don't always see in a lot of other cities. The queer community is resilient, that's what happens when you have a lack of resources and have to figure out a way to carve out a space for yourself. That resiliency made a huge impression on me.

What was bad about being a queer in the South?

It was hard because at the time people had very rigid ideas of what it meant to be a masculine person, like what kinds of people you're supposed to date. I definitely fell outside of that, I was very interested in men. I didn't fall into the butch/femme community rules, so that was something I really struggled with. I think that has changed a lot. There's a new generation of queer people there now.

What do you miss the most about living in the South?

Waffle House! [*laughing*] I mean! Let's get real. Waffle House was a 24-hour community space. I've had so many late night conversations with friends there. I also miss the seasons, and I miss my friends and family down there.

What would your porn site FTMFUCKER. com be like if you filmed it in the South?

Being a Southerner really shaped my sexuality. Having little competent sexual education and a lot of religious shame meant learning how to have sex in my body that felt affirming and good mostly on my own. I think that DIY ethic really carried over into my porn work where if something was missing or wasn't working, I figured a way to do it. I have shot a few trans guys from the South on FTMFUCKER. I love queers from the South, they are very strong and beautiful, and there's good reason people call this place the Dirty South! If I tried to shoot only in the South you would see porn made in magnolia trees, Spanish moss and old cemeteries, debutants and dapper dandies, old trucks and rough and tumble country boys... Damn, [*laughing*] why haven't I made this happen yet?

OP

ORIGINAL PLUMBING

TRANS MALE QUARTERLY / ISSUE 14 / USA $9

BOARD STIFF

DID YOU KNOW

The first modern snowboard was made by accident in 1965 by Sherman Poppen of Michigan, who fastened two skis together and attached a rope to one end for his daughters to use. They called it the "snurfer" (combining snow and surfer) and it was a hit! Poppen licensed the idea and sold half a million snurfers the following year.

COVER MODEL: Wolfe Moon;
photo by Ev Marquee

LETTER FROM THE EDITORS

THERE'S JUST SOMETHING ABOUT A BOARD

Snowboarding and skateboarding go hand in hand—they are the rebellious yet sometimes misunderstood second cousins of the sports world.

Growing up in the 1980s and 90s, skateboarding wasn't just an extreme sport—it was a booming subculture for self-identified outsiders. As kids who didn't fit in, we both gravitated toward that world—the music, the fashion, the rebellion, the injuries, and the hair. Reading *Thrasher* magazine while watching *SK8 TV* and that Christian Slater movie *Gleaming the Cube* on repeat, we felt like we were part of something big.

Even though it's been years since either of us have actually set foot on a board, we have so much love and admiration for all those that kick-push through life, who slide down hills newly minted with snow, and those who patiently paddle in the water waiting for that perfect wave. For *Original Plumbing*'s 14th issue we honor The Board and all those who embrace it. For us, The Board reminds us to live authentically, to take risks and to always be free.

Amos and Rocco

HIT US UP!

 originalplumbing.com

 twitter.com/opmag

f facebook.com/originalplumbing

 instagram.com/originalplumbing

t originalplumbing.tumblr.com

Photo by Drasko Bogdanovic

THE FAMILY THAT BOARDS TOGETHER...

Name: Chris Ellis

Preferred Pronoun: Sir

Age: 28

Hometown: New York City

First Board: Sector 9 Bamboo G-land 44" board.

Go to Trick: Cross-step.

Go to Spot: Anywhere.

Favorite Food After Boarding: Anything.

Boarding Hero: Favorite longboarder is Sergio Yuppie.

Gnarliest Injury: Gliding and burning off all of the skin on my left forearm.

Skate Shoe of Choice: New Balances.

What type of board do you ride? Any type of longboard.

How did you get into longboarding? I got into longboarding when I was living in Miami, ten years ago. Cruising is big in Miami and I chose to skateboard while my girlfriend chose a Beach Cruiser. We rode out together on the beach a lot, and I got better and better at longboarding.

What do you like most about the culture? What I like most about the culture is the downhill rush, actually feeling the wind, feeling like I'm flying, feeling so free, and board dancing.

When you think of skateboarding and the "LGBT community," do you see any representation out there? I don't think of the LGBT community when I am boarding. I do it for a peace of mind. There are not a lot of LGBT boarders and that does not really matter to me.

Skateboarders have their own language. What's your favorite word or term that's thrown around? My favorite word is "SHIT" because it takes a while to get a trick down and it hurts like hell when you mess up. So I say "SHIT" a lot, and when I do get it down, "FUCK YEAH" is my favorite phrase.

Do you board alone or do you have a crew that you board with? I board alone.

How did you get into skating? I got into skating from just being a sports person on a different level. I don't like basketball, baseball, football, or anything like that, so I took to longboarding.

What is a moment you are particularly proud of or a trick you worked on and finally pulled off? I was pretty excited when I glided for the first time.

Does skateboarding create community for you? Skateboarding did not create a community for me because I am a wild person so I meet people wherever I go.

What is your son's name? My son's name is Josiah.

What is your son's age? Seven.

In the photos I saw him on a scooter. Does he skate? And if so, what does he like best about skateboarding? My son loves the scooter, he has like 5 already. What he loves about skateboarding is me cause we ride together, we race all the time. He is scared of the skateboard 'cause he knows how much damage it does, but he does want to learn once he gets bigger and can take pain much better than he can now.

Do you have a family memory that revolves around skating? Racing with my son!

Interview by Amos Mac
Photos by King Texas / Texas Isaiah

"I GET ALONG WELL WITH PEOPLE WHO ARE ORGANIZED, EMOTIONALLY AWARE AND PUNCTUAL"
—KINNON

After Instagram-stalking this hot Canadian snowboarder with majorly impressive brain cells and creative underwear options, he visited NYC and we photographed him in a furniture studio. No real reason behind the location, we just wanted some metal worktables for him to spread out on!

Name: Kinnon

Age: 29 going on 80

Hometown: Antigonish, Nova Scotia

Sponsor: My chest surgeon, Dr. Hugh McLean of the McLean Clinic, has very generously sponsored me to compete in the Gay Games in Cleveland, Ohio.

Go to Trick: Frontside 540s in the pipe. And I will boardslide just about any rail or box in the park even if ends in a butt slide!

Go to Spot: I love Mont Tremblant in Quebec, but I'd be happy riding down a pile of garbage if it had a nice box at the end.

Are Canadians nicer? Ha! Well I haven't spent much time in America, but the times that I have, I met some very friendly people. Though East Coast Canadians are definitely very down to earth and will stop you on the street and talk your ear off.

How did you first get into snowboarding? I was a competitive freestyle skier from the ages of 11–14. I did moguls and aerials. I was also into skateboarding. When snowboarding started picking up at my local ski hill it looked so cool and fun, I made the switch!

What is your favorite part of snowboarding? In the winter every set of stairs I walk past turns into something I dream of conquering. I've spent a lot of time building jumps onto handrails and sessioning that for a few hours.

I know you were semipro, can you tell us a bit about how that happened and what it was like to snowboard on your provincial team? The tricks that I'd learned as a skier and skateboarder transferred over into snowboarding pretty quickly. I spent one winter snowboarding every weekend, practicing spins and learning how to ride a halfpipe. The next year I decided to start competing. There weren't a ton of girls competing in halfpipe in Nova Scotia, maybe about six or seven of us. I came in second place in the first contest I entered. I was hooked! I was sponsored on the Burton Snowboards Atlantic Team and I was on the Nova Scotia Snowboard Team. Two of my former female teammates are now professional riders and Olympians. I'm proud to have shared the snow with them back then.

You are a competitive powerlifter; your legs are massive! You have the nicest set of gams I have ever laid eyes on. You're competing at the Gay Games this summer, right? What do you hope to deadlift and squat there? Oh man, thanks! I'll be competing on August 10th. I just had a contest here in Toronto and I squatted 352 pounds, benched 253, and deadlifted 430. I'll be looking to do at least those numbers, but it'd be nice to add 5–10 pounds to all of those lifts. I'm so excited for the Gaymes!

What is the most memorably majestic moment you had while snowboarding? It was a bright, sunny, and relatively warm day, and I was competing in halfpipe at the Junior Nationals at the Calgary Olympic Park in Alberta. It was a really nice pipe to ride, much better quality than I was used to back home. I had, what for me was, a perfect run. I landed a 540 for the first time in a contest! I was surrounded by people who had such love for the sport. I felt so at home, even though I was technically on the other side of the country.

Since I got to spend a moment of time with you in real life, I can say you are as nice as you are sexy. How did you get

to be so sexy and so nice? Seriously though, what are your personal virtues? Do you look for those same qualities in a date? Aw, thanks man. Likewise! I had a blast hanging with you folks. I am a person with a lot of feelings so I tend to anticipate how others may feel in difficult or awkward situations. I appreciate that kind of consideration in others. My friends joke that I cling to my schedules beacuse I really take on too much, so I get along well with people who are organized, emotionally aware, and punctual. I'm lucky to have a wonderful MTF girlfriend who is always on time and puts up with my ridiculous type-A personality.

Anything else you want to tell our readers? I want to thank you so much for putting this publication together. It has really helped me feel connected to the larger trans male community all over the world. I'm such a big fanboy!

Interview by Rocco Kayiatos
Photos by Amos Mac

IT'S
FUN
TO
DISCOVER
NEW
TRAILS

RIDIN' DIRTY

with William

Name: William

Preferred Pronoun: He

Age: 34

Hometown: Toronto

Skate, Snowboard, or Surf: Snowboarding

First Board: A Burton board from '95.

Years Boarding: Since 1995.

Go to Trick: A mute or a nosegrab.

Go to Spot: HoliMont in Ellicottville, New York.

Best Boarding Trip: It's hard to say, there've been a few. I'd rather save up my money and go to a nice spot rather than ride locally. I've really enjoyed Mont Tremblant and Whistler, but actually now that I think about it, best most recent trip was at HoliMont. We just had an amazing time. Best older trip was in the 90s my friend and I went to Mont-Sainte-Anne in Quebec and neither of us could speak much French other than saying silly things like, "What time is it?" and "Where is the bathroom?" But we ended up meeting a group of super fun locals and we hung out with them a bunch and we made it work even with the language barrier. Also there may or may not have been some pot involved so it was just funny as hell.

Boarding Heroes: Terje Håkonsen, Peter Line, Devun Walsh. These guys were innovators and they were inspirational.

How did you get into it? I had been a skier first and I saw a few people riding and it looked fun and I thought, "I want to learn how to do that!"

What kind of board do you ride? Currently I ride a Forum Recon.

What do you like most about the sport? When I am riding, I am not thinking about anything else. It's fun to discover new trails and challenging yourself on hard ones.

What do you like most about the culture? I really used to love reading the magazines and seeing the awesome pics of the pros doing big jumps and tricks. I also probably owned 10 snowboarding videos that my friend and I would watch all the time to get pumped up before riding. Also back in the 90s, I loved the snowboarding gear and clothes. Back in the day I remember skiers asking funny questions while on the chairlift like, "Can you turn that thing? Can you make it stop?"

Interview by Rocco Kayiatos and Amos Mac

Photo by Drasko Bogdanovic

WOLFE MOON

Age: 27

Hometown: San Pedro, Cali.

Sponsors: Kanvas by Katin and Ripple Surboards

Snowboarding or Skateboarding or Surfing:
Skateboarding and surfing.

First Board: Original Sims skateboard my dad rode when
he was a kid.

Go to Trick: Backside 180 bert.

Go to Spot: Channel Street Skate Park.

Best Boarding Trip: When I was living in Portland,
Oregon, my buddies and I would go drink 40s at 3a.m.
and skate Burnside. It was pretty epic. I had a lot of great
sessions there when I was learning to skate bowls.

Favorite Food After Boarding: It depends on my mood at
the time, but I'm usually craving sushi or a big burrito filled
with tons of avocado.

Boarding Hero: Jay Adams! Dude is a legend, he inspires
me so much. I got the opportunity to meet him a few
years back and he had a blue mohawk. One of my most
stoked moments.

Gnarliest Injury: I was bombing a huge hill in Camas, Washington and they must've been doing road construction, but I didn't see all the gravel on the ground. I started going down and it began to rain heavily and I picked up a lot of speed and then started getting speed wobbles and saw the gravel. I tried to get low and ready to basically eat shit. My wheel caught the gravel and I flew forward. I tucked and rolled and slid across the ground, and my girlfriend at the time was filming the glorious epic stacking of all time and I got up and all I cared about was if she got the shot! I got some gnarly cement burn tore right through my hoodie but it was worth it.

Shoe of Choice: Vans. I prefer Half Cab Pros.

How did you get into it? Taught myself at a really young age and my dad showed me a few things.

How long have you been boarding? Probably since I was seven, so 20 years now!

What do you like most about the sport? The freedom I feel while I'm skating.

What do you like most about the culture? A lot of us are just a bunch of punk kids having a good time. Rad artwork and good people.

Do you board alone or do you have a crew that you board with? I like boarding alone, but I have a crew that rolls with me sometimes and we vibe off each other pushing each other past our limits, trying new things.

Do you listen to music while you shred? Totally listen to music, it pumps me up more. I dig horror punk or punk music in general or thrash metal.

What type of boards do you ride? I have a few Santa Cruz decks, Creature, Arbor, Powell Brite Lite, Sims. I'm really into vintage decks, or any board with a medium concave. It reminds me of surfing on my shortboard because of the shape and control it gives me.

What is your proudest moment after pulling off a difficult trick? The first time I ever pulled off a Powerslide and a Checkslide it was such a rush I had stoke for a week straight.

What are the stories behind your tattoos? A lot of my tattoos are wolf-related, punk, or darker. I have a few from my favorite artist, Swampy, along with a whole sleeve and part of my body dedicated to wolves because that's my chosen career path, to be a Wolf Biologist. I have waves on my right forearm to symbolize my competitive history with surfing and a Day of the Dead pitbull skull for my pup, Drama.

The one tattoo that I hold closest to my heart is my three wolves and a moon on my left shoulder. It motivates me to keep pushing forward and not give up; that I have my pack at my side.

What inspires your personal fashion? I'm creative, I like DIY, and always been into the color black. I dig skinnies and plain tees and band tees. If I think something's rad, I'll probably wear it. Or I create things to wear using random stuff I find like metal, leather, bones, fur or whatever. If it's black I usually need it. I patch my pants and hoodies constantly and paint on most of it.

Skateboarders have their own language. What's your favorite word? I like "bunk" or "gnar." It's pretty fun to throw those around.

Interview by Rocco Kayiatos
Photo by Ev Marquee

OP

ORIGINAL PLUMBING

TRANS MALE QUARTERLY / ISSUE 15 / USA $9

theselfieissue

LETTER FROM THE EDITORS

When you hear the word SELFIE you probably think of Instagram and your own self-documentation. Or maybe you think of Ellen at the Oscars, the Kardashian empire, or how this short, powerful word didn't even exist a few years back. Some may think of the SELFIE as superficial or annoying, but for our community it is an essential documentation of our existence. We've titled this 15th issue of *Original Plumbing* the SELFIE Issue not because it is filled with selfies (although you will find quite a few), but also because it represents an utter celebration of SELF.

In this issue we celebrate artists who have inspired us with their self-portraiture. We'll chat with Mr. Transman NYC, we'll hear some of the secrets behind your favorite selfies, dish about the UNSELFIE movement, and honor thy self-reflection. Hey, a little naval gazing never hurt anyone... right?

Amos Mac
Rocco Kayiatos

OP **originalplumbing.com**

🐦 **@opmag**

f **facebook.com/originalplumbing**

📷 **@originalplumbing**

t **originalplumbing.tumblr.com**

COVER MODEL: Wynne Neilly self-portrait; courtesy of the artist

#foggymirrorselfie #selfie
@amosmac

#iwokeuplikethisselfie #selfie
@roccokatastrophe

I LIKE THIS SELFIE BECAUSE IT MIRRORS
THE MAN I HAVE ALWAYS DREAMT OF LOOKING LIKE.
IT'S NOT JUST THE MASCULINE FEATURES OR FACIAL HAIR,
IT'S THE FACT THAT I FINALLY LOOK HAPPY.

—CAYDEN
@MR_CARTERRR

THIS PAST SUMMER, I RETURNED TO CAMP OUT AT A FRIEND'S IN VERMONT AND WRAP UP SOME PARTS OF MY LIFE THAT NEEDED A TANGIBLE ENDING AND BEGINNING. AS I AWOKE EARLY THE FOLLOWING MORNING AND CLIMBED RECKLESSLY DOWN INTO THE ROCKY RIVERS BED, I FELT READY TO LET GO OF THE THINGS I COULD NOT CONTROL. WHAT I LOVE MOST ABOUT THIS PICTURE OF ME IS THAT I TOOK IT IN HOPES OF CATCHING THAT FEELING ON MY FACE. IM NOT SURE IF I DID BUT I CAN REASSURE YOU THAT WHEN I SEE THIS, I SMELL CAMPFIRE, I TASTE SPRING WATER, I RECALL TRUE FRIENDSHIP, I REMEMBER FEELING HOME.

——SKYLAR
@SKYLARKERGIL

I was the king of the selfie before there was a word for it. Why did I love selfies, even when I didn't identify with my body? I loved that I was in control. I could document myself in a manner that best fit me. It was also the risk: in the days of film I risked botching an otherwise good shot and wasting money. I can dictate what is captured and shown in a selfie.

– justin adkins
@glaze0101

Fabian

Angel

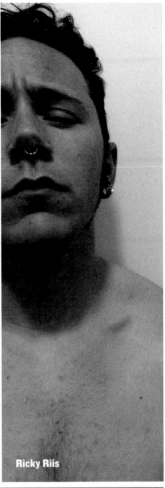
Ricky Riis

Nick Harrison

I'm a big fan of comic books and crime fiction novels. I usually post selfies online because I'm not only proud of myself, but, I like to share my joy with the world.

- Eli
@ealperin

This summer I was finally able to get my gender legally acknowledged and it's also the first time I felt comfortable enough to say "fuck it" and go swimming. **-Max @subversivethreads**

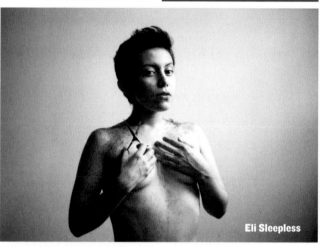

Eli Sleepless

Sawyer DeVuyst

AJ

Nicholas Schick

Kajo F.

Natty Koper

very Dutcher

MR. TRANSMAN

Interview by Amos and Rocco

Photos by Maro Hagopian, this page; Amos Mac, following page

What was your platform Mr. Transman NYC?

The "M" in "FTM" does not stand for misogyny.

Why did you decide to compete in the Mr. Transman Contest?

Two words: cash prize. I was saving up to have top surgery, and I was doing everything that I could to make that happen. I also thought I would have had gotten a tiara, though it wouldn't have been the first one that I had won.

For those that were not there, what made you stand out was your thorough platform and honest vulnerability. Can you tell our readers more about your platform and how you decided on it?

You mean it wasn't the outfits or the sweet dance moves that made me stand out? The phrase on which my platform was based was inspired by a piece by Janani Balasubramanian titled "Trans/national." I felt that it perfectly summed up what I had been witnessing in several FTM groups on social media and on message boards. Identifying as a man does not mean that we need to reinforce gender stereotypes and take on hypermasculine identities,

including adopting misogynistic attitudes and behaviors. We need to acknowledge the privilege we have when we are perceived as male, and—instead of using that privilege for personal benefit—use it as a means for change and take advantage of the opportunity to educate and challenge those around us that perpetuate misogynistic behavior.

What was your favorite part of competing?

Winning. Performing and being a giant doofus and hanging out with the other contestants was fun, but I got a lot of pleasure in winning with the platform I had and being flamboyant.

What was the most challenging part of being a part of the contest?

The most challenging part was the conflicting feelings I was having about participating in the contest and acknowledging that there is a population— trans women—who continue to be excluded from conversations and consideration in events that have a "trans" label. The second most challenging part was picking a wardrobe.

Who is your style icon?

My style varies. I'm inspired by 80s and 90s pop fashion, Joseph Gordon-Levitt in garters and thigh-highs (Google it and you're welcome), and lots of the fabulously beautiful people I see on menswear blogs and websites like DapperQ. It's hard to narrow it down to one.

Do you think it is important to have a space where trans men are on stage celebrating who they are and how good they look and feel?
Yes, but I think that it is important that every person have a space where they can be in the spotlight and celebrate who they are and how good they look and feel.

Can you share an experience that influenced the adult you've grown to be?
It's difficult to isolate a single experience. I feel like I have been greatly molded by the care, compassion, pain, humility, and resilience I have witnessed and experienced during the 15+ years of living with a chronic illness. You learn a lot about yourself and other people when you/they are at your/their lowest.

What is something in the world that you would like to see evolve?
The way that people view mental illness, the "justice" system, the American "democracy," and online dating sites.

What is something in the world that you would like to see completely disappear?
Oh, let's see. Rape culture, the patriarchy, the prison-industrial complex and police militarization, and a whole lot of oppressive –isms just to name a few.

Who is a person that has influenced the way you live your life?
My mom. She's pretty rad.

Do you have any specific career, life, or family goals?
I'm trying to figure out what my next "career" move will be. I have been working with at-risk/homeless LGBTQ youth for the past year and a half. I'd really like to focus on helping LGBTQ, especially transgender and gender nonconforming, individuals access proper healthcare and obtain entitlements. I want a job that I hope I will eventually lose because policies and attitudes will change, and my role will no longer be necessary. As far as life and family goals go, I want to put more of an emphasis on the relationships in my life and treating myself and others better. Eventually, I'd like to be an embarrassingly cool dad. I think I'm starting to get the embarrassingly cool part down. I'd also maybe like to learn how to read music, learn theory, maybe know the names of the chords I play, and notate the music I write. If I want to really dream big, I might also get my driver's license.

If your life were a song, what would the title be and what genre would it be in? Who would perform it (besides you, which is the obvious #1 choice)?
If I had to be limited to a single song, it would be titled "It's Complicated" and most likely be a very long song from a rock opera that incorporated several different styles. It would be performed by the love child of Audra McDonald and Andrew Rannells (featuring Pitbull).

Where can readers find your music online if they'd like to hear it?
Sadly, there isn't any music posted online since I've got a complicated relationship with recording equipment, the sound of my voice, and perfection. However, folks can like my Facebook page facebook.com/winterlaike and I will sometimes mention when I am playing a show. I'll also post songs up there if they ever get recorded.

OPEN STUDIOS

KING TEXAS/TEXAS ISAIAH

When did you first start making photographs?
I started around 2012. That is when I began to create.

Can you tell us in a couple sentences about the photographs you've shared with OP?
The photographs I have shared with you is a rough draft a larger project I will be starting soon.

What is the larger project?
Beginning in December, I will be working on a self-portrait series documenting memories, shadows, and silhouettes through my physical transition. I wanted to find a way to document myself without allowing others to fetishize my body. When I think of transitioning, I don't only think of the physical aspect. I think it is a mental and spiritual process as well.

You have such a strong, memorable aesthetic, it gives me chills. Do you have a specific goal in mind when you decide to make a photograph of another person? Does that differ with the goal of your self-portraits?
I don't think it differs at all. I want to document the root of a human soul and that has always been the goal. However, I never aim to photograph a person's "true self" because human beings are multilayered. To photograph a moment with someone is simply a moment, but it doesn't entirely define that person. I believe it's an important part of self-portraiture and portraiture. You get to unravel these layers and be a part of the history that is unfolding in front of your

eyes. I think it's easier to navigate when I photograph people as opposed to myself. I know my insecurities and even if I'm not aware at the time the shutter clicks, I have no other choice but to look at myself and figure it out. When it comes to portraits, there is a lot more space to create around that person in order for them to feel safe. Safety plays a major role and I don't think we speak about that often.

Do you have any pre–photo shoot rituals you do to ready yourself?
I always have butterflies in my stomach before shoots. I love it. It's a great feeling. I light some sage or palo santo and listen to music to create a good headspace about what I want to accomplish with each shoot, because it's different with each person even if I am shooting for the same project.

How many different series are you currently working on and do any of these subjects intersect?
I am working on many series, but during different times. If I am working on one series, the next series will be inspired by that one. I think it's interesting how projects share a dialogue with one another. That not only goes for the projects, but some of the people who are a part of them as well.

Do you feel there is a difference between a selfie and a self-portrait?
I don't think we can speak about selfies without talking about the power of social media. I love selfies, although I don't personally take a lot of them myself. I think they are very empowering and the interesting thing about them is we have full control over

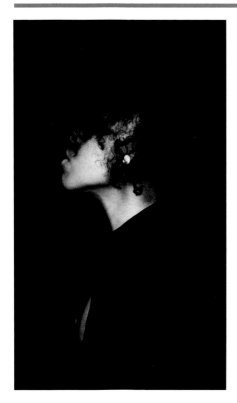

them. I don't view self-portraits in the same light. But, I do think social media warps reality a little bit and that can be a pro and a con. I think by answering this question, it has made me realize that I am still figuring out the significance of a selfie and how it may or may not relate to a self-portrait outside the context of a traditional art form.

Why is it important for trans people to share their images through self-portrait photography and instagram selfies?
Trans/GNC folks sharing their stories and images through different mediums of art is incredibly important. As I've stated before, there is power within visibility and I think it's important for us to see each other. You are here, and so am I. You are beautiful, and so am I. Why not show the world when we have the opportunity to?

Personally for me, it can be much more complicated than that. Before, I stated that within my self-portraits I was very conscious on how to photograph my own soul without allowing others to fetishize my body. It's hard to redirect that gaze in a society who is now "entering" or slightly engaging with the idea that gender is nonlimiting. In a society that pretty much condones the imprisonment and murder of black cis/trans/GNC bodies... as much as the feeling of wanting to hide completely or be completely visible wages a war within my heart... I think it is important for us to be in sight.

The power of photography within the age of society will allow us to live forever even after we are gone, and the future needs to be aware that there are so many beautiful trans/ GNC folks doing amazing work.

Is there anyone who—or anything that— inspires your photographic aesthetic?
The answer to that question changes every day, because I am surrounded by a lot of amazing creative people. However, at this point in my career, I would have to say that Toyin Odutola has definitely inspired the way I look at portraiture within the last year. Not only do I love her work but I love her mind as well. I admire how she takes the world on a step-by-step journey of her process, which is intricate and pure. Her work has showed me how a portrait can offer several viewpoints, solutions, and multiple degrees of complexity. She is a draftswoman and her work gives me butterflies.

What do you strive towards for your future as an artist?
Peace, stability, moments, patience, understanding, and happiness.

Photo Titles
6 a.m 2014
Accountability 2014
kingtexas.net

WYNNE NEILLY

Where did you grow up?
I grew up in Oakville, a suburb just outside of Toronto.

Where is "home" for you today?
Toronto. I feel like no matter where I end up, Toronto will always be "home" for me.

Do you feel there is a difference between a selfie and a self-portrait?
I do believe there is a difference, especially being a visual artist. A self-portrait for me has artistic intention and its aesthetic is planned and has a concept that functions within a body of work. A selfie is something I take with my phone when I am feeling good about the way I look that day, an expression of self-love I suppose. There can definitely be crossover between the two for me, but that is how I would categorize them.

Who inspires your artistic practice and aesthetic?
I am going to give a small list of who I am feeling influenced by currently: Leslie Feinberg, Catherine Opie, the queer/trans community that surrounds me, Dadaism, Richard Avedon.

How have other self-portraits or selfies of trans or gender nonconforming people effected the way you've felt about yourself, your life, and possibilities?
Seeing other trans or gender nonconforming people taking selfies or self-portraits gives me motivation to continue producing my work. It makes me feel like we are all adding to the positive representation and understanding of trans identities and trans or nonconforming bodies.

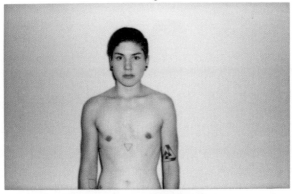

100 mg

AUGUST 30th - 3rd SHOT

What has Female to "Male" taught you about your artistic process?

This project has taught me a lot of things about my artistic process but I would say the most important lesson is that I have more confidence and patience than I thought I had. I have been very public about my identity through this project, and even though that can be scary at times, it also becomes very rewarding when I get positive feedback. This project currently has no end date so I must be patient with it and let it unfold naturally.

What do you want other trans people to know about Female to "Male"?

I want other trans people to know that Female to "Male" is a self-portrait project documenting my transition mainly through weekly photographs. I have insisted on the use of quotation marks around the word

"male" because my identity is something fluid that cannot be easily defined by use of a single word. My intent is to speak about my own experience, not trans* people in general, and my goal is to contribute to trans* representation in the media and in the art world.

Photo Titles:

August 30th 2013 - 3rd shot,
Fuji Instax Film, 2013

October 18th 2013 - 10th shot,
Fuji Instax Film, 2013

January 24th 2014 - 24th shot,
Fuji Instax Film, 2014

August 8th 2014 - 52nd shot,
Fuji Instax Film, 2014

October 10th 2014 - 64st shot,
Fuji Instax Film, 2014

100 mg

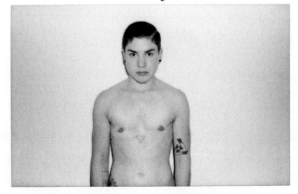

OCTOBER 18th 2013 — 10th SHOT

100 mg

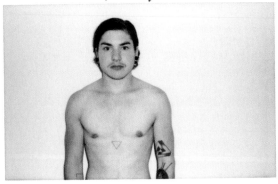

AUGUST 8th 2014 — 52nd SHOT

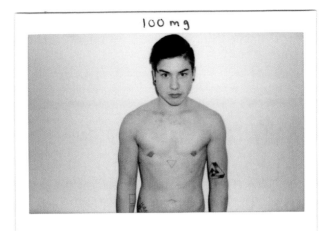

100 mg

JANUARY 24th 2014 - 24th SHOT

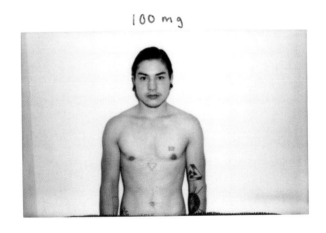

100 mg

OCTOBER 31st 2014 - 64th SHOT

UNSELFIES

By T Cooper

I realize this is not going to be the most popular thing I've ever suggested, but here goes: I don't think taking selfies is the healthiest impulse.

Outside of your great-grandmother and Jesus, who doesn't pop selfies? Celebrities and news anchors take selfies. Pulitzer Prize–winning authors take selfies. The pope and President Obama take selfies. Justin Bieber and Kim Kardashian, it's been said, will actually expire if they don't snap and post at least one selfie per hour, including during sex and sleep. And while photographer Robert Cornelius is credited with taking that first beautifully clouded daguerreotype of himself in 1839, we probably have transitioning transsexuals to thank for really perfecting and refining the art of self-portraiture.

If you're a trans man of a certain age, and you had nowhere besides tiny corners of the internet to scour for information about surgery, hormones, and tangible proof that somebody could actually transition and live to tell about it, you might recall pouring over dozens and dozens of photographs on now-defunct, obsolete resources like Transster.com and the FTMsurgeryinfo Yahoo group. Pages organized by surgeons' names, regions, and countries, all with photographic evidence of before, immediately after (bloody drains!), and then every week post-surgery, sometimes for years on end. The thing about these photos was—they

are burned on my brain, I looked at them so many times—all the heads were cropped off. Tattoos photoshopped out. Identifying household artwork, furniture, pets, and adornment excised. E-mails encrypted. Anonymity wholly preserved.

Then MySpace happened, and that was really the first time you could see guys—and girls, but I'm just talking about dudes right now because I have personal knowledge of the FTM realm—posting literally hundreds of fully identifiable photographs of themselves online publicly for all to see (friends, strangers, and foes alike). Sure, the chasers flocked, and your cousin in Tulsa and high school sweetheart in Bangor got to see what a specimen you'd become, but so did the self-appointed selfie-police, many of whom voiced concern that trans men showing their scars so publicly would make it more difficult for those wishing to live stealthily to do so (because the more photos of chest scars out there, the more folks will know about them and not be fooled by the "I had lung surgery" alibi so many of us—okay *I*—tried to float).

Boy, did those types of concerns fly out the window with the emergence of Facebook, Twitter, Instagram, and YouTube (and a lot of other places that I can't list because I'm old and don't even know what Vine and Snapchat are). Not to mention the proliferation of smartphones with state-of-the-art, front-facing cameras. And now even the paparazzi, which has brought us photos of shirtless, world-renowned trans man Chaz Bono unloading groceries from his fancy BMW in the driveway of his West Hollywood home in the tabloids (with telephoto detail of double-incision scars, even!).

It was somewhere amidst the migration from MySpace to Facebook, however, that I started feeling overwhelmingly sad about the hoards of very much not anonymous selfies fellow trans men, many of them friends and acquaintances, were posting to their accounts, seemingly in higher numbers than any cis friends I noticed did. Look, I understand completely the power of self-styled self-determination. I've taken some selfies; I'll probably take a few more. And I am so grateful for all of those brave souls who (literally) bared all so that others might feel slightly less alone and afraid when turning over our fates (and fortunes) to a medical doctor simply because we heard somewhere s/he could perform something we needed and/or wanted. And better to capture (objectify?) our bodies and our selves *ourselves*, instead of leaving others to do it for us. I mean, that's the point and power of the very magazine you now hold in your hands, right?

I get all that, I do. What a wonder to photograph yourself and actually see who and what you want to see staring back at you? Stubble, sideburns, narrow hips, broad shoulders, muscles, a flat chest from the side. And why not share that with every-body you know (not to mention everybody you don't)? But perhaps the more relevant question is *Why*?

Why do we take so many goddamn selfies and post them? Is it simple vanity? Narcissism? Loneliness? The need for approval? Because we can? Because everybody else does?

I don't know the answer, though some recent research (out of the UK) has shown definitively that most people don't like folks who constantly take and share photos of themselves. The practice of trying to connect through posting selfies on social media actually leads to less intimacy, not more, and thus negatively, demonstrably, impacts human relationships.

This is something I've sensed, but haven't quite had the language for, or really anything to explain that ennui and distance I feel after seeing hundreds of selfies from the same people online, year after year. Having two teen daughters tip-toeing into the social media world (though my wife and I have greatly limited their access to it), really underlined that discomfort, almost put it into relief for me. Unless you've stumbled upon fifty photos of your thirteen-year-old styling and posing herself in a way that completely unknowingly mimics porn culture (simply because it's something she's seen both peers and strangers, especially of the female persuasion, doing in their photos), you might not understand why it's difficult not to feel serious concern about selfies.

Selfies have become ubiquitous, as common as weeds. The problem is, like weeds, the invasion of selfies tends to block out healthier, more colorful growth (like, say, actual face-to-face, human-to-human contact). Especially in kids. Unless you're Woody Allen or Freud, the constant scrutiny of oneself never ends well. (And even with those dudes it's debatable.) Pair that lens-gazing with the compulsion to share the images and curry public favor, and you've got an unrivaled recipe for sustained emptiness.

Being a teenager is never a picnic. But being a teenager on blast, with no private space and a constant stream of criticism coming at you from the electronic ether, can start to feel something like impossible. (Not to mention lethal, in light of some mind-bogglingly tragic cases of teens committing suicide as a result of unrelenting online harassment.)

Most of the time, the selfie isn't even a selfie, but rather a reflection of all the things other people are (or, are cultivating their image to suggest they are), that we believe we are supposed to be, too. Hence the prevalence of certain "looks," like the duckface or the Miley, that become facial and body fashions. (None of these expressions, it should be noted, communicate much beyond availability.) In truth, the selfie is, by nature, exclusively about the other, a note in a bottle pleading that someone, anyone, love me. Which, I think we can all agree, isn't the best feeling in the world, and maybe something we could do a little less of.

Enter UNSelfies.

As part of We Are Changers, an empathy project for young adults that my wife and I founded around the publication of our young adult novel series, we want to ignite an UNSELFIES revolution. The mission is simple: turn the camera around and focus not on how you look, but how you feel. Instead of capturing your physical self in a photo, try to capture your emotional self. Or document what somebody else is feeling or experiencing in a photo. We are building a living, evolving gallery of Unselfies, hundreds, ideally thousands of non-self-involved little moments that moved people for whatever reason.

Anyway, this is all just to lodge one vote for the art of looking outward through the lens. Literally, to shine a light on others so that we can understand experiences and situations, lives and worlds not our own, so that we can better understand that which is not ourselves—especially of value, I think, for those of us who spent a considerable amount of time self-scrutizing, and not always loving everything we saw.

OP

TRANS MALE CULTURE

THE LIT ISSUE • NUMBER 16 • 2015 • USA $9
THOMAS PAGE MCBEE PHOTOGRAPHED BY AMOS MAC

read

Letter From The Editors

Total Trans Lit Explosion! It's obvious that we are witnessing a trans literary boom right now. What better way to showcase our favorites than to create an entire issue around the people we look towards when it comes to focusing on the evolution of trans storytelling? In this issue you'll enjoy a portfolio featuring some of the most groundbreaking poets in our community right now, words of publishing advice, interviews with some literary darlings, notes on how to get over writer's block and get those feelings out onto paper, and a ton more. Of course this issue wouldn't be complete without a shirtless photo of a writer lying on his bed in a pigeon mask.

Buy books, or rent them at the library! Reading is beyond sexy! Trust us!

Amos and Rocco

COVER MODEL: Thomas Page McBee; photo by Amos Mac

Hit Us Up

ORIGINALPLUMBING.COM

TWITTER.COM/OPMAG

f FACEBOOK.COM/ORIGINALPLUMBING

INSTAGRAM.COM/ORIGINALPLUMBING

t ORIGINALPLUMBING.TUMBLR.COM

10 QUESTIONS

ELLIOTT DELINE

Current Location:
Syracuse, New York

Favorite Memoir:
Autobiography by Morrissey

Favorite Non-Fiction Book:
*Tastes of Paradise: A Social History of
Spices, Stimulants, and Intoxicants* by
Wolfgang Schivelbush

Favorite Fiction Book:
American Pastoral by Philip Roth

Most Inspiring Trans* Writer:
Leslie Feinberg

Most Supportive Person In My Life:
My partner, Joey

My Earliest Memory That Involves Writing:
An early memory I have is reading *Harry Potter
and the Prisoner of Azkaban* 12 times between 5th
and 6th grade.

Besides Writing, I Spend A Lot Of Time:
With my cats and traveling.

**A Trans* Narrative That I Feel Is Not Written
About Enough:**
Trans people with mental illnesses

When I Get Writer's Block, I:
Figure I need to go out and experience
some more life.

STONE BUTCH BLUES
INSPIRES TRANS WRITERS

IN NOVEMBER OF 2014, TRANS AUTHOR AND ACTIVIST LESLIE FEINBERG PASSED AWAY AT THE AGE OF 65.

Years earlier, for a piece that went unpublished until now, we asked writers to share with us how Stone Butch Blues inspired their lives. We have decided to publish these quotes now, in honor of Leslie Feinberg.

Two expressions come to mind when I think of Stone Butch Blues *and the time period it conveys: "There is nothing new under the sun" and "There but for the grace of God go I." It was very special to me that the book took place in my home of upstate New York. I found myself both nodding in recognition and gasping in disbelief. It's like a different kind of genealogy—a precious record that survived against the odds. And it's one of the transgender community's (and certainly, the transgender writer's) only cultural reference points to evaluate how far, and from where, we have come.*

—Elliott DeLine, author of REFUSE

I read Stone Butch Blues *later than I should have, in my late twenties. It showed me that my struggles for happiness and equality were nothing compared to the struggle of those who came before me, battling for actual survival. It taught me about legacy and responsibility, that others fought so that I could have my very existence and inspired me to play a part in progress for future generations.*

—Nick Krieger, author of NINA HERE NOR THERE

I remember that the first time I read Stone Butch Blues, *I wept. It was like being handed a family tree I hadn't known about, a whole history of gender nonconforming people like me surviving in working class towns.*

—Rae Spoon, author of GENDER FAILURE and FIRST SPRING GRASS FIRE

I read Stone Butch Blues *in 1995. And, although Jess Goldberg's life seemed a million miles away from the life I was living in a conservative, midwestern college town, this book gave me an incredible sense of possibility and marked the beginning of my own transformative process.*

—Hank T., Assistant Professor of Psychiatry, Rush University

Self-portrait of Leslie Feinberg in the West Village in 2011.

Figures
by Emerson Whitney

Figure 1.

There's a vague light in the corner of the frame, a wave of color rising. The trunk or a chest, some kind of life. Me? This is here-ness, a durational project, personhood that will eventually be "then."

In this photo, there's a three year old holding my cheeks. I never thought I'd like someone who is three, the surprise is evident on my face. He's holding me by my cheeks and saying, you're Emerson, and I'm thinking, who?

Clearly, from this photo (judging by my gaze and the slight purse of my body) I'm a person. Clearly, a living animal person. What do I feel like when no one sees? What if we—subject and object and witness—look away for a second? What happens?

Figure 2.

I've worked hard at the light on my cheeks, feeling the pressure of "cute," afraid that someone will look at the photo and say child! Emerson Whitney looks like a child! I've pulled my shirt over my hips and am standing at an angle so as to appear boxy, less woman. I've put my tongue behind my teeth like I've been told makes a wry smile. I'm thinking: LIKE MY FACE! CLICK MY FACE!

I'm thinking Lacan: the subject is self divided or split between a wish for wholeness and the reality of fragmentation.

I'm thinking: sometimes, when speaking of myself in the third person, I am afraid to mess my own pronoun up.

I scroll through photos of objects all day, our objects, our cats on keyboards, our lunch, our cats on our lunches, trans objects too, trans subjects splayed open on the internet in various states of "alive."

What if all of us look away for a second? What happens?

Foucault says POWER: bodies, multiplicities, desires, forces.

CA CONRAD says TOO MUCH WAR

Once I asked Fred Moten how to go about not getting assimilated. He said Oh, and laughed, You already are. That's the nature of a body, a heavenly body, any body.

Sometimes I wish I had more control, that I could force myself and my body to match whatever it is you are thinking, that my identity could be an assertion and not a negotiation.

But the three year old says Emerson!

I blink into the photo.

Uncle Lynnee's Advice To Young Writers

In List Form For Busy Guys
By Lynnee Breedlove

Writing isn't a talent. It's a body of work. Here are some workout tips.

1. Write every day. Set up coffee the night before. If you're not a coffee guy, become one. If your first beverage of the day is beer, good luck. You're not Bukowski. That guy had extra brain cells. He could soak 'em all in whisky and still churn out genius. I guarantee this will not be you.

2. Get a notebook and favorite pen. I like a box of medium blue gel ink rollerballs and a leather-bound notebook. Sexy. Words come out the fingers onto the paper. But I've been known to write on a $1.29 Iron Man cardboard-lined notebook for teenage boys and a ballpoint from Office Max. Just get it out.

3. Put these tools by your bed or if you have an outside chill spot, drag that and your coffee out there. I like to hole up, write down who fucked up, why I'm pissed, or what hottie I dreamed about. By page 2 I'm writing relevant shit fit for public consumption.

4. Write at least three pages a day to dump crap clogging up your brain. Only then does decent stuff start to roll out. Counts as autotherapy. Free and private.

5. If you end up famous like Kerouac they'll posthumously publish your journals, so don't put anything down you wouldn't want anyone to know now or later. Maybe you don't want your girlfriend to find out you're boinking her bestie. That's why they used initials back in the 19th. Discretion is the better part of valor. That means keeping your indiscretions discreet or don't fuck up. If you find your significant others do keep reading your journals, you're either fucking around or not "sharing" enough with them. The beloveds like it when you talk about yourself. I think it's called intimacy. Keep the drama on the page and outta your bedroom. Lock up all writing until edits are done. A cabinet where you stash your firearms is good. Store bullets separately.

6. Rewrite and edit on a laptop. Longhand comes out more emotional. Then get in there and cut it up, ruthless, math brain, on a machine. Nobody wants to read your diary, except your love thang. Edit, edit, edit.

7. Post, blog, or read out. Get a feel for your effect. Maybe you love it but nobody else does. If you were trapped on a desert island, you'd write love letters in the sand and that would be enough. But in the world, it's an energy loop. Test your product. Change direction or stay on course based on what you and your audience like.

8. When you hit the big time, someone else will edit you. Don't be precious. Sometimes you have to refuse for a week and fold your arms and swear at the edits. Then negotiate a couple and say yes to the rest.

9. Tell on yourself. In order to get real with them, get real with you. This requires work. You snowboard the Himalayas? You're a Dharma Punk? Talk about your failures. No one cares about guys who never lose. Readers want to be inspired by how you overcame adversity. Get deep but not embarrassing; you do want to get laid. Your writing is a permanent ad for you. And like lovers, your audience wants you vulnerable, not pathetic. Change names to protect the guilty. Call it memoir fiction or wait 'til all parties are dead.

10. Be straight up journalistic about emotional shit. Steer clear of maudlin. Death, destruction, and heartbreak, yes, but just break down what happened. If it's sad, they'll cry; if it's funny, they'll laugh, without instruction.

11. Find your voice. Write like you talk, take out half the fucks, add some poetry. Read it out loud to hear whether it sounds clunky or like something you wished you'd said in real life.

12. Create content. Do shit. Hemingway went to Spain to fight a war against fascism and went down in history as a guy with integrity even though he offed himself. People believed what he wrote. Travel. Take risks. Get naked. Jump off shit. Fly or climb to great heights. Navigate land, sea and air in as many vehicles as you can master. Swim under a full moon off the coast of Mexico and wonder if there are sharks. Go where you don't speak the language and make babes laugh. Do something your parents hate and you love.

Live. Write. Cut out the boring stuff. Not easy, but simple.

Photo by Emily Jane Corbett

Poetry Corner

CHING-IN CHEN

H. MELT

SAMUEL ACE

Closed Sky

by Ching-In Chen

Morning rose empty
as pigeon, beak
on horizon.
                Cleanse.
Someone else, another body
cooks in dense air.

What song lives each
time sun goes out.

Lightbulbs then, wood
oil flames.
*

Someone cleans sea.
A body fragrant in air breaks
molecules and surface.

This body cleans
surface. A song comes
out to peck and pray.

Sun feeds on prey.
Make body alight
Rest thing which
can't stay
infection
*

A pathogen cleans fragrant
body. This body eats

skin, repeats song
in infected moring.

Whatever abnormal has

no story. I composed
my host and what they
replicate. I fear
only to repeat.
*

Pathogen clean body
fragrant a body in morning
a rose inert against its agent
sun feeds this coat

An envelope of protein.
A surrounding system
of damage. A host
makes body light
and break.
**

Look, no one cleans sea. Their
surface recombines with dirt.
Molecules another bird.

Pathogen in morning
song insect flying into sun
*

Look, sea does not want to
participate. No one on the side of
sea.
Oilslick mouth is a her.
What does not close is a skin next
to skin.

           Drops of a body birds come to
host.

After Reading Leelah Alcorn's Suicide Note on Tumblr

by H. Melt

When I was 14, I learned what transgender meant

I turn on a bath
the water is
too hot

I immediately told my mom, and she reacted extremely negatively,

I light a rainbow candle
watch the rage melt
into orange

telling me that it was a phase, that I would never truly be a girl,

the headline reads
"Boy, 17, hit and killed
by semi on I-71"

that God doesn't make mistakes, that I am wrong.

the basketball team
is planning a moment
of silence

If you are reading this, parents,

and I wonder
if they even know
who to mourn

please don't tell this to your kids.

Italicized text is taken from the suicide note of Leelah Alcorn.

There in the dusky blue

by Samuel Ace

December 22nd 5:53:02 am

There in the dusky blue   a pillow of
dark   the children pour brandy into
flower pots   eat currants and plums
run across the threshing floors toward
dawn   ten of them gather by the leaden
windows in the long factory corners
hiding from hurricanes   truck bombs
the everyday   the doctors walk toward
them   leaching minerals from their
bones   leaky hearts in the humid
barrel of coasts   they have a list

A carpeted village of what's said in the doctor's white office
a hidden secret of girls who are boys   who like baseball and
trucks   race cars and little MGs   who love mud boys   who knock
over every toy on the white coat floor   who throw their genders
across the room so maybe just maybe the doctor will die from a
hidden head injury caused by a flying Playskool bus

There is a steeple and he flies to the top where down below
the children are tiny dots   there's a campus of churches on
a street of prairie fire   an early intervention or a first lesson in
perspective

The bars on the hospital bed taste of metal   he gnaws on them
in his sleep   throws up on them in the morning when he tries
to leave   the air no longer blue   just dim with clouds   no
comfort at all   his dog lies down with him and he rests his head
in her belly of fur   he is a feather and the door a swinging force
of wind

You Didn't Even Know This Shit Was Trans*!

 A Literary List By Henry Giardina

1. Twelfth Night Shakespeare, being a badass, wasn't one to shy away from trans themes. Ever. At all. However, unlike some of the more obvious trans plays, *Twelfth Night* digs into the implications (comic and tragic) of moving between genders and bodies. It's a play about choice, with the awesome distinction that for once the choice of who to love is secondary to the choice of who to be.

2. Hamlet Yes, Shakespeare again. But hear me out. By the time Hamlet meets his tragic end, we've seen his life unravel in a giant metaphor for the trans experience. Oh, so you've come back home to find your father is dead, and you're the only one who knows the truth about it? And your mother refuses to hear that truth, or acknowledge the fact that you have emotions that she can't understand? Oh, and your friends are totally fucking useless because they don't understand you either? Oh, and your girlfriend doesn't get you

either? Yeah, we've all been there—and we've all nearly gone crazy, too. At the turn of the 20th century, the theory that Hamlet's character was born a woman was being taken so seriously that the Germans made a movie based on it, starring Asta Nielsen, and throwing in a whole crazy extra storyline in which Hamlet's problem is that he has been misgendered all along. Layers upon layers, people. It's real.

3. Monsieur Venus This is a book by a woman who referred to herself as "Rachilde, Man of Letters" and Oscar Wilde was obsessed with it. If you read it, you'll see why. A woman makes a man her lover, and then decides it's not quite enough for him to be her lover. He's got to be her mistress. So together they try to switch genders, and it totally works—so flawlessly that our hero, the eponymous Monsieur Venus, gets challenged to a duel by the end. And nothing, in 1884, is more manly than that shit.

4. Lieutenant Nun

The Autobiography of Catalina de Erauso-Hey, did you know that there is a person from actual history who began her life as a nun and then later decided, "Fuck this noise, I'm going to be a soldier?" It's not the plot of *Mulan*. It's real fucking life. In the 17th century. And it's all in this book, in which Catalina de Erauso details her life as an ex-nun who escapes from her convent to spend most of her life passing for a man in the Spanish army. None badder, none rawer.

5. Cerebus

Cerebus the Aardvark, an epic 90s graphic novel in about 300 installments, is not only a brilliant read, but features a main character who is an ass-kicking aardvark in the future, blessed with a uterus and both male and female genitalia who identifies as male, and refers to himself in the third person. Need I say more? Probably, but I'm not going to. Just read it.

6. Metamorphoses

There's just no genderfuckery like the genderfuckery of antiquity. In Ovid's poem, characters change from male to female on a whim, combine to form beautiful, intersexed deities, and give up human form altogether in favor of something way more awesome. And then there are some characters who try to have sex with trees. It's all in there, folks.

7. Mrs. Henderson

Two English schoolboys in the 50s are having a disagreement about whether or not girls have penises. One boy is making the case that they don't. To which the other says, but that's impossible, because my mom definitely has one, I've seen her pee with it. At which the first boy thinks: fucking cool. Francis Wyndham's short story is, depending on how you look at it, outrageously offensive or damned subversive. Either way, it's like nothing else ever written.

8. Attis

In Catullus's poem, the very confusing myth of the cult of Attis is partway explained. Sort of. It goes something like this: Attis's mom got pregnant by putting an almond in her cleavage (yup) and gave birth to Attis, a boy. In later life, Attis gets cursed so that he'll go mad and cut off his male genitals. After doing this she starts referring to herself with female pronouns and becomes a kind of earth mother and a cult figure. It's all worth it for the lines: "Attis runs with mad energy into the woods. He was a handmaid in these woods all his life."

9. Against Nature

This is another Oscar Wilde favorite. In Huysman's book, the decadent hero Des Esseintes meets an American acrobat named Urania, and fantasizes about a transformative bout of sex with her which would change her into a man, and himself into a woman. But real-life sex proves less exciting by far, and he dumps her. Ah, the old, familiar story.

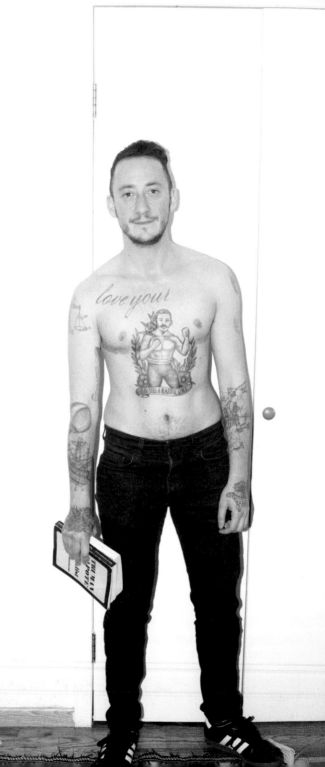

The Masculinity Expert

Thomas Page McBee
Interviewed By Amos Mac

PHOTOGRAPHED BY AMOS MAC

Thomas Page McBee is what I'd call a real writer's writer. His novel Man Alive *(City Lights, 2014)* blew my mind while simultaneously blowing the lid off of the way trans male narratives have been presented in nonfiction. His work has been published everywhere from the New York Times *to* BuzzFeed, *and he even held the title of* VICE's *masculinity expert. He is currently working on an upcoming story for* Playboy *on trans athletes, and get this—they pitched the topic to him. He also owns a really intense pigeon mask, which I quickly became obsessed with. Let's find out more about Thomas Page McBee!*

Amos Mac: I read *Man Alive* in two days. It was so poetic. I knew you in San Francisco when you were going through some of what is featured in the book, so reading about it was haunting and quite beautiful.
Thomas Page McBee: Well, I'm glad.

***Man Alive* is not the traditional trans narrative which is important, there's a lot more going on. I actually want to send it to my mom to show her the scope of the trans narrative.**
Let me know if you do and how she reacts, it seems to be a big hit with moms! My mother passed away and didn't get to read it. She read an early draft and gave me feedback about how she wanted it to be different because she's such a big part of the book. She wasn't able to read it to know that it had changed which I was disappointed about. When she died last year it was right when people were starting to read it and I was able to let her know that people overall loved her character in the book so that was really nice.

As a writer, how do you open up to this level of honesty?
I think writing the *Self-Made Man* column (therumpus.net) was helpful, and also being isolated, because I was in New England

and it's not like I was surrounded by my friends. I almost feel in a certain way I have to work harder now to write so vulnerably as opposed to before, when I felt I just needed to connect with people in a way.

It was about feeling isolated and starting to transition in a place where there weren't a lot of trans people and my instinct is to connect when I feel lost, so that's what I was doing. With the book I had already written a lot of it, but the revising is where things got kind of deep and made sense and connected. It wasn't like when I write for the internet, which I was doing a lot of, where I would be writing something and a few days later it would be online and people would react to it. It wasn't that I was less vulnerable but I do think there is a protectiveness that comes when you're doing something all the time. I think the book required me to not think about what would happen once it got into the world or else I wouldn't have been able to do it.

I feel the exact same way about this magazine. If I would've thought about it before putting out the first issue I never would've done it.
It's a certain kind of fearlessness.

It's a survival skill. If you're doing a project and you feel like it has to be done...
It's also a certain recklessness of personality, which I think I have, and I'm fine with. I take big risks in work and relationships and in life, and the way I do it is by not looking before I leap. I feel things out instinctually and say, "Does this feel right?" If it does I just do it, I don't weigh the pros and cons and get really rational and think about consequences.

In the beginning of _Man Alive_ you write, "This is an adventure story about how I quit being a ghost." Can you talk about that?
There's a whole part about "a stranger comes to town" versus "a hero goes on a journey." The book is about building a narrative, when actually life is chaos and often doesn't quite make a lot of sense, but you have a sense that there are meaningful things that have happened. Building a narrative using the tools that exist is basically what the book is about, which is why I don't think it's a book about transition or being trans. It's about becoming a person.

VICE has called you a masculinity expert. What the hell is that (_laughs_)?
That's tongue and cheek.

On a serious note I wanted to be in charge of my narrative about my transition and about being a trans man in the world, which for me personally has a lot about being a man in the world. My book is a lot about that process. There are a lot of conversations about being trans and I think that's important and I have those too, but I don't think there are enough conversations about masculinity and what being a man really means. And because I have the privilege of passing and moving around in certain worlds where people don't always know I'm trans, I think I have a way of start having different types of dialogues with men especially that other people don't always get the chance to have. Being a masculinity expert was a lot about that, and about being on top of that and pushing for that conversation.

How is your experience with dealing with the same tired and often insulting trans questions during mainstream media interviews?

I really try to model for whoever is interviewing me the way to communicate with other human beings, and I think in a way it just works with people. It's not like I'm faking it. I just try to say often in an interview, "Well, like a lot of men, I've had this experience" or "Yes, being trans is unique and a specific experience, just like a lot of other unique, specific human experiences that all exist within the human condition" and "If you've ever been though a major change, uprooted your life and done something radically different than what you've done so far, then you can connect to this story."

If other people are going to tell our stories anyway, then at least it should be in a way of empathy and connection and not from a place of "othering" and "isn't this strange."

What are you working on right now?

I'm writing a book based on stories and articles I'm writing, but I'm also writing original essays and journalism-type stories about masculinity from obviously a million different angles. The main idea is to go into all-male spaces and report back.

Can you fill me in on the spaces or topics?

White-collar boxing, because it's so strange. It's like these very rich bankers, going into amateur gyms to pay a lot of money and be trained by guys who put their bodies on the line for $500 throughout their careers and who have no money and it's a really weird vibe. I wrote a whole essay about barbershops and my experience.

I'm trying to find some MRAs to figure out about that world. Spaces like that. I want to talk to some stay-at-home dads, which aren't really all-male spaces, but it's like, men in different roles. I want to go to a fraternity. Spaces where men gather.

What are you reading right now?

The Short and Tragic Life of Robert Peace by Jeff Hobbs.

It's a nonfiction book about this kid from Newark who has a tough life and ends up going to Yale and it meets a tragic end and his roommate becomes a reporter and tells his story.

I love *In Cold Blood* by Truman Capote. Really narrative nonfiction. It's journalism but it's a novel.

Do you have any advice for young trans writers?

I think what's true for young trans writers are true for all writers. Base-level reality. I've been a writer since I was 9 and now I'm finally at a point where I'm like, "This is never going to stop."

A lot of being an artist is getting right with yourself, growing up as a person. If I could change anything at all about my own process, it would be to not worry so much about it, to reassure that I was great at this and I loved doing it. It wasn't even that the rejection was getting me down, and there was a ton of that—I'm a relentless optimist so that was fine—but it was more that my life would become eclipsed by other things in my life and I would stop.

My advice is, if it's something that you love doing, you can't stop doing it, and you can't worry about stopping. You find your way. You find the way to do it that works for you. It might not be the way it works for other people, or the way you envision it, and I don't think there's one path. I write for big pop outlets, and then I wrote a literary book, but I had no idea if anyone was going to publish it or care. Even if no one read this book or if I hadn't written it, I still would've been a writer because I write all the time. So I think that finding a way to be relentless is the thing, and being in charge of your own story. I think trans writers especially need to be conscious of that.

Cooper On Cooper Action

A Conversation with T Cooper
By Cooper Lee Bombardier

PHOTOGRAPHED BY AMOS MAC

T Cooper is the OG of trans male publishing. He is the author of seven books, including the recent nonfiction Real Man Adventures, a meditation on the subject of masculinity. His novels include Lipshitz Six, or Two Angry Blondes and The Beaufort Diaries, as well as the four-part young adult novel series entitled Changers, which he is cowriting with his wife.

Cooper Lee Bombardier: There is this myth of a "writer's life," where someone sits at a typewriter in a cabin wearing a heavy-knit woolen sweater, writing all day. What does your "writer's life" look like?

T Cooper: When I was younger and had fewer responsibilities, I could always carve out time, stay up all night if needed. And I used to go to writers' colonies for month-long stays, where I'd drop out of life and just write, like boot camp. But I don't think I would do that now.

CLB: I think the biggest thing is to have some kind of regularity, even if it is "irregular." A consistent contact with the work.

TC: Yeah. Now I just cram in work anywhere I can. This is an art, but it's also a job, so I tend to treat it as such. I write like there's a scary fucking dragon breathing fire over my shoulder all the time. And I'm not saying it's like coal mining or sewing for 17 hours a day in a windowless sweatshop, just that it's not like this joyful process, like I'm loving every second I'm creating my important and beautiful "art."

CLB: Do you feel the cold, fishy breath of the grim reaper of publishing huffing down your neck?

TC: It's hard not to. I spent all these years trying to get as good as I possibly could at what I do, but the world has changed: it doesn't value those skills as much. In fact, you can have a great deal of success these days even if you haven't worked very hard to get as good as possible at your craft.

CLB: Perhaps that is the downside to the

need for constant internet content: quantity trumps quality.

TC: And writers are getting compensated less and less for the same work. So, like species who will die if they don't adapt, I'm trying to branch out into other realms, like TV, so I can support my family, but also do work that I care about and am skilled at. A privilege, I know. I do believe writers are our cultural canaries, though. Look around, people: your canaries are dying!

CLB: Back to the coal mines. The metaphor for our conversation.

TC: With the glow of the iPhone screen lighting our way! I'm just not sure the internet is generally a writer's best friend. I value the traditional editorial process so deeply, and those sort of relationships just aren't happening as much these days. Writers need to write drafts, to let shit sit for a bit, and they need a good editor pushing them to make work as strong as possible before it goes out into the world. Publishing every random thought and impulse is diluting. If everything matters, then how can anything matter?

CLB: I agree. We should develop an app that causes a timed delay between pushing the "publish" button and the actual posting.

TC: That's such a good idea. It could use the same technology as those DUI gadgets attached to cars' ignition switches.

CLB: I think this quickness has cheapened a lot of conversations. So in what ways are you adapting?

TC: It was really fortifying to be part of a BBC America TV series, even if it got canceled last year. And I'm starting to work on another show now. I love learning a new craft, especially such a collaborative one.

CLB: And how is collaborating with [your wife] Allison (who is also a seasoned writer and journalist) on TV and the YA series?

TC: I never really envisioned collaborating on creating narrative with somebody else. I coedited an anthology and did zines, and was in a performance troupe, and planned events at a collective bookstore and all that for years—but actually writing stories with somebody, that's an entirely different bag. But when you trust the person you're doing it with, trust her skills and instincts and overall approach to the creative process, it ends up making the final product even stronger, even if there are sometimes disagreements. It's only because we both care so much.

CLB: Is there a way that that pushback between you two makes you a better writer?
TC: It probably does. I feel like I've always done that for myself, too. Meaning, there's rarely a time I've written something and been like, WOW, that is SO good, I'm awesome, drop the mic.

CLB: Totally. I hardly ever feel like that. When I started out "really" writing, it was to perform spoken word. I'd write something, perform it, then drop it. It took me years to see that the revision process is as much a part of writing as the creation process.
TC: And in collaboration, now there's a second person there acting in that role, two sets of eyes on bullshit patrol.

CLB: I love that: "bullshit patrol"!
TC: Would you say that you feel more vulnerable writing fiction or nonfiction?

CLB: Nonfiction is the most vulnerable, because I am holding a microscope up to my biggest personal losses and failures. What about you? And how are your recent forays into nonfiction treating you? I first came to know your work through the fantastic novel _Some of the Parts,_ in the early 2000s. And _Lipshitz Six_, so good. Lots of historical research and Eminem and trans-in-the-streets realness. And airplanes!
TC: Goddamn, those books feel so ancient, and I would change so much... I suppose I felt most vulnerable writing the nonfiction _Real Man Adventures_, even though it blended genres. That was the most exposed I've ever felt, because it was ostensibly about me. I've

never really been predisposed toward the autobiographical "I."

CLB: What I loved about _RMA_ was that it was such an unapologetic musing on what all this trans biz is about, and it was funny, personal, and multivalent, and really wasn't toeing some PC trans narrative line. Like, it was just one person exploring this for themselves without trying to carry all of transdom on their back.
TC: I tried to resist those impulses. I think the wider world really likes a "journey" memoir to walk you through it and explain how it is for everybody. But it's never that simple nor universal, and to me, while there's room for that type of story, I'm just not interested in writing it.

CLB: That's what I think is so excellent about this moment in trans writing. There's enough reach and audience for work to take on all manner of literary risk. Not to belittle anyone's journey memoir, because those are important books, too. But the journey always seems to end with transition, like, "Ta-da! I'm a dude now." [_Bows_] What about the rest of your fucking life?
TC: We all have missing pieces. We're all just trying to figure out what they are, and fill those gaping holes in our lives. Sometimes it's about gender, sure, but rarely gender alone.

CLB: It's interesting that we were both writers before we were trans, maybe. In some ways we are both saying that our identity is formed more around what we "do," rather than being tented up around our genders. But at the same time, my gender experiences throughout my life are certainly a lens through which I view so much that I do end up writing about. Perhaps one cannot escape his or her own location.
TC: I agree. People took me as "female" when I started publishing, and I transitioned, pretty much, in early career, and have published the last, what, four or five books as unequivocally a dude. I wouldn't say I write

about my transness (except in *RMA*), though of course many fictional characters are reflective of my interaction with the world AS who I am. Or was. If that makes sense.

CLB: It makes total sense, and the same here. It was all in my writing even when the writing wasn't trumpeting "trans."

TC: Do you tell your students you're trans?

CLB: In the university setting I do not, though it's not a secret. My purpose is to push them to become more skillful at writing, not to trot out my personal identity. What about you?

TC: Exactly the same for me, and for the same reasons. Of course they can read all about it online, and probably do, but in the classroom, it's Professor Cooper, and that's that.

CLB: Students call me Professor Cooper, too! Reminds me, recently a student asked why I didn't offer a trigger warning for *Close to the Knives* by David Wojnarowicz. They told me the book was "damaging," and I felt like saying, You know what was really triggering? Watching all of these people you love dying horrible deaths because the homophobia and ineptitude of our fucking government.

TC: Holy shit, I also had this student at Emory last semester who freaked the fuck out when Scott Turner Schofield visited the workshop to talk a little about dialogue and showing vs. telling. I didn't "prepare" the students, I mean, what would I say? "Just so you know, children, a transsexual will be visiting class tomorrow." Fuck that, they're adults, it should be no different from anybody's writing I present. Anyway, the minute Turner disclosed, this kid, who's like, seemingly pretty smart and aware, started having what seemed like a panic attack or something, and quickly gathered his belongings, came over to me and whispered, "I ca—, I ha—, I, I, I'm gonna—" and bolted out the door. Now, he could've just received a text saying his beloved Peepaw just died, but

it was curious timing, and I don't know, man. Just sit with your discomfort for a minute. If something scares you or moves you, up or down, good or bad, whatever, then sit with it a little and try to get your head around it. That's what we're all here for, right?

CLB: I just think there is a huge distinction between an act of violence—homophobia, transphobia, misogyny, racism, etc.—and a representation of those things couched in the context of a work of art. Especially when you look to how the work of art is critiquing those biases (or not).

TC: This reminds me, my guardian auntie Kate [Bornstein] just sent me a cute picture of herself wearing her gold "Tranny" necklace, and it got me thinking about language and how for me, I can't think of anything, a word or image or piece of writing, nothing that would offend me so much as to request that somebody else not use it.

CLB: I get really fucking sad when I see people attack our elders over things like word choice. Where were you when Kate, or even I for that matter, was using the T-word to refer to ourselves? I started performing trans writing 20 years ago and started T 13 years ago. After being told we are wrong by so many people for so long, why do we think it's okay to hammer other trans people's self-expression? I get that the T-word can be offensive if used by nontrans people as a pejorative, but what about trans people being allowed to have some self-determination about what we call ourselves? I have used the word privately in the past to refer to myself, but I would never call you that, unless I knew you wanted me to.

TC: You can call me that anytime. Do it now.

CLB: No. End of rant.

TC: I still prefer "transie" over "tranny" anyway. So do you think this interview will help people tell us apart from now on?

OP

TRANS MALE CULTURE

THE TATTOO ISSUE · NUMBER 17 · 2016 · USA $9

Photo by Amos Mac

LETTERS FROM
★ THE EDITORS ★

As a trans person, my relationship to my body doesn't feel precious or permanent in the way I imagine it would for a cis person. That has definitely informed my process of getting tattooed. I wanted to decorate this clunky, imperfect body with tattoos to match.

I got my first tattoo at age 17. It was something I put thought into, knew I wanted, and it had significance. After that, it was a series of impulsive decisions based on cost and inside jokes or balancing out empty space. Once I started transitioning, I started to value my body a bit more and my decision-making around tattoos changed a little, but not much. They are a road map with mile markers. I love them all but don't feel attached to any of them, just like my body in a way. I love all of it but don't feel attached to any of it.

Rocco Kayiatos

Whenever I dream about myself, I'm always tattooless. It's eerie, considering I've been covered with a mismatch of images and words for so many years. Pee-wee Herman's bowtie. Conjoined cat twins wearing a sweater. A trifecta of badly drawn noodles. Even the tattoos that I claim don't mean a thing all represent a moment in time that has shaped the person I am today.

Although I'm quick to change the subject when I'm asked to share the "meaning" behind my tattoos, I really wanted to hear the stories behind yours. I wanted to know how these moments, forever inked onto our bodies (until you cover it up, if you're into that) have shifted, transitioned, and effected the people we are and the memories we hold closest.

Amos Mac

★ HIT US UP ★

TWITTER.COM/OPMAG
FACEBOOK.COM/ORIGINALPLUMBING
INSTAGRAM.COM/ORIGINALPLUMBING
ORIGINALPLUMBING.TUMBLR.COM

LIFE ON MARS

PORTRAIT BY AMOS MAC

FOX COREY

JAKE TEDDY

TRANS AND INKED

INTERVIEW BY ROCCO KAYIATOS
PHOTOS BY CARRIE STRONG

Many of you may be familiar with this handsome inked-up dude. He's definitely Insta-famous. If you don't recognize him, you may actually already be following the account he runs, @transandinked. He has dedicated part of his online presence to representing the hotness of trans people and their tattoos. Max took some time out of his busy schedule to discuss his IG page and his tattoos.

Rocco: Why did you start @transandinked?
Max Warner: I started @transandinked almost three years ago, I believe. The goal was to have a common focal point for transgender people as well as people that support us. Tattoos are a great way to start conversations and break barriers between people, regardless of how different we each may be. There are over 45 million people in the US alone that have at least one tattoo. That means we all have at least that in common.

When did it start gaining in popularity?
It picked up surprisingly quickly—within the first few months. I knew that people loved tattoos, but had no idea that so many people in my community could get closer just because of them. The page itself has gained so many supporters even outside of the trans community.

Why do you think trans guys love tattoos?
I think most people like tattoos. The reason I chose tattoos as the topic, though, for a trans page is for us to bond over something other than just the fact we are trans.

How has your life changed as a result of running that page?
I have a very busy life in general, but I had no idea that running this page could turn into such responsibility. The bigger it gets, the more of a responsibility it becomes. I'm honored that I'm the one that gets to do it. Bringing so many people together, from so many different places all over the world, is an awesome thing to be part of!

What was your first tattoo?
I got my first tattoo when I was 19. It was my friend's lips. I got hers on me and she got mine on her, because she was the one friend that took me in when my parent disowned me.

What tattoo do you love the most?
That's tough. My favorite tattoo would have to be my "Built for Sin" script on my left arm.

It has more meaning behind it than all the others. At the time of getting this tattoo I was going through the beginning stages of my transition. Being raised in a Christian household I was taught that all the things I now stood for would be considered a sin. I decided that I must have been built for it. Built for sin.

Do you regret any of your tattoos?
I don't know if I'd say I regret a couple of them, because at the time it's what I wanted. It has more to do with my choice of artist. The work wasn't what I was expecting, so I will be getting a couple fixed or covered. It's probably the reason why I am so picky now.

Do you think tattoos make a person sexier?
Personally I think tattoos are very sexy. Now, if it's a bunch of bad tattoos, then no. But if it's nice work, then yes, definitely.

What is the weirdest way that someone has asked to see or touch your tattoos?
I have been asked far more often the meaning behind them, than to touch or see them, because tons of people assume that some of my tattoos are gang related or they become a religious subject.

Often people tell others with tattoos that they will regret them when they get old. Describe what you think you will look like as an old person.
I envision myself having tons of tattoos when I'm older. Yes, they might be blurry or wrinkled, but hey, at least I'll have badass stories behind them. I love art and creativity, why not be a canvas for someone trying to grow into a better artist themselves? ⚡

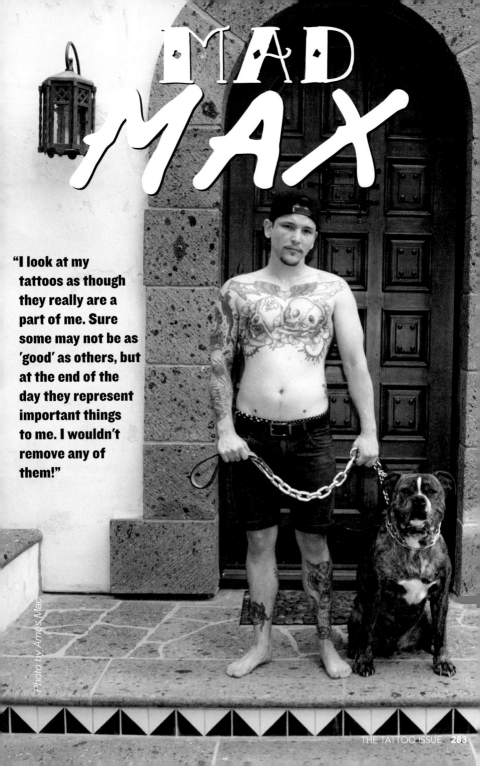

MAD MAX

"I look at my tattoos as though they really are a part of me. Sure some may not be as 'good' as others, but at the end of the day they represent important things to me. I wouldn't remove any of them!"

Photo by Amos Mac

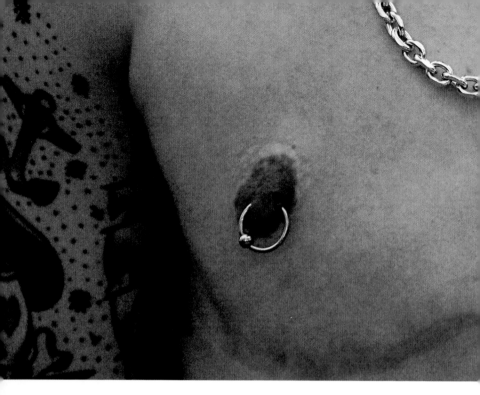

HOME

BY RYAN CASSATA

Sometimes it's hard to feel at "home" anywhere since I travel so much. I've driven across this country five times coast to coast, and have been on more flights than I could ever remember. Lots of people ask me what my tattoo means: "Is it a pocket? Is it some weird satanic symbol? Just what on earth is it?"

Elementary school was rough. My parents were divorced and I shifted houses every weekend. I didn't have many friends, and I was bullied a lot. I went home from school crying on more than one occasion, whichever "home" it was that day. I was lost. I was uncomfortable. I was afraid. I found myself in baseball. Baseball. The Red Sox. The 2004 World Series. Curt Schilling's bloody sock. Reversing the curse. Johnny Damon's grand

slam in Game 7. I obsessively started cutting out newspaper articles that mentioned my beloved Boston Red Sox and plastering them all over my bedroom walls. I memorized the starting lineup, I memorized all the players' batting averages, and I knew who the starting pitcher was for every game. I was subscribed and sometimes I skipped school to watch the games. I also started playing Little League and because at sign-ups they told me, "Baseball is for boys and softball is for girls," I played softball. I was amazingly good at it. I was nicknamed "Twinkle Toes" for my triples that should have really only been singles. I stole home, I sprinted home, and I hit an inside-the-park home run once. I was also the catcher of the team and I caught for one of the fastest

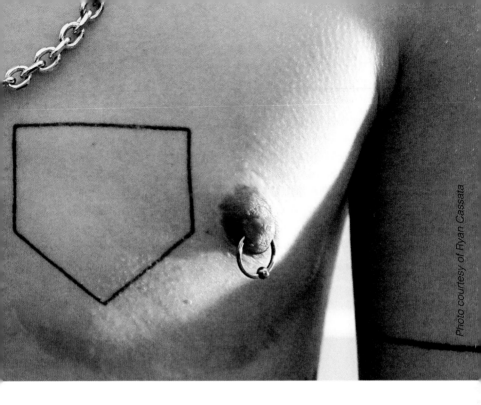

Photo courtesy of Ryan Cassata

pitchers in the league. I gave hand signals for strikeouts and I threw out steals at second. I was voted onto the All-Star Team every single year that I played. I stopped playing just after 8th grade when I lost my balance due to permanently losing my hearing in my left ear from a mystery illness. Doctors ordered that I quit playing sports if I wanted to keep the hearing in my "good ear." I decided that I better keep my hearing so that I could play my guitar and continue to write songs. I still love baseball and I still scream when the Red Sox win the World Series.

Getting moved around as a kid from Mom's house to Dad's house, and now never settling into my apartment because I'm touring too much, I've realized that "home" could really be anywhere. Home is where my mom is cooking her red sauce and meatballs. Home is where my dad and I are watching TV and laughing and sometimes crying. Home is where my brothers and I are all together. Home is where all my friends gather. Home is on the stage where I get to play in front of hundreds and sometimes thousands of people.

Although I've found home all over the country, I'll never forget the first home I had, behind home plate. That's why home plate is tattooed on my chest, right above my heart. And still I continue to run home, wherever that may be, because I know that home is where the heart is. ⚡

TATTOOS TRANSCEND GENDER

BY HUN LAW
PHOTO BY GRAY WONG

I.

I am Hun. I identify myself as a female-to-male trans/genderqueer person. For me, tattoos are a body project. Every tattoo that inks onto my body has special meaning. The first tattoo that relates to my gender politics is a koi on my left chest. According to ancient Chinese classic Shi Yi Ji, a koi is a pre-transformed dragon, which is in the dynamic state of half-dragon-half-fish. To me, koi resembles my gender status: gender is a form of transformation. Being trans is never about crossing from one sex to another gender; it is, rather, a continual process that involves the mixture of the masculine with the feminine.

I have always hated my "breasts." I choose to transform it with a koi tattoo and sculpt my body with bodybuilding rather than having chest surgery. This year, I allowed myself to compete in a bodybuilding contest. My victory challenges the cliché notion that having tattoos hurt your chance at winning bodybuilding contests.

II.

I have a Hedwig tattoo. It is a half-circle tattoo that comes from the famous trans film *Hedwig and The Angry Inch*. The song "Origin of Love" sang by the protagonist inspired me to write a poem about an imaginary world filled with a nameless organism, which is comprised of two-males, two-females, or one-male, one-female. In my poem I wrote:

You have told me an ancient legend
It is said that there was an organism that
existed long before Adam and Eve

They have two heads, two sets of arms and legs
They face back to back, two pairs of eyes have
never seen each other

They have double our field of vision

They are beloved children of God, although

They have two male, female, or one-male-one-
female bodies

They have special talents but they know noth-
ing about the world

They live in harmony in a nameless planet

They do not understand desire, love or money

They do not need emotions or thoughts

They do not undergo birth, aging, illness and
death, because they do not age

They belong to a certain illusionary eternity

They are just who they are, nothing more

However, the increasing power of these nameless organisms scared Zeus, and he used his thunder to separate them into halves, scattering them with tornados. This is how we, as human beings, come from:

We just have one head, one set of arms and legs

We only have half the field of vision, we are
unable to see each other in the dark

We lost the other self, before that

We have never seen each other, so we have no
idea on embracement

We want to find out the other self, therefore

We create a new form of language, in order to
describe emotions and thoughts

We learn about desire, love, and power

We categorize ourselves, so that we could find
out the lost one

We only have male and female

We are always cautious to fabricate the reality
that we do not belong

We are not who we are, we always stare
off into space

We are forced to separate with our other "half." The Hedwig tattoo serves as a reunion symbol with our lost "half." This is also a tattoo that marks the transness of body and gender identity.

III.

The tattoo on my left waist marks my life motto: Live out your true self. I always remember the line from E. E. Cummings, "It takes courage to grow up and become who you really are." Although true self never really exists (because our "self" is always subject to constant changes according to the circumstances around us), this motto reminds me to be as authentic as I can be. The most important thing in life is to be happy and calm at all times.

I am a poet, trans/genderqueer, a female body-builder… these identities are all important to define who I am. My tattoos endow meaning to each of my unique identities. My masculine tattoos do not erase my femininity, as I think that tattoos are rather neutral: we are the ones who give masculine or feminine meanings to our tattoos. My tattoos add new perspectives to my queer identity, and allow people to embrace the multiplicity of gender embodiment. I am proud of my tattoos, as much as I am proud of my queer identities. ⚡

OP

TRANS MALE CULTURE
THE BATHROOM ISSUE · NUMBER 18 · 2016 · USA $9

THE BATHROOM
ISSUE

*Photo by Alex Giegold
and Tomka Weisser*

LETTERS FROM THE EDITORS

I am writing this after just having left the men's locker room at the 24 Hour Fitness in Hollywood, California. Every morning I shower there and walk around topless. If you had asked me 16 years ago, when I began my medical transition, if there was a day that I thought I would feel comfortable showering in a space like that or even using the bathroom, the answer would have been a resounding "no!"

I have passing privilege, and I feel that most as my comfort with using the bathroom grows. There is rarely a moment in my life now that I even have pause around going to the men's room, no matter what state, city, or country I am in. But it wasn't always like this.

For the first part of my life, I was consistently questioned when taking care of the most basic of human needs: peeing. After medical transition it took years to shed that fear and trauma. In this issue some will address the discomfort and injustice of not being granted access to safe public restrooms, but you will also find tales of revolution and triumph, as well as the queer tradition of scandalous sexcapades and so much more.

Rocco Kayiatos

Public restrooms still give me anxiety, regardless of where in the country I am in. Traveling almost nonstop for my current field of work has made this increase, despite having transitioned a decade ago. Depending on what state I'm in during said bathroom visit, a feeling of great sadness comes across me for the humans who are most often targeted in this bathroom struggle.

Originally we wanted this issue of Original Plumbing to discuss the issues beyond the bathroom, but after our open call went out, the response was almost entirely about personal feelings regarding experiences specific to the bathroom. So you'll see that this issue touches on many subjects—from acknowledging the Pulse shooting on June 12, to the history of the Sutro Baths, and beyond.

Amos Mac

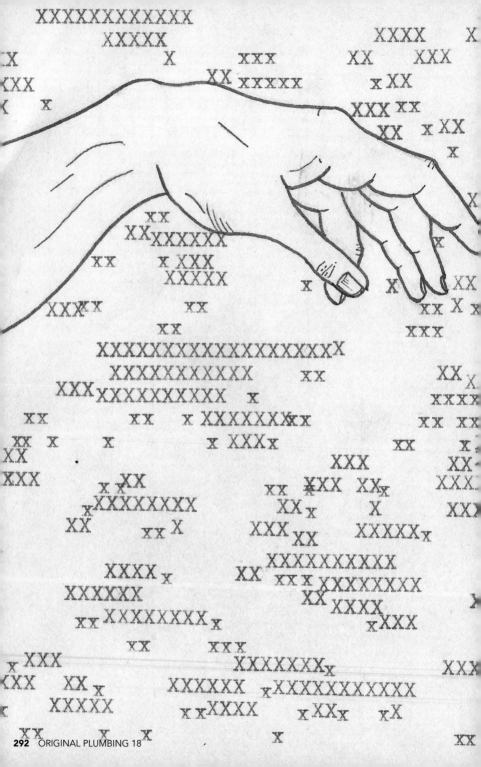

Illustration by b haywood

MEMORIES OF THE SUTRO BATHS

By J. Soto

On my twenty-sixth birthday I stayed in a bed & breakfast that had a bathroom dedicated to the Sutro Baths. Painted on the sliding bamboo closet doors were scenes depicting hundreds of two-inch-tall people swimming, jumping, and diving into light blue pools of saltwater. The people were rendered small and playfully, and the illustration seemed more fitting for a children's book than for a bed & breakfast on the California coast. The actual baths had once been magnificent, built solidly against the sea cliffs of San Francisco's Outer Richmond District forty miles south of where I was staying. Funded by the wealthy entrepreneur Adolph Sutro in 1894, they were at one time the largest public pools in the world.

I was already very familiar with what was left of the Sutro Baths as I had made it a practice to visit them frequently while living in San Francisco in the early aughts. The baths had now been reduced to their foundations, a series of interlocking cement forms that I had always found arousing. It was never pictures of their completion that immediately turned me on, made me feel

edgy and exhilarated, but their ruin, the arc of their foundations, filled up with seawater always about to breach the outer stone limits and spill out onto the surrounding sand. On these walks, without the actuality of the baths, their once-innovative steel skeleton frame architecture and glass providing airy shelter from the elements, I could dream up what they were about and how my body might enjoy them.

What was left of the baths was and still is a place between places. Between the rhythmic salty ocean surf and the cliffs above that promise nonelectric views of the Pacific or fog. As a pretransition young man and dyke in my early twenties, I would make my way through the shaggy grass down one of the worn pathways. Once there, I could trace the perimeter of each massive pool by walking along its edges, trying not to fall in by trying to not let the desire to fall in overtake me. I would imagine that the stone steps down into one pool would lead to a completely different place somewhere on the other side of an ornate metal gate. In this fantasy, I might reemerge into the next pool as a fat and hungry sheephead fish

into a room full of other fishes, breathing in and out of water, the place and I both transformed. Like many bathhouses, the attraction wasn't only about the physical act of sex, but equally about belonging to a place, to something recognizable, and about being in tune with desire and kinship on a holistic scale.

But sometimes it's the constancy of one thing that brings what is missing into sharp focus; like the sustained sixty-five degree weather along that pocket of coastline that makes you forget the seasons. I've since recognized that my imagined reality was different than the cold history of the murky pools below. The racial segregation of public spaces at the turn of the century would have meant the baths were a whites only space and fully welcoming black patrons to the baths never happened. Those that I consider part of my geographical lineage out west, the mestizos who had been living there, also would not have have been swimming in those rejuvenating pools. Further still, the desires for how my own body exists would have confounded the sex-segregated space of the public swim-

ming pool as they sometimes still do today. Belonging consisted mostly of an imagined scenario while walking along the ruins and always has.

Often we write our own waking dreams while at the same time creating them in reality on whatever scale we can. This is the complexity of being transgender, this is queer resilience, this is its magic. I would like to begin using this magic to its full capabilities and not in spite of reality. I've become more mindful of the intersections of oppression that keep the magic from coming into being.

There at the baths, the surf was dangerous and there were forgotten caves below the surface of the pools big enough to trap a person. Still, while walking, I imagined scenarios where my body was welcomed into that environment that was so deeply integrated into the earth there, that its very existence depended on the cycle of tides to fill each pool every day. Today, they are not just fantasy, but aching potential and we have grown more resolute in our steps. **OP**

PUBLIC
RESTROOMS

ERIN NATIONS

BATHROOMS ARE FOR US

By J.W. McQueen

As a trans man who also identifies as queer, I have a complicated relationship with public bathrooms.

The trans part of me struggles with them for all the reasons you might imagine—fear of being discovered as an "other," fear of violence, outrage, persecution, etc. We've all been there, you've all heard it.

The queer part of me, though. It LOVES them. Seriously. Some of my most memorable sexual moments have occurred in public bathrooms. I submit for the record:

1. Cutting class to make out with my high school girlfriend in the bathroom on the second floor of the band hall. I'm pretty sure one of my first orgasms happened there, with her eating me out on the edge of the sink. I still dream about that.

2. College.

3. The time in my early 20s when my lesbian friends and I tried to see how many of us could make out in one of the stalls at the Wild Rose at one time. I think there were like 7 of us. Yes, I realize that is not an even number. Yes, you can make out in threes.

4. The time I was back there visiting and ran into an old love interest. We made out in one of those same stalls, even though my current girlfriend was sitting at the bar.

5. I met that same girlfriend in a bathroom at a lesbian bar in Brooklyn.

6. Fingering that one reallllly hot girl in the bathroom of the karaoke bar in California.

You get the picture. Bathrooms are an often-sexy place of release for queer folks because it provides a somewhat isolated environment for same-sex interaction. This was especially true back when being gay in public wasn't as easy as it is now.[1] You know, as recent as even 8 to 20 years ago. Bathrooms were a place where you could escape the watchful gaze of society and just go have some fun.[2] Women are especially able to get away with this because they are socialized to want to go into restrooms in groups for moral support or whatever. Best believe I took full advantage of that shit back then.[3]

Adding alcohol or drugs to the mix often ups the stakes, and the added Thrill of the Possibility of Being Caught™ just made it that much more exciting.

So, after transition, when I allowed myself to try dating men after years of thinking about it, I was bound to return to my comfort zone.

It was at a dive bar in Hollywood. There was a burlesque show on that I had gone to with some friends. One friend in particular, who had designs on me, was trying to put the moves on. In an attempt to rebuff her without actually having to do so, I drop in conversation that I am only seeing men at the moment.[4] She's shocked. She doesn't believe it. I tell her yes, truly. I may be meeting one tonight. She gets quiet and goes to get a drink. Whew.

But it was true, I was meeting one. Ian. We'd met on Grindr a few months earlier. We'd hooked up twice. It was always really good—fantastic, even. We clicked. We turned each other on. The kissing was awesome right away.

I had casually texted him to tell him I was near where he lived (half true) and that he should come see the show. To my surprise, he said he would. He brought two friends. They were lovely. We were all standing there, watching the show (I had totally forgotten my sad lady friend had left and never came back), and then Ian grabs my hand. We held hands for a second, and then he puts my hand on his dick, which was hard. "Let's go," he whispered.

He pulls me across the club toward the bathroom. I smile because I see where this is going. But then I panic. Oh shit, it's a men's room at a straight bar. It's not the ladies' room at the dyke bar. Men's rooms barely even have doors on the stalls, let alone a safe space for two men to have sex. Especially not a trans man. Oh God, what if I get caught being gay and trans at the same time? I stopped in my tracks. He looks back at me and gets a genuinely concerned look on his face. I can tell he sees why I am freaked out.

"Don't worry. I checked it out." He gives me a smile that makes that line sound less creepy. It was sweet, I swear.

He leads me through the door and we make a beeline straight into the stall, door latched. This is not his first rodeo either. It is hot, it is strong, it is fast, and it ended with a "CAUTION: Wet Floor"–worthy splash on the dirty linoleum. And then we are back out as fast as we were in.

I'm all smiles the rest of the night. **OP**

—

1. I am not suggesting it is "easy" now. I realize in many places, for many people, it is still not, nor will it ever be easy. What I mean is that the few places we have where we can really be ourselves in public were even fewer and further between, even in "liberal" places. Forgive me?

2. Yes, I know that further back in queer history, bathrooms were often the only place where queers could meet for sex, and yes, I realize how fucking sad that is. I also acknowledge that bathrooms were a place of entrapment and great persecution by vice squads, and that the lack of a safe space for sexual release created places where sexually-transmitted infections and even more serious, the likes of HIV were spread. Perhaps all these things play into the psychology of why the bathroom hookup feels so dangerous, and leads to the thrill?

3. And now so many are wondering, "How many times have I seen my female friends go into a bathroom in a group? Were any of them fucking, too?!" You'll never know, but now you'll always picture it when you see it in the future. You're welcome.

4. Not really sure of the appropriate term for what I have been doing with men, but I'm sure dating is not accurate.

BASIL SOPER IS TRANSILIENT

Transilient Co-Founder and Writer
New Orleans, LA

This summer, my partner and I embarked on a cross-country trip doing work for a project called Transilient. We are interviewing trans and nonbinary people about their lived realities in hopes of changing the mainstream trans narrative. I am originally from the Carolinas and live in the Southeast. I spent eight years living in North Carolina and five doing trans activist work there. HB2 and the Mississippi law really impacted me. I decided that the best way to take care of myself in response to bathroom issue, and traveling while trans, would be buy a STP packer I could pee out of at urinals. When we were in NYC we painted a friend's living room for some cash so I could buy the packer. I bought it. It didn't work. I pee all over myself every time I use it. It was awful! This all happened right after the Orlando shooting and I was feeling really dysphoric while grieving, while simultaneously trying to remain upbeat and hold space for people during interviews and drive across the country with my partner and our dog, it was challenging! I had to up my meditation and stretch game for sure. I pray a whole lot. We went to Nebraska and I peed in a bar where the men's restroom only had two urinals and the walls were plastered with naked photos of women. I can pee standing up with my pants around my ankles so I did that. My bare booty was out in that bathroom. Haha. The next day, we visited Brandon Teena's grave in Lincoln, Nebraksa, and I held ceremony for him. All I can really do right now is stay connected to the big picture, do my best to stay grounded, keep giving others a platform, and keep peeing and fighting! **OP**

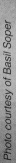

Photo courtesy of Basil Soper

A reprinting of the **2002** zine *Piss & Vinegar*,
followed by an interview with Dean Spade.

Interviewed by Rocco Kayiatos

Comic by D Soltis

Dean Spade stars in:
Just When You Thought it Was Safe to Pee

In February, 2002, the World Economic Forum met in NYC. (The WEF is a weekend conference (cost: $25,000 per person) where corporate leaders talk about global economic and political policy.)

Naturally, anti-globalization protesters turned out in force.

This is Ray, the guy who runs the list I told you about

Nice to meet you

Z and I went to his friend Dean's house to meet up with a bunch of other activists, put together flyers, stickers, and first aid kits (in case of tear gas), and plan what we wanted to do.

One of the things we discussed was how we felt about getting arrested should civil disobedience opportunities arise.

I can't get arrested, because they'll probably deport me

I'm not looking to get arrested, but I wouldn't mind so much if I am. I don't have a record.

I might be interested in getting arrested, if a good opportunity comes up

I said

I'd rather not get arrested. The thought of being sex-segregated makes me nauseous.

Dean said

I have better things to do with my time than sit in a jail cell. But my ID says I am female, so they'll put me with the other women--which is physically safer, at least. It wouldn't be the end of the world. Assuming they didn't strip-search me or anything.

Z and I ended up staying pretty late, doing the whole trans bonding thing.

Yeah, like you're supposed to try to look all normal in order to pass

And you can't wear flamboyant clothes, or talk with too much inflection in your voice

I had a hard time with a lot of transguys, who didn't respect that I don't want to take T, or look the "right" way

Or have a punky haircut

The worst was when people got mad at me for being into gender theory and having fun with gender. Like it's all supposed to be so serious--transsexuals are supposed to suffer. And something was wrong with me because I think it's fabulous to be trans.

We stayed so late, in fact, that we promptly overslept our meeting time. By about four hours. By the time we arrived in midtown...

small knot of protesters behind layers of barricades

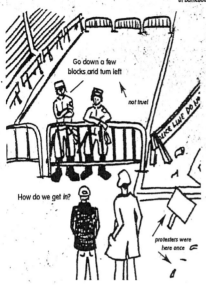

Go down a few blocks and turn left

not true!

POLICE LINE DO NOT

How do we get *in*?

protesters were here once

...Dean and his friends were heading home.

A few hours later--by then Z and I had found our way into the protest, milled around for a while, come home and made dinner--

Hey Dean, this is Z -- just calling to say we're sorry we missed you, but we were both late -- anyway, we got home fine, didn't get arrested or tear-gased or anything...

Z got a phone call.

You're gonna be crying when you *lose*

Whatever, dude! I'm going to scoop up your little pathetic, quivering, losing remains!

uh-huh...
ok...
uh-huh...
what's the number?
ok...

Dean's been arrested for using the men's room!

The Story

(dramatized by the author, who wasn't actually there.)

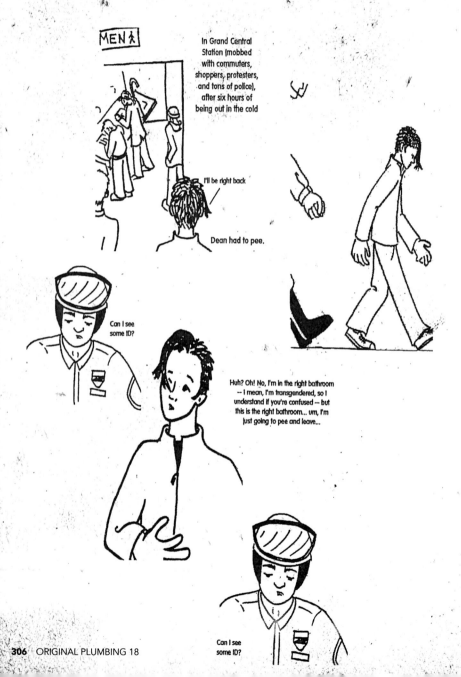

MEN

In Grand Central Station (mobbed with commuters, shoppers, protesters, and tons of police), after six hours of being out in the cold

I'll be right back

Dean had to pee.

Can I see some ID?

Huh? Oh! No, I'm in the right bathroom -- I mean, I'm transgendered, so I understand if you're confused -- but this is the right bathroom... um, I'm just going to pee and leave...

Can I see some ID?

Dean Spade is an Associate Professor at Seattle University School of Law. He teaches Administrative Law, Poverty Law, and Law and Social Movements.

In 2002, Dean founded the Sylvia Rivera Law Project. That same year, he was arrested for using a public restroom. We had the pleasure of talking with Dean about activism since the early-aughts and how the movement has changed.

Rocco Kayiatos: Can you tell me what happened to you in Grand Central in 2002?

Dean Spade: In February 2002, I attended the protest against the World Economic Forum meetings that were being held in New York City. It was a large anti-globalization protest, similar to the protests that had happened in 1999 in Seattle against the World Trade Organization, in Quebec City in 2001 against the proposed Free Trade Area of the Americas. These were all protests against summits where the rich and powerful gathered to plan economic policies that harm most people and the planet. It was also very shortly after the World Trade Center bombing on 9/11/01. The New York City government prepared for the protest by turning out the police in outrageous numbers. I participated in the protest with friends, and then we left. On our way home we decided to go to Grand Central Station to use the bathrooms because we had been out in the streets for hours and were in need. I went into the men's, a cop followed me, stopped me and asked for my ID. I explained that I was in the right place and I just needed to use the bathroom, and the cop started to arrest me. My friend Craig saw the cop follow me in and went in to see if I was okay. He and our friend Ananda who was nearby in the corridor both tried to intervene and advocate for me, and they were arrested

too. Others of our friends who were with us tried to get to us and were held back by a line of riot cops who showed up. We spent about 24 hours in jail. When we were transferred from the jail where we'd been to the cells at the court, a random court-appointed lawyer came to talk to me about my arraignment. I had recently graduated law school but had never represented anyone in criminal court and didn't really know what was going on or what was going to happen to me, or even whether or not I could actually be convicted of something. The lawyer who came to talk to me asked me about my genitals and when I told him I did not think it was relevant, he was mean and dismissive. It was really scary to see how even though, in so many ways, I was so privileged in this situation being a white, employed, fancy-educated person, I felt really vulnerable in this system facing transphobia from the cops and the lawyer.

What kind of action came as a result of that incident?

The story of my arrest circulated as one of the news items about the protest. I got emails from people all over the country who had had similar experiences in bathrooms being falsely arrested or harassed, and also from people who had been beaten in bathrooms. There were also a lot of people in my local community in New York City who wanted to mobilize about what had happened. The connections I made and the information I gathered during this time about what was happening to trans people at the hands of the police and the inability of trans people to get effective legal help was important in building up to the founding of the Sylvia Rivera Law Project, which opened in Fall 2002. One of the first projects SRLP did was creating our 30-minute movie, *Toilet Training*, and the activist/educator toolkit that goes with it. This movie was the first about this issue and has been used in all kinds of institutional settings by people trying to change bathroom access. It is still being used a lot, but it seems a bit dated now (finished in 2003) so we are in the process of making a new version with the brilliant trans artist and filmmaker who made the first version, Tara Mateik.

Another influential thing, for me, about this experience that I think may be of interest to OP readers was that many trans people said negative things about me online after this arrest. Many people wrote that I must not pass and this must have been the cause of my arrest, so I was at fault for the arrest. It was a difficult moment of seeing the internalized transphobia in trans communities, and it felt like a betrayal. We made a zine, authored by "the Anti-Capitalist Tranny Brigade" as part of our organizing after the arrest called *Piss and Vinegar*. The title references the vinegar-soaked bandanas activists wore to the protest to protect against police teargas, as well as the phrase "full of piss and vinegar" meaning full of youthful energy, boisterous, rowdy. In the zine we wrote about how this policing within trans communities

harms us all. It was very important to me in my work at SRLP and all my work going forward to try to build shared analysis in trans communities that rejects gender policing of all kinds, by cops and between trans people, and is committed to a vision of gender self-determination where no matter how a person looks, dresses, speaks, or what medical care they seek, no one should be put in a cage.

Had you considered yourself an activist before that all happened?
Yes, I was already a part of activist work in New York City. I had been part of multi-issue queer work going on in NYC when Giuliani was mayor that was focused on pushing back against his administration's brutal treatment of welfare recipients, its increased policing (especially of public parks and bars that were queer & trans gathering places), its attacks on sex workers and

immigrants, and its criminalization of poor people. I got into that anti-Giuliani activist work because I was working at Meow Mix and other queer bars and at the gay bookstore A Different Light, and the other working class queer and trans people I met in those spaces were being affected by and organizing against Giuliani's policing of night life and sex workers. I was also part of activist work to push back on how the lesbian and gay rights movement was increasingly pushing a conservative pro-military, pro-police, pro-marriage agenda. In 1998 I co-organized, in a group called the Fuck The Mayor Collective, the first Gay Shame event which took place at a queer performance and living space called Dumba, and focused on articulating a queer agenda that would be the reverse of what we saw at corporate pride. For this event, we made a zine called Swallow Your Pride, also focused on building an anti-racist, anti-capitalist, feminist queer and trans resistance to the mainstreaming gay politics. This stuff feels like ancient history now, since that mainstreamed gay agenda is so ultra visible now and embraced by the US government and a lot of the 1%.

My passport photo from 2002.

How did your activism change as a result?
The kinds of responses I got from people who had experienced similar police harassment and bathroom issues and problems trying to get legal help spurred me to start the Sylvia Rivera Law Project. I could see that there was a huge need—trans people were and are targets of legal systems that enforce rigid gender norms, especially on poor people and people of color. And I could also see that there was building momentum for racial and economic justice-centered trans resistance. I started the Sylvia Rivera Law Project as a space for both these things. I started it with a grant to be one lawyer providing legal help, but immediately we put together a steering committee to create a collective structure that could capture the energy of the community and work to provide more help than we would ever be funded to provide, given how invisible and unpopular

trans issues were at the time. SRLP is now 14 years old, still providing free legal help to trans people facing violence in prisons, foster care, public schools, psychiatric hospitals, immigration proceedings, and more.

What was the climate of understanding around trans people back then as opposed to now?
Trans issues are more visible now—a mainstreaming process is underway where certain trans lives are more visible in particular ways, and we are seeing a lot of backlash because of that. From the perspective of the people who come to SRLP for services, though, things are not getting much better. Providing actual help to trans people in need is still not popular with funders so the work is still always on a shoestring, always with a waiting list of people who need services, and the conditions facing trans people in need are worsening. The immigration system, policing and prison systems have grown significantly since the project was founded, poor people are poorer, and benefits systems have been cut.

Probably more people in the US would now say they know about trans issues or don't hate trans people because they are seeing more media representations of trans people, but I think we have to really question what that mainstreaming changes. Mainstreamed media representations tend to show us what a "good" or "deserving" person from a marginalized group is and tell us to have sympathy for them. They don't tend to disrupt narratives

Me and Ponyboy, an activist/photographer. Photo by Ponyboy, 2002.

about who is "bad" and "undeserving." So maybe some people who oppose the terrible bathroom bills would say that it is bad if a white, masculine, middle class trans man can't use a bathroom, but do they feel the same about a disabled trans woman of color with a criminal record? I think a lot of the acceptance that happens when images of "deserving" trans people circulate is very conditional and rarely actually changes what the most vulnerable trans people are going through. My life as a white trans professor might get better, or I might experience some new acceptance because of the mainstreaming, but conditions are still horrific and getting worse for SRLP's clients who are locked up or who experience ongoing police profiling and harassment, exclusion from jobs, education, and health care, and possibly increased vulnerability because they are the ones who will get caught up in the backlash.

What is the most heartening thing you have witnessed in regards to progress being made for trans people in bathrooms?
I think, overall, it is heartening that there are so many more people working on this than

there were in 2002. Also, it feels like there are just more trans people and I love that. I think the key thing for us now is to think carefully about what we want our movement to look like. Are we fighting to just have a privileged few of us take our places in the existing racist institutions of the US, or are we part of a broader struggle that would actually benefit all trans people and everyone who is harmed by the enforcement of gender norms? One way this comes up is about the bathroom and sex-segregated facilities. We need to make sure the conversation is not just about the bathroom, but that we take that conversation and use it as a way to talk about how trans people are experiencing violence in all the places where gender norms are enforced through sex segregation, especially prisons, jails, immigration facilities, psychiatric hospitals, group homes, and shelters. The most vulnerable trans people facing the most violence are in these spaces, and if we stick to only thinking about bathrooms and/or mainly imagining the ability of white trans people to access bathrooms at school and work, we will miss the chance to intervene on the most significant sites of violence in trans lives.

OP

TRANS MALE CULTURE

THE ART ISSUE • NUMBER 19 • USA $10

art issue

*"I find inspiration in a lot of
unexpected places and circumstances."*
—Torie Leigh

Letter from the editors

*Upon first thought, some may not think of art as anything more than a beautiful drawing, painting, or photograph. But art is so much more; it is essential to life! For those of us who are a part of a marginalized community, the artist is also a documentarian. They are the messengers of hope, the illuminators, the mouthpiece of the revolution. They provide context, humor, and visibility. In moments of political unrest, one may lose the ability to accurately verbalize their feelings. It is almost an impossibility to translate our surroundings or climate with anything **but** art.*

While the artists on the pages of Original Plumbing's *19th issue represent just the tip of the iceberg of trans talents, they are nothing short of miraculous. We focus on ideas around **art as activism** as well as those who share new trans perspectives in the fine art world.*

We hope this issue leaves you inspired to create and put your own work out into the world. Trans people making art is a revolutionary act!

—Rocco Kayiatos   *—Amos Mac*

COVER ILLUSTRATION: Xavier Schipani self-portrait; courtesy of the artist
OPPOSITE: *Skunk with Flower* **by Torie Leigh**

I KEEP TRYING TO FIND THE MAGIC WORDS

BUT KNOWING THE PEOPLE WHO NEED TO KNOW THAT,

THAT WILL ACTUALLY CONVINCE
THEM OF OUR HUMANITY.

@KETCHWEHR

I JUST DON'T KNOW IF THAT
KIND OF MAGIC EXISTS.

XAVIER SCHIPANI

By Amos Mac

Where do you call home?
Austin, Texas, for now but I am definitely an East Coast guy.

When did you first start to create?
I feel like I was always interested in making things. My mother recently told me a story about covering our apartment in plastic construction sheeting and letting me paint the whole thing, and when we didn't have paint she'd send me outside with a bucket of soapy water and I would paint our balcony. I was around 2 years old.

Was illustration always your preferred method?
I like to work on a large scale, it feels good to be active while I am working. Illustration is definitely what I rely on more consistently for work and I do identify with the culture of design that surrounds it.

Your work solidifies timely moments across politics, pop culture, and smaller movements, highlighting people doing the work in marginalized, often LGBTQ communities. What's your process like around this?

I think that my work definitely shifted after the election in a more political direction. I was inspired to create work almost as a form of journaling or documentation to help cope with cultural/societal highs and lows. I started a drawing-a-day project the day after the election and focused a lot on the LGBTQ community, as I feel like it is important to give voice to those who may not always be represented in mainstream media.

Was there a moment when you struggled as an artist, trying to find your "voice," so to speak? If so, how did you break out of that and find a focus?
I definitely struggled finding my voice as a "trans" artist. I was having issues with being labeled, but also felt it important to represent myself honestly. I think as I have gotten older I have become more comfortable with myself, and my "voice" as an artist has been informed by that confidence.

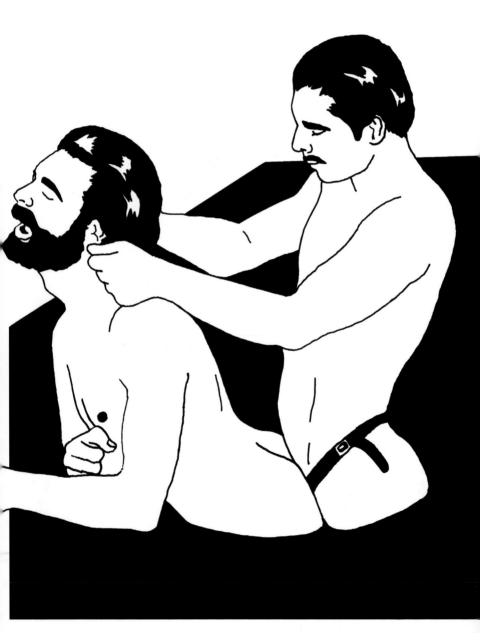

*Some of these images are from my zine **Doggy Style** and they all fit into a body of work that I would consider to be 'Social Realism'. elevating and highlighting trans/queer identities social consciousness .*

- XAVIER SCHIPANI

Your work is very accessible through social media and other spaces, like murals. What is the most memorable piece of work you've made lately?

I have been working on a project that isn't accessible yet. It is a series of paintings of individuals that I know or have asked for permission to paint that have transitioned. The paintings capture the individual's current self interacting with a past self. It is titled "Thinking of You" and it explores the themes of honoring the different parts of a transition, even if it is difficult.

How did you get involved with Refinery 29´s 29rooms? What kind of feedback have you received from your room?

I have worked with Refinery29 in the past doing freelance illustrations. They approached me in late spring and asked if I would be interested in collaborating with them for 29rooms and I was super honored. I have received really positive feedback, lots of personal messages from folks expressing that they really connected with the space and felt inspired by it, which is the best thing I could hear.

Which artists inspire you?

I am inspired by a lot of different artists, a lot of times its just the right painting at the right time, like hearing a song exactly when you need to. I am a fan of Nina Chanel Abney, Kerry James Marshall, Sara Andreasson,

David Hockney, Myla Dalbesio, Celeste Dupuy-Spencer, Juliana Huxtable, Henry Taylor, Deana Lawson, Lyle Ashton Harris, Julien Nguyen, Cauleen Smith, Toyin Ojih Odutola, Jonny Negron, Orion Martin, Cy Twombly, Barbara Kruger, Caitlin Keogh, Tom of Finland, Carl Andre, Eric Yahnker, Jordan Kasey, Ridley Howard, Laura Krifka… This question I could answer infinitely.

Where can we look forward to finding your work next?

I was super exited to take part in the new 29Rooms in Los Angeles this December, and I have work in a show in Baltimore now. Other things TBA for the spring!

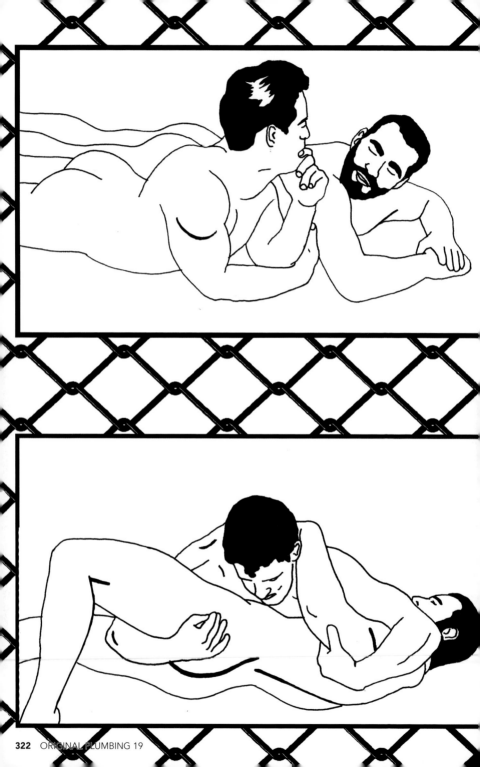

ETHAN X. PARKER

By Amos Mac

Pronouns:
xe/they

Where do you consider "home"?
I'm originally from Houston—born and raised—but I live in Austin currently. I never consider Texas my home, and I've yet to find somewhere to put down some roots.

Why is it important to create autobiographical comics around your nonbinary transition?
I feel that with "transgender" being a media buzzword in the past few years, it has created a binaristic way of viewing gender when it comes to transgender people. Folks are seen as either MTF or FTM, and there is no in-between. The more I looked and searched for nonbinary representation in transgender communities, the more I was met with people wanting to impose binary roles (specifically cisheteronormative binary roles/expectations) on the way I show up in the world. I am also agender. That seems to blow people's minds that I can be transitioning not to woman or man, but to void. The concept seems impossible to people, yet here I am living my agender trans life. So I began creating because there wasn't content that I could find, and I know I couldn't possibly be the only human in the world with this experience.

What type of materials do you prefer to work with when you're creating?
In a perfect world I would create using pen, brush, and ink. I really enjoy the simplistic beauty of black & white illustration.
Lately I've moved into digital art because I have access to infinite supplies and resources, and as an artist on a serious budget it helps me be able to continue creating without limitations.

Has the political climate inspired you to create art?
Politically, not so much. But socially, yes! I don't feel like I need to draw a picture to let people know that the country's leadership

Innis, 2017

doesn't care about trans people; I feel like that's common knowledge. I create art to support and empower queer and trans people that I see slugging through the muck on a daily basis. I create for the front-runners who are out there putting their careers and lives on the line so that the trans community can get the access we need to survive. I create for the people who can't be visible with their trans identity because it's not safe. I create art for my people, who don't often get a voice in the greater conversations about transgender rights, though Black trans women and TWOC literally paved the path toward queer and trans liberation.

Do you have artists you're most inspired by?
I am inspired by all artists and all art, so picking a few in a hierarchical way, I feel, does a disservice to the others. I am most moved by art that reflects the times, art that carries the voice of a people and delivers it to the masses in the most unapologetic way that it can.

What is the art tool you can always count on?
My mind.

Any upcoming projects we can look forward to seeing?
I've got a comic coming up in an all trans anthology called *We're Still Here*, about navigating fashion and self-expression as a non-binary trans individual. Additionally I am working on a portrait series featuring Black trans/GNC people who identify as masculine, but are actively subverting and queering what it means to embody Black masculinity. I've got a couple other things in the works but I can't speak on them just yet. All I can tell you is that they're going to be amazing!

Khye, 2017

KRIS GREY:
PROCESSION

"The dominant narrative for transgender experience focuses on transition from one binary gender to another. I reject this organizational framework by using hormones and technology of the medical industrial complex to craft a defiant body. Rather than 'transitioning' from one sex to the assumed 'opposite,' I am hybridized and self-designed to occupy a position outside of this binary. I am particularly drawn to alternative 'transition' narratives and self-fashioned outcasts hidden from history. Procession animates one such figure, Jean Carroll (1910–69), the Bearded Lady of Coney Island, who later in life chose to permanently transition to the Tattooed Lady in order to maintain her financial independence and to be able to wed her suitor of 15 years. Procession queers the ceremony of wedding by deconstructing the costume, tradition, and union associated with marriage. The charac collapses gendered signifiers through a mysterious ritual."

KC CROW MADDUX

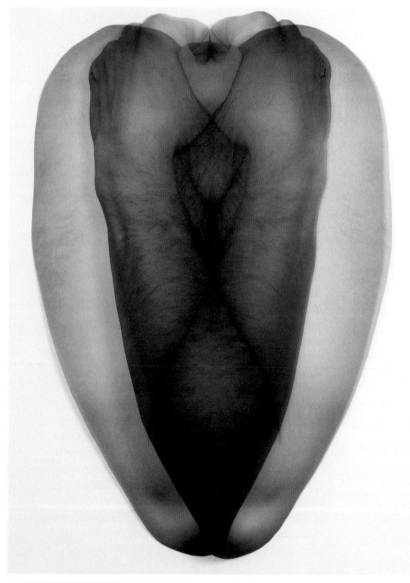

Untitled, 2016, digital photo prints on clear film, nails, 30" x 30" x 1"

"The current political climate has driven me to work louder, harder, less subtly, and more ambitiously. As a trans person, I feel like my artwork has an important role in humanizing this experience for people who don't understand us."

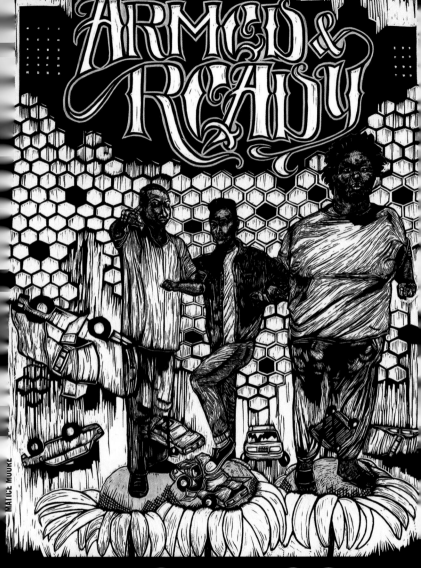

ARMED & READY

MATICE MOORE

MATICE MOORE

"The phrase *Armed & Ready* is a way of articulating our fierce commitment to each other and to standing up against gender policing."

ROMMY SOBRADO-TORRICO

Pronouns: They/them/Rommy

How do you identify?
Lost and sad, illegal, qtpoc brown kid.

Who—or what—inspires your art?
It depends on the content of the piece but typically it's stories—mine or that of the folks I'm honoring in my work. The resiliency, power, and complexity of the lives of undocumented migrants, femmes, working poor class folks of color, brown and black trans and queer siblings deserve to be represented in rich and dignified ways, in ways that celebrate our existence. I always go back to the stories and they always inspire the many layers in my work.

BAMBY SALCEDO

D'LO

ZOE LUNA

HINA WONG-KALU

GEENA ROCERO

SHANE ORTEGA

MICAH BAZANT

is an artist who lives in the Bay Area.

I create art as a practice of love and solidarity with racial justice movements. As Miss Major says, "When Black trans women get free, we all get free." Art helps us remember that the "impossible" is possible, and imagine the world we need to build together.

I am inspired by our transcestors known and unknown who dreamed themselves into existence. I am inspired by the great freedom struggles of our time, the Black Lives Matter movement, and the Indigenous resistance at Standing Rock, by the artists of these movements, and all the regular folks who put everything on the line to fight for a different world.

Look out for the Trans Day of Resilience art project. My organization, Forward Together, is working with ten trans artists and writers of color to create a new body of work that will all be released in November. And this spring we'll be creating a trans art kit, that will be like a trans art event in an envelope, so folks in more isolated places can experience the art together in person, and use it to create more beautiful healing community spaces. Check tdor.co for updates!

Ky Peterson, a young Black trans man in rural Georgia, was arrested for defending himself during a transphobic sexual assault. After a year in jail with no legal support or trial he was forced to take a plea deal. Ky was sentenced 20 years in prison

FREE KY

Free Ky. Created by Ky Peterson, Pinky Shear and Micah Bazant, 2016.
Trans Life + Liberation Art Series. Watercolor, pencil and photoshop, 12x12.

COBI MOULES

◀ *Drug Free School Zone* is a lot about childhood obsession, boyhood, and youthful queer desires. NKOTB [New Kids on the Block] played such a significant part of my childhood, particularly during that stage when friends began to group off and separate based on gender, and crushes became more intense. It was a very confusing moment and because I wasn't able explore these feelings to the fullest in the real world I imitated my surroundings and focused all of my fantasies onto the New Kids. So by re-creating and altering NKOTB posters, trading cards, and magazine clippings I delved into my childhood obsession, taking inventory of my youthful desires while reconstructing them with an empowered hindsight. Wanting to be both one of the boys and with the boys, I explored the range of possibilities of love, lust, and friendship.

▲

Bois just wanna have fun is a fantasy world in which I have multiplied myself throughout the Grand American landscape. Reflecting on mid-19th century American landscape painting, this series is embracing the beauty of nature while shifting the weight of its representation through the exaltation of my own existence within it and as part of it. The landscape, based loosely on the work of the Hudson River School, is a stand-in for my own Christian upbringing. As a queer and trans person, I seek to renegotiate my relationship with this upbringing and disrupt the notion that I am unnatural through such Christian lens.

MARIUS MASON

By Cindy Crabb

Marius Mason is an environmental and animal rights activist currently incarcerated in Texas. Prior to his incarceration, Marius worked for three decades doing aboveground activism to stop the systematic exploitation and destruction of the natural world. In 1999, in the name of the Earth Liberation Front (ELF) he set fire to a lab at the University of Michigan that was conducting research on GMOs. In 2008, after Marius's husband turned state's-evidence, Marius was threatened with a life sentence for the arson. With little financial stability and fear of dragging his family into a costly legal battle, Marius pled guilty and was given an extreme sentence of nearly 22 years. No one was ever harmed in any of his actions.

Marius came out as transgender in 2013. After a three-year battle to win the right to medically necessary care, he is, we believe, one of the first trans men to begin medical transition while in federal custody.

Since coming out, Marius has initiated an annual Trans Prisoner Day of Action: an international day of action in solidarity with trans prisoners.

How did you come up with the January 22 Trans Prisoner Day of Action, and what do you hope it will accomplish?
I wanted to try to reach out to other trans prisoners, to try to connect them with the one thing that has gotten me this far down the road—a sense of community, a connection to people that cared and understood both as allies and as fellow trans and queer folks. What I really hoped for by asking people to host all kinds of events for this date—everything from a couple of friends getting together for snacks and letter-writing, to a huge dance party, to demonstrations and teach-ins—was

to raise awareness that there were trans people in prison who might need different kinds of advocacy and services than other prisoners that many communities of resistance were providing to their fallen comrades. The events have sparked the creation of a few newsletters, in Austin and Australia, that have been especially helpful in bringing trans prisoners in contact with each other, and bringing their stories to light, as well as introducing more people to the work that great organizations like Black and Pink and Trans Initiative. And maybe most importantly, connecting individuals to each other, helping trans folks feel included and seen.

What have you come across in the fight to begin transitioning in federal prison?
For me, personally, transitioning in prison has both easier and harder than I ever imagined. I did a lot of legal research before I came out to the psychology department here. I went through two separate assessments to get my diagnosis of gender identity disorder/gender dysphoria. The Bureau of Prisons (BOP) policy was continuing to change, even as I was going through my assessment, and for the first time, it seemed that medical transitioning would be policy, even if you began your process after incarceration. I am anxiously awaiting the next phase of my transition, when I will have been on hormones for a year and can then request surgical affirmation.

Have you experienced hurdles and pitfalls particular to transitioning in prison?
It has from time to time "sucked," when the shot did not come when it was supposed to or I had to beg the officers to call about it or when other inmates would sneer and scoff. I was not used to being pathologized or objectified, to being vulnerable to abuse (at least

Self-portrait, acrylic paint on paper

We've been following your development as an artist with your Trans Hero series. Do you consider yourself more of an activist or an artist? Or do you feel they are intertwined?

Before my incarceration, I considered myself much more of an activist than an artist. I was a singer-songwriter and played out, mostly in conjunction with reading my poetry, at local open mics. My "art," such as it is and was, is usually just another way to communicate an idea that relates to my activism. I like the word you used "intertwined" as it conveys the image of how these two ways of interacting with my community supported and related to each other. Right now, I work mostly in acrylics and somewhat less in watercolors and pencil. I am not very accomplished, so the ability to control (and correct) my images in acrylic works better for me right now.

Who are your artistic inspirations?

I was completely floored when I read about the life and work of an artist, Chiura Obata. His works depicting Yosemite are intensely graceful and colorful, showing his deep appreciation for the natural world as a teacher and a healer. I feel like the works of Frida Kahlo, Vincent van Gogh, Diego Rivera, and Lucian Freud also are important to me and how I see painting. They used images in the same way that I would like to: to share a vision, an opinion, and to invite a conversation about the world.

I was inspired to do a series on trans folks when I realized that most of the images that I had seen (and granted, I am so limited in what I get to see of all that's out there) were in memory of folks who had been brutalized, murdered, or incarcerated. That is a great use of the medium of art, to mourn our lost comrades and to galvanize support for those who need to be defended. But I wanted to also pay tribute to some of the trans people that I was reading about who were doing interesting projects. I wanted to show that there are a million ways to be and to live as a trans person.

not as an adult). But it has been an important lesson in what many marginalized people go through, and since my "differentness" is not always visible, I could compare and contrast how I was treated by some staff who "knew" and some who did not, who just interacted with me based on their own assessment. Having been an educated "white" person without any visible group heading that would have attracted prejudice before—I can learn how this constant "othering" has an effect on its target.

The use of female pronouns and honorifics, of being constantly characterized as female, is depressing. I have advocated for myself directly, asking for help from my doctor when the issue involves staff or medicine access. I think my transition was timed to go with the policy changes in the BOP. It was the final thing that made me feel like I could come forward. I still feel very fortunate for all of the trans prisoners before who pushed the policy debate forward so that there could be some premise for people like me to begin a transition in prison.

OP

TRANS MALE CULTURE

THE ISSUES ISSUE • NUMBER 20 • 2019 • USA $10

The Issues Issue

The Final Letter

Dearest Reader,

Welcome to our twentieth and final issue. Perhaps you sensed something was up when you looked at the cover and saw the two of us staring right back at you. (Hey, this could be our final shot at being cover models!) Or maybe you've read the news about our grand finale on social media. Whatever made you pick up this magazine, we're so happy you're here with us today. *Original Plumbing* changed our lives, and we wouldn't be here, ten years later, if it wasn't for you.

In September 2009, a rapper and a photographer with zero background in publishing decided to make a print publication! You might ask, "Who the hell were you to make a magazine?" The answer is simple. We were (and still are) two creative, passionate artists who waited our entire lives to see trans male reflections in the media. When the struggles of being the "token trans guy contributor" for mainstream projects became exhausting for both of us, we knew it was time to carve out a space ourselves. Enter the birth of *Original Plumbing* magazine!

OP started as a result of Amos making Rocco's portrait for what he hoped would be a simple color-xeroxed zine of trans guys photographed and interviewed in their bedrooms. As he explained the idea to Rocco, their conversation naturally expanded on the potential of this as an ongoing, serialized magazine. Our brainstorming grew until we decided to dedicate a year to this project just to see what we could create while gauging if there was a need for a magazine for and by trans guys. Those early days are memorable: sitting in coffee shops for hours, ideating in what we'd call "hot air balloon sessions." Our friendship and the project grew in tandem.

We don't think anyone saw *Original Plumbing* lasting a decade.

From the moment we launched a Facebook page to promote the first issue (yes, this was back when Facebook was the place to be for social media), it was clear that there was an overwhelming need for *OP*. Emails poured in. Notes from readers, writers and artists wanting to contribute, parents and educators of trans kids thanking us, academics wanting to write dissertations on us, and people from around the globe just saying hello still show up in our inbox to this day. Once *OP* hit its stride a few issues in, we committed to produce twenty issues. Here we are.

We want to thank you, dear reader. If it wasn't for your outpouring of love and championing of our work over the years, we would've felt so alone in this. Your support proved that *OP* isn't just *some magazine*—it is a time capsule of trans male culture during a major turning point in the trans civil rights movement. *OP* showed the world that trans guys are allowed to take up space and aren't afraid to make some noise – and pose for a few cute photos while we're at it.

We hope you don't see this final issue—the Issues Issue—as a sad moment. We couldn't be more thrilled to end this project on a high note. We will always be proud of what was put into the universe through the vessel of *OP*. The magazine opened doors for countless projects to follow, from hyper-visible Hollywood media moments to homespun DIY projects. Thanks to *OP*'s reach, many eyes landed on the work we've done outside of the magazine. It lifted us up, giving us a platform beyond the trans community. After ten years, it's time for us to make time to focus on new work in a world that has shifted so much since the launch of *OP*.

It's been an honor to create this space for the community. Don't think of this as an end or a cliché goodbye. Look at this moment as an open door. In fact, maybe someone can create a new doorway. Maybe it's time to rip the old door off the hinges and create something completely new.

Love,
Amos and Rocco

COVER MODELS: Amos Mac and Rocco Kayiatos; photo by Alex Schmider

LEON WU

Interview by Rocco Kayiatos
Photos by Amos Mac

Suiting up for the future.

Introduce yourself and tell our readers about the work you do.

I'm Leon Wu and I'm most widely known as the Founder and CEO of Sharpe Suiting. At Sharpe, we make fine custom suits and clothing for all genders. I founded the company five years ago and during that time we have designed and constructed nearly a thousand suits for the LGBTQ community and beyond. The last 5 years of running this company while transitioning has been a ride. I remember throwing one of our first launch parties jointly with *Original Plumbing*, so it's quite an honor to be featured in the final issue. I will remain a founder and part owner in Sharpe, but I will be making a departure shortly from this company I love. My life calls me to other paths.

In my spare time, I take every opportunity to share whatever I've learned with my community. Whenever asked, I speak in conferences to empower the people in

the LGBT community to advance professionally (StartOut, MBA programs, SXSW, universities, a campsite in Colorado, basically anywhere I can). I also teach financial planning workshops on how to plan for a stable financial future and retirement. Many of us didn't even have the headspace to do such a thing until now. But I always teach that it's not too late! Every day is a start to a new, exciting, and opportune path!

Who was the first trans man you ever met?

Around the age of 21, I realized I was transgender when I met my best friend Max Madrigal. We performed together in a drag king troupe called The Lost Boys. I knew he identified as transgender and within a few years of becoming friends with him, I saw him undergo his medical and surgical transition. At that particular time I was just getting used to allowing myself to dress masculine-presenting offstage. My girlfriend at that time thought it was sexy and in a lot of ways she helped me come into my own, buying me boxers and boxer-briefs as presents. What I witnessed watching and listening to Max through his ups and downs on testosterone and his top surgery was beautiful. Over time, I began to imagine myself in the same experience.

Do you have any role models?

Buck Angel was the most visible trans man in the public eye during my twenties. Over a decade later, after I started Sharpe Suiting, he came in for a custom suit. My starstruck turned into friendship. He's still a great role model to me.

In the past decade, what's one of the biggest changes you've seen for trans men?

Health care! I paid for my top surgery two years before it was widely covered by most health insurance plans. Social media and me-

dia in general helped provide a major forum for trans visibility. I'm so grateful for all of these changes.

What does community mean to you?

A deep sense of belonging due to common struggles. Any group of people who band together for a positive change, a solution, or challenge, or just an inherent understanding of each other and exchange of that sentiment.

What is your biggest hope for the trans community?

Achieving equality together rather than sabotaging each other individually. I truly wish cyberbullying and trolling would stop. Some of us are on covers of men's magazines for the first time ever. Some of us have families. Some of us are healers or provide service to our community. No matter who we are or what we do, every one of us is important to move our community forward. I wish there was more support and understanding for one another instead of fear, envy, or jealousy. We need to build and foster safe spaces, like Camp Lost Boys, a separatist sleepaway camp for men of trans experience created by Rocco Kayiatos and Justin Chow. We need to continue learning from each other instead of hating on or letting ourselves be triggered by one another.

Be you and be simple. Complexity has been a burden on all of our lives. Recently through deep daily meditation, as well as getting to know other trans men and their thought processes, I've realized that peace and serenity is really in the mind of the beholder. Not our external society nor anything exterior from a person's being or soul can ever provide us what we already have within. Find yourself, hold yourself up, and uphold your community brothers, sisters, and siblings.

MALCOLM RIBOT:
FTM TRAVELER

"Our community is beautifully loving, generous, and welcoming. We truly are a family. The vast majority embrace connection, and sharing love with others— with open arms."

GAVIN GRIMM

Interview by Amos Mac | Photos by Scout Tufankjian/ACLU

Gavin Grimm is a name already solidified in the trans history books. His journey into the spotlight began in 2014, when he was 15 and his family told his school that he was transgender. A nightmarish uproar by some parents and students followed, inspiring the school board to bar Gavin from using the boys' bathrooms, and adopted a policy requiring students to use the bathrooms for their "corresponding biological genders."

With the ACLU's help, Gavin sued his school district for violating his rights under the constitution and Title IX. In February 2017, just one month after Donald Trump took office, the Department of Education withdrew the guidance.

Now living in California, Gavin attends college and has dreams to become a middle school English teacher.

You're in California now! Does any part of you want to move back to Virginia?
I will never again live in Gloucester County, VA. But I love the East Coast, I'd love to end up back on the East Coast. I'd love to be able to teach in Washington, DC, or somewhere around there, but I don't know what my life will be like in three years when I've completed my education. By that time will I settle down here? Throw some roots down? I only know I'll never live in somewhere like Gloucester again.

You're no longer in high school. What's going on with the case and how involved are you still?

The case is now at district-court level and active. I'm still a part of it. If it takes ten more years, I'm here for it. I'm all in.

Can you remember the first trans guy you saw in the media or online who inspired you?
I didn't know that you could transition until I was maybe 11 or 12. And I discovered it because I watched the show *Naruto* a lot, I was a big fan. On YouTube there was an individual who would dress up as one of the characters on *Naruto* and he posted videos. He always had short hair and dressed very masculine, and he had costumes, but in some videos he appeared a bit more feminine, and in other videos he appeared assigned male at birth. When I was 11 I wondered what was happening. What I realize now is that I was seeing videos he had recorded a year or two apart from each other. I didn't know that when I was watching. I wondered if one video was his brother. I felt a mix of confusion and emotion. More than anything else there was the feeling of, "I can do that?" That was exciting, and that was the first time I'd ever thought about the concept of actualizing the way I felt inside.

What's a piece of advice you'd tell a trans child in school who's having issues navigating through?
No matter who tells you you're wrong, or who tells you you can't join the Boy Scouts or go to the bathroom or you can't do this or do

that—if you're a trans boy and they're telling you you have to wear your hair long, or you're a trans girl and they're making you wear a suit—none of that treatment invalidates who you are. You are valid. It is okay that you are trans. It is wonderful that you are trans. It's not something that anyone can take away from you. Even if they try to tell you you're wrong, that's an inalienable part of you and not something anyone can take away from you.

Have you seen the world change for trans people since you first came out?
Yeah! I feel like it's different for my generation than it is for young trans people now, even though there was a lot of awareness around language and terminology and a lot of that happened when we were teenagers and young adults. The big change I'm seeing is an increase of children who never have to go through the wrong puberty. The trans narrative that everyone is so familiar with, "Oh yeah, I went through a traumatic puberty, I have to fund top surgery"—a lot of these things are out of the narrative for younger kids because they've never experienced it. That is awesome, you know? To have the joy of knowing trans kids who will never have to have their Adam's apple shaved down if that's what they choose to do, or they'll never have to have a double mastectomy if that's what they choose to do? These are things they don't have to worry about because people listened to them when they were young—and they had the language when they were young. Even from my age group, very few people my age had access to language and information before puberty. But now awareness is being raised every day. Kids are being believed and affirmed.

This reminds me of the Philly Trans Wellness Conference. So many kids attend! Have you been?

Yes, I went last year. I don't recall if I spoke or was on a panel, but I did participate. I helped with the parade while I was there. It was the most magical thing I've ever experienced. It was so purely joyful with no baggage attached. The kids, you know, the more gender creative ones, the trans boy, the trans girls, none of them cared to exclusively choose gendered objects. Everyone was like, "Fairy wings? Yeah! Eye patch? Sounds awesome." They weren't in a space where they felt they had to justify who they were. My heart was swelling. It was so fantastic to see.

What is something your followers might be surprised to learn about you?
I don't know... people love the "I'm just a kid" narrative. People love to ask me that question. I've told so many things in that vein. I can't think of anything. I like Dungeons & Dragons. There we go. That's something I haven't said.

What's an issue in the trans community rarely discussed in the media that you wish had more of a platform?
I think the biggest open secret in the trans community—something everyone in the trans community is aware of this, I think—is the substantially elevated rates of violence against trans women of color. Intersectional identities are not nearly as often presented to the media. And they should be. We should be hearing the voices of the most marginalized before anyone else. We should be hearing the voices of trans women of color, we should be letting them lead the charge. Increasingly we have heroes like Janet Mock and Laverne Cox, so there's more public visibility. It's awesome. And even if trans people of color are cast in the media there's still never a platform for them to say, "Because I'm a trans woman of color, I'm at a higher level of danger." There's just not that platform. And I'd love for there to be that platform.

ZANDER KEIG

Interview by Rocco Kayiatos
Photo by Evelyn Hockstein

This social worker, writer, and Coast Guard veteran is rewriting what it means to be a man.

What are the biggest challenges trans men have faced in the past decade?

The two biggest challenges for trans men, that I am most aware of are: 1. The number of guys getting phalloplasty, and 2. The negativity directed towards "binary" trans men. Back in 2008, when I got my phalloplasty, I can recall, vividly, the negative comments from other FTMs about the surgery, the outcome, and the meaning behind why one would want a penis. Many guys told me they would never get a phalloplasty, because they "did not hate their body" or "didn't need one to be a real man." While I would never tell another guy what he needs to do to be his authentic self, I was appalled at the general lack of compassion expressed by those making negative comments. What I have noticed, very recently, is that many of those same guys are now postphalloplasty or have surgeries pending. I don't at all find that surprising, as many live in states or work for employers where insurance now covers the surgery, but I do find it bothersome that none of them have come back around and said, "You know what, I was a real dick to you a while back. I'm sorry." The reason I'm not surprised is because early in my transition I was very against getting phalloplasty and talked about it at FTM meetings. I now make a concerted effort to share that part of my transition journey, because it resonates with others and provides me with an opportunity to make amends for the way I spoke during that time period. As for the binary vs. nonbinary tension, I'm not sure why that developed

and how to remedy it. I feel the split has weakened our community, as we were once much more unified and able to advocate from a stronger position. Early in my transition, which medically began in 2005, I was non-binary identified, so I can relate to the identity, but I never felt marginalized by transsexual men and once I was blending as male 100% of the time a nonbinary identification ceased to be worth asserting, because people saw and treated me as a man. I found it exhausting to constantly correct people. I had the same experience pretransition as an androgynous dyke. I would get called "sir" all the time. For about ten years I corrected people, angrily, most of the time. Eventually, I just gave up, but I never really liked it until I began to embrace a transgender identity, which was eight years before I started testosterone. I hope that the binary vs. nonbinary divide dissolves or we find a way to reorganize our community in a way that honors both identities. One thing I have noticed is the number of nonbinary FTMs attending FTM groups, even in cities where nonbinary groups are available, which then results in the binary guys dropping out of the group, leaving fewer and fewer guys to mentor those early or new to transition. If no nonbinary group exists, by all means attend a general FTM group. But if both groups are available in your city my appeal to you is, if you are nonbinary, let the binary guys have their space to discuss their transition too.

When you first came to your trans identity, what was the biggest challenge you faced as a trans man? Now what is the biggest challenge you face as a trans man?

The biggest challenge I faced as a trans man early in transition was shifting from relating, almost exclusively, to women to welcoming men into my social sphere, especially non-queer men. Since I was entrenched in lesbian separatist circles from age 16 to 36, I had

very little social interaction with men, unless they were gay. I had to learn how to relate to/with men in social situations. I cannot say I have mastered that task yet, but I feel much more comfortable with/around men, and have even discovered that I really like the company of men and participating in particular male activities: attending retreats, lectures, and seminars, and reading books, articles, and magazines by and for men. My favorite resources for all things male are: the Art of Manliness website and podcast, *Men's Journal*, the Mankind Project and Male Survivor website. The biggest challenge I now face as a trans man is much more personal. I recently dealt with a life-threatening bottom surgery complications ordeal that included the highest level of physical pain I have ever experienced, five nights in ICU and two weeks bedrest. Thankfully I am an optimist, because I was able to maintain a positive outlook throughout the ordeal, but it definitely tested my resolve more than it's been tested before.

What is an achievement for trans people you couldn't imagine you'd live to see?

Out, serving and transitioning active duty transgender service members in the US military. I have a front seat to the change, because I was appointed to be the Clinical Social Work Case Manager for the Navy Medicine West Regional Transgender Care Team (TGCT) on October 31, 2016. My region encompasses Asia, Pacific Islands, Pacific Fleet, and Western USA. I have enjoyed working with the service members (Navy, Marine Corps, and Coast Guard), their primary care providers, their Chain of Command, the other TGCT providers and individuals from the US Army and US Air Force. As a military veteran (US Coast Guard, 1986–88), who served during the pre–Don't Ask, Don't Tell (DADT) era, hiding and being silent were the only options to avoid detection and discharge. Of course DADT

I hope that the binary vs. nonbinary divide dissolves or we find a way to reorganize our community in a way that honors both identities.

was repealed in 2012, but it only covered sexual orientation, so transgender service members were still made to hide and keep silent. I had a suspicion, and there was some unofficial scuttlebutt (military lingo for gossip), that President Obama would lift the "transgender ban" before leaving office, so I set about landing a civilian social work job with the military in order to offer my services/expertise, should the occasion arise. At the time, I was a social worker with the Veterans Health Administration (VHA) Healthcare for Homeless Veterans Program. I had been with the VHA since September 2012. I started with the US Navy on May 30, 2016. One month later the Department of Defense released the In-Service Transition for Transgender Service Members Instruction (DoDI 1300.28), and two weeks later I was in a meeting, with all the top brass on-base, discussing how to develop what was to become the TGCT. Of course, there have been some ups and downs, for some service members, since the Presidential tweets in July 2017, but no change in official policy permitting gender transition. It has been an honor to be part of such a momentous sea change!

What do you feel is the biggest issue the trans community faces today?
I believe the lack of a national standard regulating insurance coverage for medical transition has caused many in our community to seek dangerous or less reliable routes to access cross-sex hormone therapy, genderaffirming surgical procedures, and other transition-related care. I am not advocating for a single-payer universal healthcare system. What I am arguing for is a federal Department of Health and Human Services policy that mandates no insurance company may exclude gender-affirming care for trans US citizens and legal residents. I am not even sure that would be possible, legally, but I'm shooting for the moon here. There is currently a disparity across the USA, with regard to which states have successfully lobbied for the removal of insurance carrier exclusions and those that have not. That disparity directly impacts the lives of trans people not living in or able to relocate to those states: not everyone has the capacity to or interest in packing everything up and moving to Oregon or Colorado or Pennsylvania or any of the other states that prohibit trans exclusions.

SKYLAR KERGIL

"Many people use YouTube for different things, but I believe the impact of storytelling and personal narrative being shared across the world was crucial for the trans community. Like my experience, I've heard from others that YouTube helped them so much with feeling less alone, and helped them share information and resources rapidly. Many trans men have told me that my videos were the ones that helped them realize they were transgender and that they could be who they were and are. It warms my heart each and every time."

Photos by Reed Wetmore

ALEX BLUE DAVIS

Interview and photos by Amos Mac

Alex Davis plays Dr. Casey Parker
on *Grey's Anatomy*!

It's safe to say you're playing the most famous trans doctor on TV today, but you've been in the business as a musician and actor for years. When you first started your transition, did you ever expect there to be such a visible role like Casey on network television in your lifetime?
Yes, I imagined it happening in my lifetime because growing up, I saw other marginalized groups slowly get represented on TV. Maybe we'd get to be a part of that? I watched a FTM character, Max, transition on the cable show, *The L Word*, then there was silence on TV. Years later there was buzz about trans women on cable and streaming. And some trans men followed. So, I thought, maybe there would be some cool cable roles for us, but network might take a little more time. Then Scott Turner Schofield, a trans guy in a trans role, booked *The Bold and the Beautiful*. And now we have *Grey's Anatomy*. It's so awesome to see this all happen.

How has your life changed since Casey first appeared on the screen?
I love my job. That's the biggest direct change. I have never loved a job in my life. (Sorry other jobs!) Being a working actor on a show I respect, with smart, joyful people is such a dream! The people on set truly respect each other and have been so welcoming to me. It's been an ideal working environment. Also, because of it, I started playing music again. I'd taken a break from being a singer-songwriter to focus on acting because the music business broke my heart a bit. Since I booked *Grey's* though, I've been inspired to play just for fun, which was so hard for me in the past. I'm very grateful for that change in my life. It's like I get to share this awesome experience with my old best friend, who can also help me handle it all and keep things in perspective.

What do you wish was around (in the media, or otherwise) for trans men ten years ago?

At that time we were all just kind of figuring it out. It would have given me hope to see stories about trans men who were happy, in happy relationships, and doing something that they loved. Back then, I had the feeling that transitioning would mean I'd be alone, most stories I heard had some painful element of loss and loneliness. But now that's changing, and maybe I can be that example for someone out there? I'm still neurotic and self-doubting, don't get me wrong, but I'm happy, I have a healthy marriage, family, and a job I'm passionate about. I want people who want that in their lives to know it's possible, because for so long I didn't think it was.

Was there a person in your life that opened your eyes to the larger trans community?

His name is Kyle Lasky. I met him in Northern California and we discovered we had a lot in common. He introduced me to Joe Stevens. I saw a photo of Joe and thought, oh wow—I need to meet him. I saw his band Coyote Grace play a show here in LA and and he was so friendly and forthcoming and seemed happy to be gigging and living his life. He introduced me to other cool peo-

ple and that was it. I was on my way. Thanks Kyle and Joe!

What do you feel is your biggest success so far?

Staying alive and being in a healthy relationship. Every day I'm shocked by it.

How has the parenting journey you're on with your wife inspired other areas of your life? What is one thing about parenthood you were not expecting?

I was not expecting to be able to handle it at all! I'm terrible at multitasking for the most part, and I have a hard time keeping track of stuff, and I've been known to be bad with time management—all of those things are incredibly important as a parent. It's been amazing to see myself take care of them, even when I'm exhausted—I do it—and I want to do it because they are magical kids.

Is there anything you're working on outside of *Grey's Anatomy* that we can look out for in the future?

Check out my EP of covers, *Songs for Surgery*, out now on iTunes. Also follow me on Instagram @alexbluedavis.

CHASE STRANGIO IS THE ACLU LAWYER WE ALL LOVE SO VERY MUCH

Interview by Amos Mac

Photos courtesy of Chase Strangio

Can you pinpoint a singular moment or person that inspired you to become a lawyer?
Growing up I definitely did not want to be a lawyer. There were lawyers in my family and I associated it with being stressed out, working a lot, and wearing uncomfortable clothes. I also developed a vision of social change that looked to the legal system as a source of oppression, not liberation. But after graduating from college and recognizing the access and privilege that I had, I started to see law as an intervention that I could use to disrupt the system. Dean Spade and then later Gabriel Arkles were both inspirations in guiding me into law and then framing and examining my role as a lawyer.

What is your proudest success so far?
Sometimes I am just most proud of being alive and working on being a kind and accountable person every day. There were so many times in my youth that I didn't know how to imagine a future, and I am proud to just be living one. In terms of work, I feel so lucky to get to work with our beautiful trans community and every time we push the

boundaries of what seems possible feels like a truly liberatory success. One concrete thing that I am very proud of is the veto of the antitrans bill by the South Dakota governor in 2016. We worked really hard to stop that bill, and I think that was a turning point in our legislature work to start telling trans stories and fighting back against each and every attack on trans lives in state legislatures.

Does being a parent influence your professional work?

Being a parent influences every little thing that I do. In my work, I am driven to help create a more beautiful world that my kid can live in and I have a changed understanding of caretaking responsibilities and pain that impacts the way so many of us go through the world.

When fighting anti-trans legislation, have you ever interacted with someone who disagreed with you, but had a change of heart after hearing you speak about your trans experience?

In my work I am constantly interacting with people who disagree with me. Some people are brazen and comfortable sharing how much and why they disagree with me, others are more reserved about it. I experience this disagreement in hostile places but also in more friendly ones, where people are still trying to understand and grapple with their own internalized transantagonism. Putting my experience out there publicly has made a huge difference in moving people but it also taken a toll on my health and well-being. It is exhausting to use your own story of trauma and your body as a tool to teach people that you are human. I am so amazed by the many young people who do it regularly in the states where we work. Every day, fighting to be held in their full truth.

If you could have dinner, or a nice brunch, with trans people living or dead, who would they be and why?

Well, what first comes to mind is Flawless Sabrina because I miss her so much. She was a guide to me and I would give anything to share some more time with her. Other people I would love to engage with are the trans people who I have worked with who were and still are incarcerated. I wish I could host a feast and share in festivities with the people who have given me hope and life, but who continue to have so much taken from them every day.

If there specific anti-trans legislation or issues you wish more people knew about? What is something we could do to fight it?

Coming off a big win in Massachusetts in November to preserve explicit legal protections for trans people in public accommodations under state law, we can expect attacks to escalate in other states across the country when legislatures convene in January. My hope is that our movements stay committed to state and local work even as we are experiencing tremendous assaults from the federal government. It is in the states where we see repressive tactics tested out—voter ID laws, anti-immigrant laws, anti-trans laws, carceral expansion laws and policies—and we must stay vigilant. In all this work, we can build power if we fight together by sharing our resources—financial, emotional, logistical. So many people are under attack and if we give money or art or skill-sharing, we can help challenge the oppressive regimes that want to extinguish our beautiful, complex lives.

BUCK ANGEL

"Language is a powerful tool.
It is how we make a change."

FIGHTING FOR OUR RIGHT TO RECONFIGURE ORIGINAL PLUMBING

By Willy Wilkinson
Photo by Cody T. Williams

Apparently I'm a trans elder. When I announced that I was Willy at age nine in the early 70s, there were no trans-affirming schools or resources to help my family get with my name change. There was no conversation about trans issues, no community, no empathy, no discrimination protections. It was 1972, the year Title IX was enacted, which was designed to ensure equal access to education for women and girls. But the idea that Title IX could protect trans folks, or anyone discriminated against for their gender expression, was a long way off.

After we won discrimination protections in San Francisco in the mid-90s, I began training public health providers on transgender issues. Some resisted the idea that trans people were full human beings worthy of respect, and few could wrap their minds around complex gender identity.

I identified as third gender. There were very few of us. The FTM community, as we called it, was very transition-focused; what we now call "nonbinary" was an anomaly. I circled around medical transition for years, flirting with it, dreaming of it, smitten in the throes of desire, but I repeatedly decided not to go there. I was living with a debilitating chronic illness and wanted desperately to transition to a healthy body—maybe testosterone would take me there. But I was third gender, my mixed heritage inextricably linked to my gender identity, and staying in a female body seemed like the best option for an imperfect dilemma.

But years later when I became a dad, all the pink and blue of parenthood—all the wrong assumptions about my gender and my relationship to my kids—drove me nuts. Suddenly I was slammed with a torrent of emotion, and I felt a sense of urgency. The time had come. I jammed that needle in my ass like a down and dirty dope fiend, and began the next twist in a very long transition. It was the Year of the Dragon, the only animal in the Chinese zodiac that is a mythical creature. A dragon year is a blessing, a time to make a major transition in one's life, a good year to take calculated risks. This is the year when we may be able to achieve what seemed impossible before. Besides, I was forty-nine, and I knew I wasn't going to fifty in a female body.

Six months on T and I was getting read as male most of the time. After a year I began to wonder what it would be like to have a body that truly reflected who I was. Honestly, I didn't want to get killed in the locker room as a small Asian trans guy. I wondered what it would feel like—emotionally, physically, sexually, and psychically—to have a dick.

Of everything we've gained over the years—growing awareness, people who truly care about trans issues, legal protections, a multitude of resources, a vibrant community—there is nothing that compares to the changing landscape of health care access. When I launched the Health Care Access Project at Transgender Law Center in San Francisco in 2004, it was the first program in the nation to provide transgender cultural competency training for providers, educate community members about their rights in health care settings, and advocate for comprehensive access to care. At that time, I never could have imagined that we would one day have health insurance coverage.

Historically, trans people have been discriminated against in health insurance in four ways:

denied a policy simply for being trans; denied coverage for transition-related care; denied coverage for sex-specific care, such as gynecological services for trans men or prostate screenings for trans women; and especially egregious, denied coverage for anything the insurer claims is related to being trans. For example, the insurer would deny coverage for a broken bone because the person was on hormones and that affected their bone health. So, "too bad you broke your arm; we don't cover trans care."

But the Affordable Care Act and regulations in some states made these transgender exclusions illegal for most health care settings nationwide, though trans and gender-expansive folks across the country are still trying to find doctors who treat them with respect, and get access to care covered by insurance. In California the landscape changed in 2013 when the state required HMOs, PPOs, and Medi-Cal to cover transition-related care, including surgery. Immediately we began holding forums on phalloplasty and how to get your surgery covered. It was a timely confluence of health insurance access and the influx of medical expertise. The sessions were packed with curious trans men.

As trans men, we have had to contend with a long legacy of negativity and misconceptions about our junk—that it's inadequate, not functional, not man enough, a travesty—whether or not we opt for genital surgery. With phallo, there is the myth of the Frankendick, which seems to perpetuate even today despite medical advances in blood flow, nerve sensation, and urethral lengthening. True, it's complex to make a penis. Most of us get a complication, and most of us get past it. Everyone's experience is different, but I, for one, think it's a phenomenal surgery process. In California I have witnessed how access to transition-relat-

I Got A Zit Constellation For My Gender Galaxy

I'm An Old Ass Mofo In Puberty

Aarp Is Coming After Me

I'm An Old Ass Mofo In Puberty

From *Born on the Edge of Race and Gender:
A Voice for Cultural Competency*

ed surgery covered by insurance—top surgery, metoidioplasty, phallo—has transformed the mental and physical health of transmasculine folks who want these surgeries. In my experience, patient satisfaction rates are high.

Yet our victories are in jeopardy as those in power prey on us once again. Recently the Trump administration announced its plan to roll back the rule in the ACA that protects against discrimination, not just for trans people, but anyone who does not fit traditional gender stereotypes. They say that ACA protections against "sex discrimination" don't apply to trans folks, just like they announced

in February 2017 that Title IX's sex discrimination protections don't protect trans students, though the law hasn't changed and trans kids have continued to win their cases under Title IX. But know this: even if this mean-spirited administration rescinds these Obama-era regulations of the ACA, it will still be illegal to discriminate against trans people in health care settings and insurance.

If you experience discrimination, contact an LGBT-friendly legal organization and file a complaint with your state's human rights agency. We all have the right to affordable, culturally competent health care.

CONTRIBUTORS

SAMUEL ACE is the author of several books, including *Our Weather Our Sea*, *Meet Me There: Normal Sex*, and *Home in three days. Don't wash*. He teaches poetry and creative writing at Mount Holyoke College.

JACOBY BALLARD is an herbalist, yoga teacher, and meditation teacher based in Salt Lake City. He is a founder of Third Root Community Health Center in Brooklyn, a worker-owned cooperative holistic health center. He has specialized in holistic transgender health for over 13 years.

DRASKO BOGDANOVIC is a Sarajevo-born Serbian Canadian artist, portraitist, and photographer of homoeroticism.

COOPER LEE BOMBARDIER's writing was recently published in *Foglifter*, *Put A Egg On It*, *Ninth Letter*, *NAILED*, and *The Rumpus*. His work has appeared in the Lambda Award–winning anthology *The Remedy*, as well as in *Meanwhile, Elsewhere*, winner of the 2018 American Library Association Stonewall Book Award.

JUNIOR BRAINARD teaches English at Community College of Philadelphia and enjoys spending time with his partner, Tina, and their 3-year-old, Tony.

LYNN BREEDLOVE is a writer, performer, activist, and transportation entrepreneur. He's fronted Tribe8, The Homobiles, and COMMANDO; founded the nonprofit ride service Homobiles; and authored *Godspeed*, *Lynnee Breedlove's One Freak Show*, and *45 Thought Crimes*.

RYAN CASSATA is a singer-songwriter, actor, performer, writer, and LGBTQ activist. Cassata has appeared on *Larry King Live* and *The Tyra Banks Show*, and won the first ever Harvey Milk Memorial Award. He's been featured in *Rolling Stone*, *Billboard Magazine*, and the *New York Times*.

CHING-IN CHEN is author of *The Heart's Traffic*, and coeditor of *The Revolution Starts at Home* and *Here Is a Pen*. They have received fellowships from Kundiman, Lambda, Watering Hole, Callaloo, Can Serrat, and Imagining America. "Closed Sky" was included in their latest book, *recombinant*, which won the 2018 Lambda Literary Award for Transgender Poetry.

T COOPER is a best-selling author (of nine books); a journalist; television writer; English and creative writing professor; and most recently an award-winning filmmaker (of *Man Made*, a feature-length documentary tracing the lives of four transgender men who step on stage at the only all-trans bodybuilding competition in the world).

CINDY CRABB is the author of the long-running feminist autobiographical zine *Doris*. She is the author of *The Encyclopedia of Doris* and *Learning Good Consent*. She is a therapist and somatic experiencing practitioner in Pittsburgh.

JAMES DARLING is a queer and trans performer, photographer, and video artist from the South.

SEAN DORSEY is a San Francisco–based trans and queer choreographer, dancer, writer, and activist. Sean Dorsey Dance has toured to 30 cities across the US and internationally. He is founding artistic director of Fresh Meat Productions, which invests in the creative expression and cultural leadership of trans and gender-nonconforming communities.

ELLIOT FOXPRINCE is an American photographer and digital artist living in the UK.

HENRY GIARDINA is a writer and editor based in Los Angeles. His work has appeared in the *New York Times Book Review*, NewYorker.com, and the *Paris Review Daily*, among others. He is a 2016 MacDowell Fellow and a 2018 Edward F. Albee Fellow.

ALEX GIEGOLD is a photographer from Jena, Germany.

KRIS GREY is an NYC–based genderqueer artist whose cultural work includes curatorial projects, performance, writing, and studio production.

beck (b) h. is a 24-year-old conceptual artist living in northwestern Ontario. beck finds community through documenting existence as a tender queer, trans, disabled person through multiple forms of art. beck spends their time exploring, learning about woodworking/plant husbandry, being the best cat-dad they can be, and daydreaming about space.

IAN HARVIE is a stand-up comedian and actor.

TEXAS ISAIAH's work explores gender, race, and sexuality by inviting the sitter to participate in the photographic process. The invitation constructs a space to engage in collaborative visual dialogues about legacy, self-empowerment, emotional justice, protection, and topophilia.

CHASE JOYNT is a moving-image artist and writer. His first book, *You Only Live Twice* (coauthored with Mike Hoolboom), was a 2017 Lambda Literary Award Finalist and named one of the Best Books of 2016 by *The Globe and Mail* and CBC.

HARVEY KATZ spent 15 years traveling the country performing as Athens Boys Choir, which is how he met Rocco and Amos and the loveliest weirdos from coast to coast. He retired from life on the road in 2017 and is currently finishing a nursing degree.

SHARON KILGANNON is a photographer based in Brighton, UK. She has been photographing the queer community for nearly 10 years.

JOSHUA KLIPP is an attorney, musician, disability access specialist, tree lover, and casual writer. He lives in a wee apartment in San Francisco with his amazing wife, two energetic dogs, and an incredibly social bunny rabbit named Canelo.

ASHER OUNZUMBA KOLIEBOI is a minister, organizer, and lover of small dogs.

A native of New York, NICK KRIEGER realized at the age of 21 that he'd been born on the wrong coast, a malady he corrected by transitioning to San Francisco. He is the author of *Nina Here Nor There*, winner of a Stonewall Honor Book Award and an Independent Literary Award.

SIUFUNG (HUN) LAW is a genderqueer advocate, professional bodybuilder, and transgender researcher from Hong Kong.

His/her tattoos symbolize his/her self-discovery journey as s/he believes that we are a body of art that involves continual processes of becoming.

SETH LIST lives and works in the high-tech sector in Austin, TX. In his spare time, he runs the Austin chapter of the nonprofit Equality Texas.

BRANT MACDUFF is a taxidermist and conservation historian living in Brooklyn. He walks very fast and hates bell peppers.

KC CROW MADDUX is a trans artist whose work is intentionally difficult to categorize. His pieces layer photography, installation, painting, and sculpture together to create a "trans" format.

EV MARQUEE is a fashion and portrait photographer from LA who splits her time working between Southern California and the Bay Area. She is a self-taught queer photographer who loves working with everyday women, unconventional beauties, and the POC and LGBTQ+ community.

H. MELT is a poet, artist, and educator whose work proudly celebrates Chicago's queer and trans communities. They are the author of *On My Way to Liberation*, *The Plural*, and *The Blurring*. H. Melt works at Women & Children First bookstore.

MATTEO MONTONE is a professional body piercer from the East Coast who loves his dogs and riding his motorcycle cross-country.

MATICE MOORE is a Black queer gender-nonconforming artist from Arizona.

COBI MOULES is a Brooklyn-based painter whose work navigates his queer and trans identity. Through play and humor, he explores multifaceted notions of the self, autonomy, and gratification.

ERIN NATIONS is the writer and illustrator of the comic book series *Gumballs*. His work has appeared in *Full Bleed* and the *We're Still Here* anthology. He is a frequent contributor to the quarterly comics newspaper *Vision Quest*. He lives in Portland, OR.

WYNNE NEILLY is a Canadian queer and trans-identified visual artist and award-winning photographer who is based in Toronto. Wynne focuses on portraiture and editorial work, using its personal nature to reflect the development of identity and the complexities of human gender expression. His work seeks to normalize and validate the queer and trans body.

CATHERINE OPIE lives in LA and is a professor of photography at UCLA. Opie's work has been exhibited throughout the US, Europe, and Japan, and she has won numerous awards, including the Queer Art Prize in 2017 and the Smithsonian's Archives of American Art Medal in 2016.

ETHAN X. PARKER is a community-taught artist making works centering life at the intersection of being Black, queer, and trans. Xe took up visual art in 2015 as a form of healing from trauma, and through that xe discovered xyr trans identity. Ethan creates art documenting the collective experiences of nonbinary and trans folx of color as a way to honor QTPOC communities unpacking and decolonizing gender.

KY and SOL PLATT live in NYC, where Sol is a busy third grader. She is on the New York State gymnastics team, a merit scholarship recipient in jazz and classical piano, and studies modern dance and choreography 4 days a week.

XAVIER SCHIPANI is a painter and illustrator living in Austin, TX. His work explores gender, identity, and sexuality with much emphasis on "maleness" and "masculinity" in crisis. His subject matter is heavily figurative, represented in a world where gender "norms" are relaxed and space for self-exploration appears.

E-J SCOTT is a curator, academic, queer cultural producer, and fashion historian. His work includes curating Queer & Now, Tate Britain (2018), producing West Yorkshire Queer Stories (2018–20), founding and curating the Museum of Transology (2017–), and curating Brighton Trans*formed (2014).

BASIL VAUGHN SOPER is a writer, photographer, Southerner, and the founder of Transilient. Transilient's objective is to create a platform accessible to all people, in and out of the trans community, through traveling and truthfully capturing interviews and portraits of trans and nonbinary folks.

J. SOTO is a queer Chicano transgender artist, writer, and arts organizer. His collaborative writing project Ya Presente Ayer can be found in Support Networks, Chicago Social Practice History Series. His projects include the Latinx Artists Retreat and the Latinx Artist Visibility Award.

CHARLIE J. STEPHENS is a high school English teacher and creative writer living in Northern California. Charlie's written work has appeared in *Rappahannock Review* and *Cold Creek Review*, and can also be found in *Nothing Short of*.

CARRIE STRONG is a self-taught photographer and retoucher based in Oklahoma City.

HANK T. is assistant professor in the Section on Population Behavioral Health in the Department of Psychiatry at Rush University Medical Center. His research focuses on uses of information communication technologies to improve health outcomes and access to care, particularly for marginalized populations.

COURTNEY TROUBLE has an MFA in studio arts, had a healthy obsession with Tori Amos as a teenager, and dreams of living in an abandoned church with art studios. They've been interviewing artists about queer topics for over a decade.

CHRIS E. VARGAS is a video maker and interdisciplinary artist originally from LA and currently based in Bellingham, WA. He is the executive director of MOTHA, the Museum of Transgender Hirstory & Art, a conceptual arts and *hir*story institution highlighting the contributions of trans art to the cultural and political landscape.

REED WETMORE is a Boston-based transgender portrait and landscape photographer.

KETCH WEHR is a transfeminist artist working as an illustrator and designer in New York. In addition to loving up too many rescue beasts, he is usually making comics and illustrations all the time.

EMERSON WHITNEY is the author of *Heaven* and *Ghost Box*, and teaches creative writing at Goddard College and gender studies at the University of Southern California.

WILLY WILKINSON, MPH is a writer, public health consultant, and long-term cultural competency trainer from Oakland. He is the author of the Lambda Literary Award-winning book *Born on the Edge of Race and Gender*.

CODY T. WILLIAMS, who likes sharing time exploring and experimenting, is that little creepy photographer in the background spending his free time storytelling through imaging the space in between.

GRAY WONG is a photographer and graphic designer.

THANK YOU

Rocco and Amos in 2009 posing with a post office receipt after their first massive mailing of *OP*'s first issue.

We couldn't have produced this magazine for years without the help of so many generous and inspiring humans.

1984 Printing in Oakland was our first printing press, our first home—Amy, thank you for holding our hand during those early days and showing us what a true love for independent publishing looks like.

FTM International—thank you for existing.

Joshua Klipp—thanks for the early advice and producing the first-ever *OP* fundraiser that helped catapult the magazine into the world.

Gay bars across North America that hosted our events—especially the Stud, Make-Out Room, Sugarland, and Wreck Room—you created a physical space to build community, and we'll never forget those nights.

Every person who volunteered with love, whether you sat with us and packed issues into envelopes, tabled at events, assisted with photo shoots or line edits, or provided us with advice—you donated your time for the sake of trans visibility and for that we are indebted. Special love to Sawyer DeVuyst, Mars Hobrecker, JM Jaffe, Hailey Laws, Scout Rose, Calvin Kasulke, Jamie DiNicola, Isaac Andrade, Emet Tauber, Ali Liebegott, Beth Pickens, Darin Klein, Diana Tourjée, Layne Gianakos, Majda

Jones, Winter Laike, Young Emmett, Just Shannon, and the NY Art Book Fair crew.

Derek Morris—you helped elevate *OP*'s design, and we are forever grateful for your keen taste, thoughtful eye, and, most importantly, your friendship.

Michelle Tea—thank you for seeing the cultural value in *Original Plumbing* back in 2009, lifting it up, and years later making a home for this collection through your very own Amethyst Editions.

Jamia Wilson, Lauren Rosemary Hook, Drew Stevens, Jisu Kim, and Nick Whitney at the Feminist Press—thank you for taking on this monster project, for believing in our vision, and for accepting us—late deadlines and all! You've made a very big dream of ours come true.

Amos Mac would like to give special thanks to:

Sam Early for showing up for this project (and all the other ones) and helping me even when I refuse to ask for it—you are truly otherworldly.

Carole Alfe for being a loyal fan-mom and teaching me the importance of art at an early age.

David Alfe for all your support and letting me turn your basement into *OP*'s "East Coast storage facility" without question.

Rocco Kayiatos would like to give special thanks to:

Tricia Kayiatos-Smith for endless support.

The Kayiatos family for nurturing my queerness and creativity.